W9-BWJ-257

The Board Book

ALSO BY WILLIAM G. BOWEN

Equity and Excellence in American Higher Education
(with Martin A. Kurzweil, Eugene M. Tobin)

*The Shape of the River: Long-Term Consequences of Considering
Race in College and University Admissions* (with Derek Bok)

The Game of Life: College Sports and Educational Values
(with James L. Shulman)

Reclaiming the Game: College Sports and Educational Values
(with Sarah Levin)

Inside the Boardroom: Governance by Directors and Trustees

Performing Arts: The Economic Dilemma (with William J. Baumol)

The Board Book

AN INSIDER'S GUIDE
FOR
DIRECTORS AND TRUSTEES

William G. Bowen

W. W. Norton & Company New York | *London*

CARL CAMPBELL BRIGHAM LIBRARY
EDUCATIONAL TESTING SERVICE
PRINCETON, NJ 08541

Copyright © 2008, 1994 by William G. Bowen

Previous edition published under the title
Inside The Boardroom: Governance by Directors and Trustees

All rights reserved
Printed in the United States of America

For information about permission to reproduce selections from this book, write to
Permissions, W. W. Norton & Company, Inc., 500 Fifth Avenue, New York, NY 10110

For information about special discounts for bulk purchases, please contact
W. W. Norton Special Sales at specialsales@wwnorton.com or 800-233-4830

Manufacturing by Courier Westford
Book design by Brooke Koven
Production manager: Julia Druskin

Library of Congress Cataloging-in-Publication Data

Bowen, William G.
The board book : an insider's guide for directors and trustees /
William G. Bowen.
p. cm.
Includes bibliographical references and index.
ISBN 978-0-393-06645-6 (hardcover)
1. Boards of directors. 2. Directors of corporations. 3. Corporate governance. I. Title.
HD2745.B62 2008
658.4'22—dc22

2007048476

W. W. Norton & Company, Inc.
500 Fifth Avenue, New York, N.Y. 10110
www.wwnorton.com

W. W. Norton & Company Ltd.
Castle House, 75/76 Wells Street, London W1T 3QT

1 2 3 4 5 6 7 8 9 0

*To the colleagues
with whom I have served on boards —
and from whom
I have learned so much*

Contents

The Board Book

Preface

BOARDS OF directors and trustees matter greatly. That simple truism is understood far better today than ever before. The full effects of "good" versus "bad" governance can be hard to calibrate and are the subject of active debate, but no one doubts that they are real. When things go wrong at major corporations such as General Motors (never mind Enron), there are serious consequences for society at large, as well as for the workers, investors, and communities directly involved. The directors are accountable to these various constituencies, and it is up to them to ask probing questions about the organization's strategic directions as well as the quality of leadership and, if need be, to replace the CEO or recommend other managerial changes. In the nonprofit sector, too, the media are increasingly critical of boards that seem to be "snoring" while performance deteriorates.[1] Boards of directors and trustees are, after all, the steering devices for complex organizations—with the potential to guide them down right or wrong paths. Their job is by no means only to help organizations avoid serious missteps; they also need to be proactive partners in working with the CEO/president to achieve highly positive outcomes.

Any reader of the daily press knows that interest in corporate governance has increased in recent years—a phenomenon fueled in part by widely publicized scandals and ever-increasing shareholder activism.[2] The business sections of leading newspapers have become as full of drama, and of dramatic revelations, as the sports pages. At the same time, good performance tends to go unnoticed—an aggravating but inevitable asymmetry. The widely publicized instances of foolishness, if not outright bad behavior, have led commentators in the media and institutional shareholders alike to demand that boards open themselves to ideas from outside the boardroom, and even change their structures and habitual forms of operating.

Yet, though the explosion of interest in board governance is undeniable, how boards actually work remains mysterious to many people, including many of those elected to serve on boards. Where power resides, how it is distributed and exercised, and how it is limited and controlled often remain obscure. This black-box perception of boards is a serious problem in and of itself, because all of us have a stake in the effective functioning of organizations that affect our lives and our society in so many ways.

Approach Taken

It was more than a dozen years ago, in 1994, that I published my first book on the workings of boards of directors and trustees in both the for-profit and nonprofit sectors (*Inside the Boardroom: Governance by Directors and Trustees*). In the intervening years I have seen some of the propositions that I outlined then tested in real-time situations. I have also learned new lessons from my participation on the boards of corporations such as American Express and Merck, as well as through active involvement in the governance of TIAA-CREF and the Mellon Foundation in the nonprofit sector. In addition, I have continued to benefit from the experiences, insights, and candid comments of friends who have served on many other boards, including those of such radically different entities as WorldCom, Enron, the Smithsonian Institution, and Harvard.

Much has changed over this period—but certainly not everything. Governance remains a fascinating subject. At bottom, it has to do with power and accountability—with who exercises power, on behalf of whom, and how the exercise of power is controlled.[3] It involves complex webs of personal as well as institutional relationships. It provides the voyeur with insights into human frailties at the same time that it provides the student of abstract organizational structures with conundrums. Governance also *seems* to be a relatively accessible subject. As one highly experienced board member, John C. Whitehead, puts it, "When it comes to governance, everyone is an expert."

One of the most important current topics in the for-profit sector is the ever-evolving relationship between boards and their CEOs. In the mid-1990s some corporations had begun to consider having a non-executive chairman or a "lead director," but this topic commanded not nearly as much attention then as it does today. Lead directors are found frequently now in the for-profit sector (especially at large companies), and some well-informed students of corporate governance have said privately that they have had something of a conversion when it comes to what many consider the more radical option of separating entirely the role of CEO from the role of chairman. I am skeptical that there is any one "right" model for all situations, and one of my principal objectives in this study is to parse out in some detail the pros and cons of different approaches before suggesting when one model or another is most appropriate. This book, then, is about CEOs as well as boards, and how to structure the most effective partnerships between them.

The Board Book: An Insider's Guide for Directors and Trustees pays close attention to nonprofit organizations as well as to for-profits. I am interested in boards of trustees as well as boards of directors. Of course, there is a wide variety of types of organizations within each of the two broadly defined sectors: Although useful for many purposes, for-profit versus nonprofit is often too gross a classification system. At the minimum, we must distinguish for-profit companies that are publicly owned from the increasing number of for-profit companies that are privately held. In addition, small start-ups are very different from large, multinational companies.

In the nonprofit sector, charitable nonprofits (which are eligible to receive tax-deductible contributions) need to be distinguished from other nonprofits, such as labor unions and trade associations. Within the charitable group, it is important to distinguish service providers and grant seekers from grant makers (foundations). Charitable nonprofits differ according to their size, their dependence on earned income, their entrepreneurial characteristics, and their respective missions. Museums are very different from civil rights organizations, which in turn differ in fundamental ways from hospitals, environmental entities, and colleges.

Many other distinctions could be introduced within both sectors, but in this book I focus primarily on (1) large, publicly owned and widely traded for-profit corporations; and (2) service-providing, grant-seeking nonprofits, including colleges and universities. I will, however, also comment on governance within the growing private-equity part of the for-profit sector and within grant-making foundations when there are instructive comparisons to be made.

My own fascination with how boards function is long-standing and dates back to the late 1960s, when I was much involved in efforts to think through the governance of universities in the aftermath of Vietnam War protests and other campus controversies.[4] My thinking about corporate governance issues can be attributed originally to the takeover movement in the 1990s, the rise of the institutional investor, and the appearance in the business world of the "Watergate style" of investigative reporting.

Subsequently, a series of rather gripping personal experiences intensified my interest in for-profit companies. For whatever reasons (my wife thinks I am a virus, and that wherever I go there is trouble!), I have been a direct participant in some highly charged events. These have included the takeover of NCR by AT&T, the resignation of James Robinson as CEO at American Express, the sale of Rockefeller Center to a Japanese company, the forced change in leadership of the Reader's Digest Association, and, most recently, the election of a new CEO at Merck and the legal challenges associated with Merck's voluntary withdrawal of VIOXX from the market. Anne Armstrong, a colleague on the American Express board and on the Smithsonian board of regents, observed that it was her participation in several "revolutions" that had caused her to reflect on the topic of governance. My own sequence of experiencing and thinking is the same as Ms. Armstrong's.

My tenure as president of the Andrew W. Mellon Foundation from 1988 until July of 2006 gave me the opportunity to learn about the daunting challenges that face boards in both the foundation world and the nonprofit sector in general. The workings of the board of the Mellon Foundation gave me new insights into how such boards can stimulate and even inspire new approaches. But interactions with potential grantees also provided examples of problematic board performance—it was distressing to see opportunities missed and resources wasted.

My own mix of experiences in the for-profit and nonprofit sectors has led to one of the distinguishing characteristics of this book: its comparative approach. I am convinced that we can learn much by contrasting presumptions and practices in the two sectors, and there is more than a little room for improved performance all around. Contrary to general impressions, nonprofit boards are sometimes better positioned than many of their corporate cousins to deal with recurring problems faced by all boards, including achievement of the optimal relationship between the board and the CEO. Nonprofit boards, in turn, have much to learn from disciplines characteristic of corporate boards—especially the routine use of benchmark data and the constant monitoring of discrepancies between planned outcomes and actual results.

Although this comparative orientation is not the usual approach, I believe that some of the most vexing questions are seen in a new light when a conscious effort is made to understand why different models predominate in one sector or the other. An apt analogy is foreign travel. When I visited the People's Republic of China in 1974, shortly after the Cultural Revolution, I came back not only with a new awareness of the problems and opportunities facing that vast country, whose history and culture are so different from our own, but also with a heightened sense of what was special about the United States and its institutions. Today, countries like China, India, and Russia (as well as the developing world in general) have a great need for more effective governance of their evolving corporate sectors, since the risks of investing in such countries are compounded by concerns about accountability and oversight. As the United States seeks to improve its own governing mechanisms, it would be splendid if the best features of board governance in this country could be "exported" in appropriate ways. Comparative approaches can—and should—lead to knowledge transfers in all directions.

In writing this book, I make no claim to having made a full scholarly review of a considerable, rapidly growing body of literature.[5] Nor have I conducted new empirical research. As I have already indicated, the raw material underlying the text consists primarily of a combination of lessons that I learned while serving on a variety of boards and extensive discussions with others who have served in similar capacities. In commenting on these experiences (mine and those of other people), I do not attempt to repress a personal tone.*

I have also felt no reluctance to present normative propositions, although in this book I have avoided proposing specific norms, in part because I have wanted to avoid sounding preachy. In addition, I am increasingly aware that there are exceptions to almost every rule, and that it is dangerous to be too formulaic. Still, in discussing many topics, I am prescriptive. For example, I feel strongly that it is unwise for a former president or CEO to stay on the board of an organization that he or she once led. Similarly, I am an advocate of mandatory retirement. My allegiance to these general propositions is clear; however, several commentators have made me aware of special situations in which it can make sense to set aside these strong presumptions. Accordingly, my approach has been to state what I believe the general rule should be and then to identify, as best I can, the high hurdles to be cleared in order to justify taking another approach.

Personal experiences (especially when they are gripping) can help one see simple points with unusual clarity, but they can also lead to erroneous generalizations—which is a principal reason why I have been helped so much by criticisms and suggestions offered in response to drafts of this manuscript. In working and reworking this material, and in reviewing and discussing the comments of others, I have become increasingly aware of how autobiographical many of us are when we discuss governance. What has worked, or failed to work, for each of us in our own settings takes on a special aura.

In the spirit of full disclosure, the reader should know the associations that have informed many of the comments that follow—and, by inference, the kinds of experiences that I have *not* had, since I am as conscious

---

* One other matter of style should be mentioned. In the years that have elapsed since the publication of my earlier book on boards, I have found no new solution to the pronoun problem and have chosen, generally speaking, to continue to use "he" when I want to refer, generically, to an individual of either sex who might be the CEO or chairman of an organization. (I also prefer not to use "chair" or "chairperson," though I sometimes do.) The reality is that the corporate world still contains few women in these top positions. There are many more women in senior positions in the nonprofit world, and far more now than there were in 1994, although there is certainly room for further progress in opening up opportunities for women in both sectors.

of the deficiencies of my preparation as I am of the rich array of opportunities I have had to learn at first hand about governance.

At one time or another I have served as an outside director of five for-profit corporations: American Express, Merck, NCR (until its acquisition by AT&T), Reader's Digest, and the Rockefeller Group. I have not served on the boards of small for-profit start-ups, and I cannot speak from first-hand experience about the burgeoning private-equity world—though I do feel that I know enough about developments in this sector to comment about their general implications for governance.

In the nonprofit sector, I have served as an outside director of six entities: the Center for Advanced Study in the Behavioral Sciences, Denison University, the Public Broadcast Laboratory of National Educational Television, the Sloan Foundation, the Smithsonian Institution, and the Wallace-Reader's Digest Funds. In addition, as president (CEO) I have served ex officio on the boards of Princeton University and the Andrew W. Mellon Foundation. As a result of Mellon Foundation initiatives in the field of digital technology, I have also served (and continue to serve) on the boards of three independent nonprofit spin-offs: JSTOR, ARTstor, and Ithaka.[6] Furthermore, in part as a consequence of the Mellon Foundation's larger interest in the health of the nonprofit sector, I am familiar with organizations as diverse as the American Antiquarian Society, the Barnes Foundation, the New York Botanical Garden, the Population Council, the New-York Historical Society, Duke and Harvard universities, and the Martha Graham Dance Company.

In the course of writing this book, I have benefited enormously from access to a special resource: numerous colleagues and friends who took the time to comment, often at length, on the topics discussed here. Many of their observations were so perceptive, and so well stated, that I have incorporated them directly into the text, with or without attribution as seems appropriate. What started out as personal impressions evolved into an unusual kind of collaborative work, with layers of commentary, and occasionally comments on the commentary, interspersed through the text. In this regard, if in no other, the final product has a kind of Talmudic character. Kevin Guthrie, founding president of JSTOR and now president of Ithaka, has reminded me that, in this regard, my work product resembles a book project initiated at MIT called "We is smarter than me."

The active involvement of so many sharp-eyed and sharp-tongued commentators in the construction of this manuscript, along with the interactive character of much of the text, has become a distinguishing characteristic of the book. Because of the importance that I attach to the contributions of the commentators, I list them here, with some of their principal affiliations. In the text, I provide brief identifications of commentators when I first cite their views, but I hope that readers interested in knowing more about the individual commentators will return to the fuller list of their affiliations provided here. Some of these individuals commented on only the draft of this book, others commented on both this book and its predecessor, and still others commented on only the first book.

Commentators

The Honorable ANNE L. ARMSTRONG, executive committee chairman of the Center for Strategic & International Studies; former ambassador to the Court of St. James's

BRUCE ATWATER JR., former chairman and CEO of General Mills

ROBERT L. BANSE (deceased), former senior vice president and general counsel of Merck & Co.

LEWIS BERNARD, chairman of Classroom, Inc.; advisory director of Morgan Stanley

HENRY S. BIENEN, president of Northwestern University

JOHN BIGGS, former chairman and CEO of TIAA-CREF

W. MICHAEL BLUMENTHAL, president of Blumenthal Partners; former partner at Lazard Frères & Co.; former chairman and CEO of Unisys; former secretary of the treasury

DEREK BOK, former president of Harvard University

FREDERICK BORSCH, professor of New Testament and chair of Anglican studies at the Lutheran Theological Seminary at Philadelphia; former bishop of the Episcopal Diocese of Los Angeles

LARRY BOSSIDY, former chairman and CEO of AlliedSignal; former chairman and CEO of Minneapolis-Honeywell

JEFFREY BRINCK, former partner of Milbank, Tweed, Hadley & McCloy; CEO of TIPHYS Fiduciary Enterprises and of Poseidon Services Inc

McGEORGE BUNDY (deceased), former president of the Ford Foundation; former national security advisor

GLENDA BURKHART, former senior vice president of the Reader's Digest Association; chairman of the Women's Commission for Refugee Women & Children

DAVID M. CULVER, chairman of CAI Capital Corporation; former chairman and CEO of Alcan Aluminium

D. RONALD DANIEL, former treasurer of Harvard University; former managing director of McKinsey & Company

RALPH D. DeNUNZIO, former chairman and CEO of Kidder, Peabody Group, Inc.

NICHOLAS DONATIELLO, president and CEO of Odyssey Ventures

CHARLES W. DUNCAN JR., investor; former secretary of energy

CHARLES E. EXLEY JR., former chairman and CEO of NCR

RICHARD B. FISHER (deceased), former chairman of Morgan Stanley

KENNETH C. FRAZIER, executive vice president and president, global human health, Merck & Co.

RICHARD M. FURLAUD, former chairman and CEO of the Squibb Corporation

ELLEN FUTTER, president of the American Museum of Natural History; former president of Barnard College

LOUIS V. GERSTNER JR., chairman of the Carlyle Group; former chairman and CEO of IBM; former chairman and CEO of RJR Nabisco

ROBERT GOHEEN, president emeritus of Princeton University

WILLIAM T. GOLDEN (deceased), corporate director; trustee

HARVEY GOLUB, chairman of the board of Campbell Soup Company; former chairman and CEO of American Express

HANNA HOLBURN GRAY, president emeritus of the University of Chicago

GEORGE V. GRUNE, former chairman and CEO of the Reader's Digest Association

KEVIN GUTHRIE, president of Ithaka

JOHN M. HARRIS, former president and CEO of Rockefeller Financial Services

ROBERT KASDIN, senior executive vice president of Columbia University; former treasurer and chief investment officer of the Metropolitan Museum of Art

NICHOLAS KATZENBACH, former senior vice president and general counsel of IBM; former US attorney general; former undersecretary of state

FREDERICK J. KELLY, former dean of the Stillman School of Business of Seton Hall University

JOHN C. KENEFICK, retired chairman and CEO of the Union Pacific Railroad

DONALD S. LAMM, former president and CEO of W. W. Norton & Company

RICHARD LYMAN, former president of the Rockefeller Foundation; former president of Stanford University

EDGAR M. MASINTER, retired partner of Simpson Thacher & Bartlett

ROBERT McCABE, president and CEO of Pilot Capital

MARY PAT McPHERSON, president of the American Philosophical Society; former president of Bryn Mawr College; former vice president of the Andrew W. Mellon Foundation

MICHAEL S. McPHERSON, president of the Spencer Foundation

ARJAY MILLER, former dean of the Stanford University Graduate School of Business; former president of the Ford Motor Company

THOMAS NEFF, chairman of Spencer Stuart U.S.

STEPHEN P. NORMAN, secretary of American Express

STEPHEN OXMAN, advisory director of Morgan Stanley; chairman of the executive committee of the Princeton University board of trustees

LOUISE PARENT, executive vice president and general counsel of American Express

ALAN PIFER (deceased), former president of the Carnegie Corporation and the Carnegie Foundation for the Advancement of Teaching

FRANK POPOFF, former chairman and CEO of the Dow Chemical Company; former chairman of Chemical Financial Corporation

W. TAYLOR REVELEY III, dean of the Marshall-Wythe School of Law at the College of William & Mary; former partner at Hunton & Williams

FRANK H. T. RHODES, president emeritus of Cornell University

BARBARA PAUL ROBINSON, partner of Debevoise & Plimpton

NEIL L. RUDENSTINE, chairman of ARTstor; former president of Harvard University

HAROLD SHAPIRO, president emeritus of Princeton University

JAMES SHULMAN, executive director of ARTstor

DENNIS T. SULLIVAN, president and CEO of the Church Pension Group, Episcopal Church of America

SAMUEL O. THIER, MD, professor of medicine and health care policy at Harvard University; former president of Massachusetts General Hospital

FRANKLIN A. THOMAS, former president and CEO of the Ford Foundation

SARAH TURNER, associate professor of education and economics at the University of Virginia

MICHELE S. WARMAN, general counsel and secretary of the Andrew W. Mellon Foundation

RAWLEIGH WARNER JR., former chairman and CEO of Mobil Corporation

SIR DENNIS WEATHERSTONE, former CEO and chairman of JPMorgan

CLIFTON WHARTON JR., former chairman and CEO of TIAA-CREF

JOHN C. WHITEHEAD, former deputy secretary of state; former senior partner and co-chairman of Goldman Sachs

HERBERT S. WINOKUR JR., chairman and CEO of Capricorn Holdings; former chairman of the finance committee of the board of directors of Enron

EZRA ZILKHA, investor; corporate director and trustee

HARRIET ZUCKERMAN, senior vice president of the Andrew W. Mellon Foundation; professor emerita of Columbia University

Organization

Chapter 1 begins by posing what is almost the primordial question: Why do we have boards at all? I examine the principal functions of boards of directors and trustees, their similarities and differences across the for-profit and nonprofit sectors, and the extent to which changes in the general business–social–political environment have altered both the issues facing boards and the behavior of boards. Finally, I consider two questions not addressed often enough: the extent to which external constraints preordain outcomes, regardless of what boards do or don't do, and whether these external checks are more significant in for-profit than in nonprofit settings.

Chapter 2 deals with the question of leadership—specifically the relationship between the board and the CEO of an organization. I call attention to the increasing number of "lead directors," "presiding directors," and "non-executive chairs" in corporate America and attempt to explain the factors driving this trend. I start from the premise that the days of the imperial CEO are (and should be) over. I then argue, at the conceptual level, in favor of separating the roles of CEO and chairman before identifying practical considerations that may favor maintaining the combined chairman–CEO model or adopting the lead director approach, especially as a transitional model.

Chapter 3 focuses on the increasingly lively topic of CEO compensation (as illustrated by the challenge posed to compensation committees by no less a figure than the president of the United States, "to pay attention to the executive compensation packages that you approve")[7] I suggest ways in which corporate compensation committees can exercise greater independence and enjoy more success in linking pay to performance. In the nonprofit sector, the compensation (and benefits) of presidents and executive directors has also become much more actively debated, but here I argue that compensation is often inadequate rather than overly generous. Trustees do need to be careful, however, to exercise properly their important oversight function—especially in regard to "perks."

Chapter 4 discusses the marked increase in terminations of CEOs, especially in the corporate sector, and the kinds of evaluation processes that a board needs to have in place in order to decide when to make a change in the leadership of the organization. I discuss specific examples—in the nonprofit sector as well as in the for-profit sector. One question that cuts across sectors is whether the length of "the leash" given to CEOs should differ for nonprofits and for-profits.

Chapter 5 covers CEO transitions, and the first topic discussed is succession planning—a function that badly needs improvement. How the search process itself is conducted is an enormously important subject in both sectors, and there are certainly lessons to be learned from recent experiences in recruiting new CEOs and new presidents. One central question is the role of search firms, and another concerns the criteria that should be emphasized in looking for a new leader. I also address the need for "graceful" exits of departing chief executives, and how to ensure that new leaders have full opportunity to chart their own paths.

Chapter 6 discusses building the board, which is seen increasingly—and properly—as an ongoing developmental process in both the for-profit and nonprofit sectors. Size itself matters, and characteristic sizes of boards differ in the two sectors, for reasons that will be made clear. Nonprofit boards are, nonetheless, often too large to be effective. Fortunately, the process of recruiting new board members has become much more professionalized in almost all settings, with independent directors of companies exercising much more authority than in previous years. Systematic attention needs to be given to the mix of qualities needed on boards, and achieving and maintaining diversity continue to be important in both sectors. In addition, the independence of board members is a more serious issue today than it was earlier—key questions include how to define independence and how to achieve it in fact and not just in appearance. I argue that independence should not be defined in too formulaic a way. In electing board members, it is also important to think through the proper role that shareholders and other constituents should play (the so-called majority-vote issue in corporate America).

Chapter 7 focuses on board "machinery," including committee structures, the frequency of board meetings, board dynamics (how to encourage open discussion of the most important questions), and the proper use of executive sessions. I address the management of conflicts of interest (which it is naïve and even unwise to think can be eliminated altogether), the contentious issue of what to do about board leaks, and the relatively infrequent but gripping issue of when directors/trustees should choose to resign. I also consider how boards can "prune their trees," removing directors or trustees who either are unwanted (for justifiable reasons) or simply have served long enough, whether boards should consider greater use of term limits to ensure freshness, and how mandatory retirement should be viewed. Finally, I suggest how boards can do a better job of evaluating their own performance than many do at present.

Chapter 8 is titled simply "Themes." In it, I return first to the critical importance of the partnership between the chief executive officer and the board, and especially the CEO's relationship with the board chair. Another recurring theme is the absolute necessity of having board members who possess courage and the will to act—at the same time that they recognize that board decision making is a collective responsibility and a "team sport." I next reiterate the desirability of investing significant time and energy in governance questions up front, before a crisis is at hand. I also discuss the convergence of governance patterns in the nonprofit and for-profit sectors, and the important question of the desirable degree of convergence. Finally, I end the book by speaking briefly about the rewards—especially the intangible rewards—of board service.

Acknowledgments

I could never have written this book had it not been for colleagues and friends who, over many years, gave me the opportunity to work with them on boards of directors and trustees. These experiences have taught me so much, and I cannot overstate my debt to those who never hesitated to welcome my participation both in discussions of issues of every kind and then in taking actions. The actual writing of this book has been a lesson in collaboration, par excellence, and I want to reiterate my thanks to the legion of thoughtful and dedicated commentators who have done so much to improve the argument of the book. These cheerful critics have sharpened my thinking, often by challenging propositions that deserved a more careful weighing of pros and cons than I had initially understood. I have already listed these commentators, with identifications, earlier in the preface, and it seems invidious to single out individuals.

I cannot fail, however, to say a special word of thanks to those who provided not only substantive comments but also much encouragement and advice all along the way: Kevin Guthrie and James Shulman (chief executives of nonprofit start-ups with which I am involved on a day-to-day basis); Stephen Norman and Kenneth Frazier (officers of the two companies, American Express and Merck, that have provided the richest opportunities for me to learn about how boards work in the for-profit sector); and Lewis Bernard, Nicholas Katzenbach, and Paul Volcker (old friends who are simply wise).

Susanne Pichler, the exceedingly able librarian at the Andrew W. Mellon Foundation, has been my collaborator throughout the process of writing this book. She has worked tirelessly to suggest new materials, to locate obscure references, and to clarify both the text and the notes in countless ways. Susanne has been helped, in turn, by Lisa Bonifacic and Ellen Nasto. Johanna Brownell, my assistant in the Foundation's New

York office, has been an active participant in improving the manuscript and, more generally, in simply moving the project along. Her support has been critically important. I am grateful to John Hull, chief investment officer and financial vice president of the Andrew W. Mellon Foundation, and James Bailey and his colleagues at Cambridge Associates, who assembled information about private-equity firms and their governance.

My wife, Mary Ellen, has, as always, provided the support and encouragement essential to staying the course.

Finally, I want to acknowledge the unusually helpful role played in this project since its earliest days by Drake McFeely, president of W. W. Norton & Company, and his chief assistant, Brendan Curry. These two outstanding publishers took a personal interest in the book, and that has made a real difference. They also identified a talented copy editor, Stephanie Hiebert, who caught more errors than I ever imagined I had committed.

All of this help notwithstanding, I end with the usual acceptance of full responsibility for whatever faults remain. Warts and all, I hope that this book contributes in at least a small way to the governance by boards of directors and trustees of some of our society's most important institutions.

William G. Bowen
July 2007

I

Roles of Boards—and the Constraints They Face

SOME YEARS AGO, a onetime student of mine who had gone on to accomplish a great deal came to tell me that he had been invited to join the boards of two public companies. This was a new kind of opportunity for him, and he asked what factors he should consider in deciding whether to accept either invitation. Our impromptu conversation helped me appreciate an obvious point: many things that some of us have been fortunate enough to learn through experience, and that are available to us as subconscious background, are not necessarily generally known. Recognizing that there might be others, like my friend, for whom an overview would be useful, I summarize in this framing chapter some very basic propositions about boards: how they function, how they have been affected by changes in the context within which they work, and how for-profit and nonprofit boards are subject to somewhat different sets of constraints.

Why Are Boards Needed?

It is helpful to ask, right at the start, "Why do we have boards of directors and boards of trustees at all?" Why has this particular oversight mechanism seemed preferable in so many instances to other modes of governance? The simple answer is that the corporate form of organization is highly advantageous, and it requires boards. Nonprofits as well as for-profits benefit from the legal protections of the corporate form, especially limited liability, that distinguish it from the partnership or the unincorporated enterprise. In addition, it is easiest for nonprofits to satisfy regulatory requirements by incorporating and operating with the usual kind of governing board.

There is also a deeper set of considerations. Both for-profit and nonprofit entities operate in inherently complex settings in which matters are rarely cut-and-dried. The exercise of collective responsibility through the mechanism of a board can slow down decision making, but it can also dampen the enthusiasm of the aspiring autocrat. A properly functioning board provides checks and balances by adding layers of judgment and protections against abuse of power, self-dealing, favoritism, and just plain foolishness. More positively, the existence of a board encourages the development of a shared sense of institutional purpose and an awareness of the broader social, economic, and political context within which decisions are made. Nonresident directors and trustees can approach issues from a broader and more disinterested vantage point than can those immersed in day-to-day responsibilities. They can bring fresh perspectives to bear on tough questions at the same time that they can testify to outside constituencies on behalf of a company or a college.[1] In both for-profit and nonprofit sectors, boards can serve as valuable connectors between the work of a specific company or social-service provider and the external world that conditions the success or failure of the organization in so many ways.

To be sure, boards are more useful in some settings than in others. Derek Bok, former president of Harvard and a longtime member of nonprofit boards of various kinds, has pointed out that boards can be most useful when the organization is small and lacks a depth of staff expertise. In addition, boards can be most effective when at least some of their members have enough knowledge of the genre in which the organization works to contribute substantive ideas or raise big warning flags. Finally, small organizations that are in start-up mode, in either the for-profit or the nonprofit sector, are especially likely to benefit from the ideas and intuitions of wise directors or trustees. Venture capital firms typically insist on one or more board seats to monitor their investments and provide strategic advice. There are direct analogues in the nonprofit sector. In my own experience, trustees of JSTOR, ARTstor, and Ithaka—all small, entrepreneurial start-ups—have been enormously helpful in discussing both strategic directions and ways of getting things done.

Granted these advantages, boards are far from perfect instruments. Still, for most complex entities I remain convinced that the idea of a board of directors or trustees, when translated into an effective decision-making mechanism and populated with well-chosen members, is preferable to any known alternative.

What Do Boards Do?

At the most general level, all boards can be said to share a single overarching responsibility: *to build an effective organization.* Everything else is derivative. The late Kenneth Dayton, a major figure in both the forprofit and nonprofit sectors in Minneapolis, insisted that "governance is governance." Yet another wise and experienced observer, Nicholas Katzenbach, former US attorney general and onetime general counsel at IBM, has argued that for-profit and nonprofit boards differ fundamentally in what they are and in what they do. This is not a debate that can be settled in the abstract. Both perspectives have value.

Essentially all boards serve eight principal functions, though some are more important in one setting or another:

1. Select, encourage, advise, evaluate, compensate, and, if need be, replace the CEO

Walter Bagehot, an early editor of the *Economist*, once described the constitutional authority of the monarch as "the right to be consulted, the right to encourage, the right to warn."[2] In this context, we add the right to elect, to set compensation, and to dismiss. Although electing, compensating, and dismissing are actions that need to be taken collectively, encouraging and warning are often done by individual board members, as well as by the board as a whole. I will have much more to say about the electing, compensating, and dismissing functions in Chapters 3, 4, and 5. There is no way to exaggerate the importance of active board involvement in making decisions about CEO leadership and tenure.

A sometimes underappreciated (and less understood) function of boards is to give informal advice to the CEO or president outside of board meetings. A number of commentators regard this as the most important function of directors and trustees. Anyone who has been responsible for leading an organization certainly recognizes the need for candid advice from truly knowledgeable and concerned people who are at least somewhat above the fray. Of course, CEOs must be receptive to advice if it is to have value, and often those who need advice the most are the most reluctant to accept it.

2. Discuss, review, and approve strategic directions

In both for-profit and nonprofit organizations, this central task involves a more or less constant questioning of basic assumptions and priorities. Boards have an obligation to take a long-term view and to resist any tendency to place excessive emphasis on short-term considerations, whether quarterly earnings or an unexpected shortfall in donations. Both sectors are putting more and more emphasis on the strategic-planning function of boards, and this is all to the good—as long as process is not elevated over substance. There is a risk, which seems especially pronounced in the nonprofit sector, that merely extrapolating trends and building spreadsheets can become a substitute for thinking about priorities, hard choices, and what actually drives behavior.

There is also a danger of confusing participation in the direction-setting process with actual policy making. Boards in both sectors almost never make policy in any thoroughgoing way. Rather, they raise questions, debate policy choices, and eventually adopt or reject recommendations brought to them by the president or CEO. As Katzenbach has observed, the very thought of a board actually making policy, from scratch, is frightening in the extreme. Chaos would surely result. Policies need to be formulated thoughtfully, over time, through the sustained attention of full-time officers and competent staff.

Boards can, however, participate effectively in the policy-making process: first, by asking the right questions, which are almost never purely financial in nature; second, by making sure that each realistic course of action has been identified and that a good faith stab has been made at weighing the costs and benefits of the main options; and, third, by occasionally introducing new approaches. When a board is functioning well, this process is easy, interactive, and iterative. It involves discussions among board members, the CEO, and perhaps other senior officers, with exchanges of ideas frequently occurring outside meetings as well as in them. Often no one is sure, finally, who first introduced an idea. A seamless process is a compliment to all concerned.

3. Monitor performance

Once the right leadership is in place and strategic directions and priorities have been set, the board's responsibility is to review regularly the progress of management in achieving agreed-on goals. Almost all corporate boards understand this responsibility, and they are accustomed to reviewing ongoing results against plan on a regular basis. Indeed, the real danger in the for-profit sector is that too much time and attention may be given to reviewing and parsing out small variations in outcomes from quarter to quarter instead of focusing on broader trends and emerging challenges. In the nonprofit world, on the other hand, it is surprising how frequently no real planning occurs—and it is even more surprising how frequently plans that were adopted are not tracked in even the most rudimentary fashion. In several specific situations, it proved impossible for staff at the Mellon Foundation, when reviewing grant proposals, to determine whether previously established goals were ever achieved.

In these respects, many nonprofits have much to learn from their corporate cousins. Being explicit about objectives and time frames, and paying attention to even simple benchmarks, can reduce the risk of big surprises. It should be recognized, however, that the monitoring task in some parts of the nonprofit sector is complicated enormously by both conceptual issues (what are the most important outcomes to measure, and how can they be measured?) and special accounting conventions.[3]

4. Ensure that the organization operates responsibly as well as effectively

Goals must, of course, be achieved in the right ways. Thus, an important obligation of all boards is to encourage the establishment of the appropriate "tone at the top" and to ensure the adequacy of policies and procedures for compliance with legal and ethical standards. Proper discharge of this important responsibility includes protecting the organization against conflicts of interest and being sure that proper controls are in place to monitor the expenses and the exercise of perquisites by management.

5. Act on specific policy recommendations and mobilize support for decisions taken

Whatever role boards play in developing and monitoring strategic plans, they have a clear-cut responsibility to act on specific recommendations that are operational as well as strategic. In both for-profit and nonprofit contexts, votes by boards on major policy issues serve the function of legitimizing decisions—and giving them a degree of finality—so that the organization can get on with its business. Although boards also review and sometimes approve decisions that are more managerial (for example, appointments of officers or salary increases for an array of staff members), board actions on recommendations in the strategy and policy arenas are especially significant.

As a corollary to the need to act on recommendations, boards need to mobilize support for decisions made, especially controversial ones. In nonprofit organizations, this is an absolutely critical function. To cite an experience of mine in the university world, Princeton's trustees voted, in 1969, to adopt a recommendation that Princeton become coeducational—a decision that seems so obviously right in hindsight that it is hard to recall how controversial it was at the time. This action by the trustees, which followed a lengthy process of study and debate, imposed closure on an issue that had to be settled and allowed the university to move ahead in an orderly way.[4]

6. Provide a buffer for the president or CEO—in the vernacular, "take some of the heat"

In parts of the nonprofit world, in particular, boards need to protect a president or executive director from the temptation to indulge idiosyncratic demands and self-serving pressures, including actions that serve only to placate a noisy constituency. In some situations, presidents may need to promise individuals—doctors on a hospital staff, faculty members in a university, or prospective donors to museums—that a matter will be presented to the board for consideration, even if the president has quite a clear sense of the likely (negative) outcome. It should be acknowledged, however, that in some situations board members themselves are the sources of strong pressure exerted on behalf of special interests. In a college or university setting, athletics is the most obvious example. Several commentators have remarked that special pleading by trustees can be a particularly serious problem in the foundation world, especially if a kind of "senatorial courtesy" is allowed to prevail. One experienced trustee (John Whitehead) has referred, ruefully, to "pork barrel reciprocity."

7. Ensure that the necessary resources, both human and financial, will be available to pursue the organization's strategies and achieve its objectives

All boards have a collective responsibility to act on the key staffing recommendations that are so important in shaping the human resources available to for-profits and nonprofits alike, and, as discussed at length in Chapter 5, to strengthen succession-planning processes. Board members can also assist the CEO in motivating and encouraging members of the management team by paying respectful attention in formal meetings when officers other than the CEO make presentations and by getting to know these other officers in informal settings. In addition, board members can provide valuable support simply by being visible at ceremonial events and large-scale, quasi-public, managerial meetings. Woody Allen is right: there is much to be said for "just showing up."

Boards of nonprofits dependent on contributions must also devote a great deal of time and energy to raising money and mobilizing volunteers. Individual trustees need to be responsible advocates, to make meaningful personal financial commitments, and to accept fund-raising responsibility. But board members of nonprofits also need to have a clear sense of when they should turn down proposed gifts, especially gifts in kind, offered unexpectedly. There are obvious dangers in taking on new responsibilities without both a clear programmatic case for doing so and a reason to believe that the resources needed over the long term can be secured. Kevin Guthrie, one of my colleagues at JSTOR and now president of Ithaka, has suggested that in many cases the wise advice is "Don't take the Jaguar." His reference is to a game show situation in which a participant wins a Jaguar and may be tempted to take the "free" prize without thinking carefully about what it will cost to maintain the car and pay insurance—never mind the income tax payments to come.[5]

In addition to generating new support, boards of nonprofits with significant endowments or other monetary assets must oversee the investment of the funds entrusted to the institution. Typically, nonprofits with large endowments depend on trustee investment committees and recruit board members with investment expertise. These boards also depend on in-house staff either to oversee the selection of money managers or to manage some assets themselves.

8. Nominate suitable candidates for election to the board, and establish and carry out an effective system of governance at the board level

Increasingly, boards in both for-profit and nonprofit sectors are assuming direct responsibility for the composition of the board and for the way the board discharges its duties. A board committee on governance is often the vehicle used to carry out this important function, which includes making sure that the board contains individuals of talent and integrity who contribute a range of perspectives. A sometimes unpleasant but necessary duty is to orchestrate the removal from the board of a director or trustee who needs to be replaced.

Return on Mission

Broad similarities notwithstanding, there are also deep-seated differences between the characteristic concerns and mind-sets of boards in the for-profit and nonprofit sectors. Mission is a particularly strong driving force in the nonprofit sector. In brief,

> *For-profit boards concentrate on developing and carrying out broad strategies for enhancing shareholder values; nonprofit boards are much more committed to the particular "missions" of their organizations.*

For-profit boards have no obligation whatsoever to pursue any particular line of business, and they may consider openly a wide range of strategic alternatives. The objective of the enterprise is not to continue doing any particular thing indefinitely, but rather to find the best way of deploying the company's capital and other resources. Mergers, acquisitions, and divestments are natural activities. Indeed, a key responsibility of for-profit organizations is to identify businesses that should be sold off, as well as to probe the desirability of striking out in new directions. The name "General Electric" (GE) tells us very little about the wide range of business that GE conducts today. As one person put it, the idea of being faithful to any product line either on the basis of sunk costs or tradition is "to sow the seeds of decline."[6] Of course, many for-profits have an interest in maintaining historical ties to particular fields of activity—a world in which Ford does not make cars would seem strange to many—but there's no escaping the rude truth that in 2004, the fiftieth year of the Fortune 500, only 71 of the 1,877 companies ever to have appeared on the list had been there since the start.[7]

The directors of nonprofits, in contrast, have not only the same legal duties of care and loyalty as board members in both sectors, but also what Daniel Kurtz calls a duty of "obedience."[8] This additional obligation commits trustees and directors to "act with fidelity to the organization's stated mission, within the bounds of the law." If a nonprofit board wishes to alter the fundamental objectives of the organization, "the participation and assent of some representative of the general public—for example, a state attorney general—and the agreement of a court may be required."[9]

In the nonprofit world, "organization itself has to be an outgrowth of mission and purpose," as Hanna Gray, a distinguished former president of the University of Chicago, explains:[10]

> There are basic reasons why academic institutions are organized and governed as they are, in the service of education and research and of excellence in these pursuits. Faculty are not just "professionals" with a commitment to their professions outside the institution as well as to the institution, . . . or odd types who tend to want collegial and complex decision-making. They are individual talents and intellectual entrepreneurs, demanding developers of their disciplines . . . who have in fact certain constitutional rights in the process of governance and who hold the most important authority that exists in a university, that of making ultimate academic judgments. And boards exist in part to ensure this freedom and creativity and to protect the processes and the health of the environment that make them possible. In short, they exist for the sustenance of a mission, for the perpetuation of an institution in which it is embodied over time in such a way that the future is not mortgaged to the present and, by fiduciary obligation, for the direct care and preservation of corporate assets entrusted specifically for the pursuit of a particular mission and its related goals.

In short, the governance of an academic institution is derived directly from its mission and from the way in which that mission is carried out by faculty. Other charitable nonprofits would define themselves in entirely different ways. It is no more likely that a nonprofit dedicated to improving the neighborhood on the south side of Chicago would become a university than it is that the University of Chicago would forget why it was created. Nonprofits are such a variegated lot precisely because each can be expected to have a strong attachment to a particular mission—an attachment that often lasts for generations. Harvard University is the oldest "corporation" on the American continent and has been a leading institution of higher education for more than three centuries. The American Philosophical Society was founded in 1743, and the New-York Historical Society celebrated its two hundredth birthday in 2004.

Nonprofits may, and often do, extend their reach—wisely or

unwisely—for either programmatic or financial reasons. What is today the Foundation for Child Development has been in existence for over a hundred years and started out as the Association for the Aid of Crippled Children. Whereas for-profit corporations can return capital to their shareholders, the "nondistribution constraint" prohibits nonprofits from even considering the option of returning any excess funds to "owners"— and thus inclines them toward expansion.

John C. Whitehead, on the basis of extensive experience at Goldman Sachs in the for-profit sector and as a trustee of numerous nonprofit organizations, including the International Rescue Committee, has provided a succinct summary of the central point:

> A for-profit board has an obligation to get out of a bad business while a nonprofit board may have an obligation to stay in, if it is to be true to its mission.

Focusing on mission is not, however, a simple matter; and nonprofits often face the difficult task of choosing among a variety of worthwhile activities within their area of emphasis. Then, in choosing among a multiple set of options, they need to seek what Kevin Guthrie calls "maximum return on mission." In Guthrie's words,

> Lots of people like to talk about how nonprofits must pursue a double bottom line. And how that is more complex. This doesn't get totally at the issue. It is also a question of primacy. The nonprofit must use financial resources to serve its mission. It deploys financial assets, strategy, etc. to deliver a social benefit. A for-profit organization also pursues non-quantifiable objectives, but at the end of the day its objective is to maximize shareholder return.
>
> It follows that a nonprofit must come up with ways to measure not its financial return on invested capital, but its return on mission. This is really hard. How does it know it is having an impact? How does it measure its progress? Assessments of impact must be expressed not only in terms of the achievement of goals, but in terms of how leaders are measured. Successful nonprofits can lose sight of this and begin to evaluate themselves solely on the basis of financial results.

At the end of the chapter I will return to this key distinction in discussing the ways in which constraints on nonprofits differ fundamentally from those that operate in the corporate world. First, however, I want to discuss changes over the last several decades in the contexts and constraints that have affected the for-profit sector generally, and, by extension, the nonprofit sector too.

Changing Contexts and Constraints

Boards in both sectors operate within the settings that the world gives them at any point in time. There is simply no denying that the scandals of the last half dozen years, the attendant media attention, and the regulatory consequences have changed the assumptions and presuppositions that affect board behavior.

Scandals and Their Consequences

The Enron and WorldCom debacles are widely seen as markers of an era characterized by arrogance, greed, and outrageous corporate behavior. The collapse of Enron in late 2001 and the subsequent WorldCom bankruptcy had devastating effects on shareholders, employees, vendors, and whole communities. The dramatic failures of these two companies attracted an unprecedented amount of attention that led to the publication of books and reports, the making of movies, and criminal charges for some corporate officers.[11] Other widely publicized cases include Tyco, Fannie Mae, and the handling of Richard Grasso's exit package at the New York Stock Exchange.

There are lessons aplenty in both the unraveling of once proud corporate giants and the travails of some nonprofits—lessons that speak directly to core questions of board governance to which we will return throughout this book. In noting these cases, I do not mean to suggest that bad behavior is anything like the norm in either sector; on the contrary, I agree with those who have found much to praise.[12] Bad behavior is truly exceptional. Still, there is no denying that abuses and outright criminality have had major effects on the regulatory climate and on how the public at large views the work of boards. These developments have also contributed to a genuine shift in the balance of power within many large corporations.

By far the most consequential regulatory response was the near unanimous passage of the Sarbanes-Oxley Act (SOX) on July 30, 2002, in the immediate aftermath of the Enron bankruptcy and right at the time that the full extent of the WorldCom collapse was being reported. SOX requires public companies that are regulated by the Securities and Exchange Commission (SEC) to meet new standards. It calls for full disclosure of financial reports, including off-balance-sheet transactions; requires that these reports be certified by the CEO and the CFO; insists that management establish and maintain an effective system of internal controls; requires companies to tell the SEC what happened when a director resigns; and stipulates that there must be a truly independent, financially literate audit committee. This committee must include at least one "financial expert" among its members. It is responsible for engaging an outside audit firm that, with the committee, will assess the effectiveness of internal controls and ensure that any "material weaknesses" in those controls are made public.[13]

Any piece of legislation this far-reaching is bound to generate debates over whether its requirements go too far or whether the benefits of the legislation outweigh the costs of compliance. It is well beyond the scope of this study to assess the validity of these criticisms. From my own experience as a (long-suffering) member of the audit committee of American Express both before and after SOX, I can attest to the dramatic increase in workload that accompanied the new legislation. In keeping with others, I, too, wonder if there are not ways in which the objectives of the act can be achieved without so many bells and whistles. In any case, SOX is now, for better or worse, a major regulatory constraint on how companies regulated by the SEC must operate.[14] As Ezra Zilkha (a wise man and an astute investor who has served on many boards) observed, "Sarbanes-Oxley would not have been needed if everyone had remembered what they were taught as children: 'Don't lie, don't cheat, don't steal.'" But he then added, "Nonetheless, Sarbanes-Oxley was needed because people are who they are."

One effect of SOX has been to make managers and owners of publicly traded companies more amenable to offers by private-equity investors to take over their firms. Even though this is not the primary reason for the explosive growth of the private-equity movement, which has been driven principally by the ready availability of cheap debt and the buoyancy of equity markets, it is easy to see why managers and directors alike might prefer to be freed from both the costs and the bother of what they may see as the excessive regulation that results from being a publicly traded company.[15] At the same time, as several commentators with experience running private-equity funds have emphasized, freedom from SOX cannot be a license to ignore financial controls. Independent directors, chosen by the private-equity firms, are often relied on to be sure that proper controls are in place.

An even more ominous deterrent to bad behavior than SOX may be the threat of criminal prosecutions. In an editorial that appeared the day after the Enron verdicts, the *Wall Street Journal* opined, "If anyone still thinks corporate chieftains are above the law, yesterday's 29 guilty verdicts against former Enron CEOs Jeffrey Skilling and Kenneth Lay should put that myth to rest." The editorial continues, "WorldCom CEO Bernie Ebbers is now facing 25 years . . . We think these convictions of individuals—some 30 in the Enron case alone—will do more to deter future corporate crime than anything in Sarbanes-Oxley."[16]

One presumably unintended consequence of the combination of SOX, criminal prosecutions, and the demise of Enron's accounting firm, Arthur Andersen, is that the accounting industry is widely perceived as having become much more conservative—too conservative in the minds of some. In the words of one commentator, "I think accounting firms, now fewer in number with more power than ever, are running scared in a way that is not productive." It has been alleged that accounting firms sometimes put their own interests ahead of the interests of their clients, though this is of course hard to judge. Indeed, one problem is that the power of accounting firms is insidious, in large part because tenets are not always clearly stated and may not be subject to open debate.

Several other commentators, including Herbert "Pug" Winokur, who served on the board of Enron, have said that this entire set of experiences has led directors to ask a troubling question: how is a director to know when he or she is being lied to—either by management or by accountants and lawyers retained by the firm? This basic question of integrity, and how it can be assessed, is one that we will return to in

Chapter 5. Let me anticipate that discussion by noting Winokur's conclusion: like it or not, directors simply have to be more proactive in probing the bona fides of all those on whom they rely for information.

Beyond Sarbanes-Oxley, there are other important changes in the context within which for-profit boards operate. First, there has been an unmistakable increase in scrutiny of the behavior of publicly traded companies—and of the effectiveness with which boards monitor this behavior. Investors, especially institutional investors, have become more aggressive in challenging the managements and boards of for-profit companies, and there are increasing references to "shareholder activism" and its effects. In a recent article, Institutional Shareholder Services (ISS) reported that thirty-one of fifty-one proxy fights that they studied ended in settlements, not votes, with concessions usually involving the award of one or more board seats to the challengers. Activists are not reluctant to launch fights, and they intend to keep the pressure on.[17]

One longtime observer of the corporate scene, Stephen Norman, secretary of American Express, notes that the average tenure of CEOs is shortening (see Chapter 5). Norman suspects that growing activism among shareholders has a great deal to do with this trend. Shareholders—and boards—simply will not put up with disappointing performance or evidence of a serious lack of judgment. The departures of Phillip Purcell at Morgan Stanley, Henry McKinnell at Pfizer, Robert Nardelli at Home Depot, and Richard Grasso at the New York Stock Exchange are frequently cited as cases in point.

Intensive scrutiny, especially by the media, has clearly become a more important constraint—and one more and more relevant to changes in corporate leadership. No one likes to be ridiculed or embarrassed, and many of us also prefer not to be challenged too aggressively by the media. This is certainly true of the members of governing boards. In recent years, the media have been much more active in tracking down questionable behavior and then sustaining a drumbeat of criticism. Stories in the *Wall Street Journal* and *Fortune* kept the pressure on executives at Enron, and apparently it was the press coverage more than the underlying business problems that bothered Ken Lay. The head of PR at Enron was quoted as saying, "I'm working for a delusional chairman who thinks all the company has is a PR problem that can be solved with a press release."[18]

Highly publicized debates over the leadership at Morgan Stanley, Pfizer, and Home Depot were certainly fueled by extensive press coverage. But perhaps the most striking example of the power of the media to affect the fate of a sitting CEO is the demise of Richard Grasso as the head of the New York Stock Exchange. As Professor Luigi Zingales at the University of Chicago Graduate School of Business observed, "In the case of Grasso and the NYSE, the SEC began to ask the NYSE board about its compensation practices after news of Grasso's compensation was published in the *Wall Street Journal*. The publication of that news and ensuing public outcry forced the same directors who voted for his compensation package to fire him . . . Although all directors of the NYSE had voted in favor of his compensation, once the information became public—and even the most pro-business newspapers characterized Grasso's compensation in a very negative light—many directors changed their position."[19]

Freedom from intense, day-to-day public scrutiny is another appeal of going private. The purchase of Chrysler by the private-equity firm Cerberus will provide a good test of whether the world of private investment will in fact allow management to "focus with greater intensity on the day-to-day business of producing better cars."[20] A real advantage of private-equity ownership is that management and directors are able to spend more time on key business issues (rather than on process questions) and do not have to worry about how analysts and investors will react to small blips in quarterly earnings—which are, after all, not reported. The focus is value creation. This emphasis on business performance presumes that at least some of the individuals named to the boards of private companies have real operating skill and knowledge of the industry. As several knowledgeable people noted, there is a danger that investors who are "financial engineers" will dominate these boards and be more concerned about capital structures and quick returns than about building economic value.

Several other broad changes in context have occurred. One has to do with what it means to be a shareholder. Increasingly, economic interests are being separated from formal ownership interests by the use of derivatives. In addition, the growth of index funds, which involve indirect ownership of a great many companies, complicates enormously the exercise of ownership responsibilities. Should index funds give back to owners the right to vote, as brokers do in the case of stock held in street names? These are not new issues, though they may well be more complex now than in earlier days. There is even speculation about the possibility of selling the vote, since mutual funds, for example, are generally not interested in voting their shares, whereas hedge funds might well be willing to pay something to control more votes.

The ironies of deciding who really represents ownership interests were brought home to me some years ago by Charles Exley's experiences at the time of the AT&T takeover of NCR. Although Exley himself had tens of millions of dollars of his own at risk, he nonetheless found himself challenged by representatives of institutional shareholders who had, as he put it, "not a nickel of their own money at stake." Even more interesting is the conundrum presented by index funds at that time—before they were as important as they are now. How were funds that held large amounts of both AT&T and NCR stock, and thus faced real conflict issues, to vote?[21] These were major complications that the NCR board, working with Exley, had to consider in deciding how to respond to the overtures from AT&T.

The rapid growth of pools of private equity and the increasing number of firms that are privately held illustrate one response to such issues.[22] Ownership interests are clearly represented in the case of privately held companies, including start-ups financed by venture capitalists and other firms taken private or kept private. In these situations, the interests of the real owners and the managers are closely aligned—much more closely than one finds in the publicly traded part of the for-profit sector. Both board members and managers have real "skin in the game." The opportunities for skilled executives to make large amounts of money leading privately held firms (assuming they are successful!) has had another effect on publicly traded companies: it has increased the competition for talent.

The growing use of governance rankings and governance quotients issued by Institutional Shareholder Services and other monitors of board performance presents yet another issue for board members. The way these organizations weight the various parameters included in their measures is often obscure. What is a director to think if his company's governance index is 39 and his competitor's is 93? As one commentator asked, "Should he execute his governance committee?" My own view is that boards should take seriously such rankings, but at the same time the board should not be the prisoner of an outsider's view of what constitutes good governance. There is nothing wrong with standing one's ground in the face of adverse rankings if, after careful consideration, that seems the right thing to do.[23]

Next I want to examine the spillover effects of these shifts in context and constraints on the nonprofit sector. This discussion will lead into an examination of the differences between the sectors in the kinds of external constraints that limit board options.

REGULATORY AND MEDIA CONSTRAINTS

In the world of the charitable nonprofits, there is no real counterpart to the scandals that have beset companies such as Enron and WorldCom. I cannot think of a case in which a major university, museum, or nonprofit service provider has been forced into the equivalent of bankruptcy. Of course, there have been controversies and instances of questionable behavior among nonprofits, but their effects have been less consequential.

Most commonly, issues in the nonprofit world have centered on the compensation, expenses, and perks of presidents and executive directors.[24] There was, for example, the spending scandal at American University in 2005, where lavish spending by former president Benjamin Ladner provoked an investigation by the Senate Finance Committee and led subsequently to major changes in governance. The Getty Trust in California found itself enmeshed in a number of highly publicized disputes, which ended in 2006 with the departure of CEO Barry Munitz, after numerous press accounts of questionable expenses and lack of adequate board oversight. The secretary of the Smithsonian, Larry Small, resigned in 2007 after an internal audit and congressional committees raised questions about expenses that he had charged to the Smithsonian.

Heightened scrutiny of compensation practices and perks has led trustees of nonprofits to reexamine both their policies and their oversight mechanisms. Many in the field have discussed whether to adopt SOX requirements voluntarily, since SOX applies only to for-profit companies that register securities with the SEC. A number of nonprofits have established separate audit committees and formalized processes for reviewing the compensation and expenses of presidents/CEOs, although few nonprofit boards have adopted SOX fully.[25] Many nonprofits depend on fund-raising mechanisms that raise questions about independence and conflicts that, although important, differ in major respects from the corresponding questions in the for-profit sector. Furthermore, nonprofits may be reluctant to divert scarce resources to pay for the elaborate monitoring of functions, as well as the complex reporting, required of for-profit companies.[26] For these and other reasons, I agree with those who oppose a mechanical application of SOX to nonprofits.

My own view is that lawmakers should resist the temptation to respond to every instance of perceived bad behavior by passing a new statute. Jon Small, a former lawyer at Debevoise & Plimpton, and more recently the chairman of the Nonprofit Coordinating Committee of New York, noted that ninety-two of ninety-four abuses mentioned in a recent Senate study were already illegal! It is ironic that much of the pressure for more detailed regulations stems from the Internal Revenue Service's failure to invest enough resources to make sure that existing standards of right behavior are enforced.[27] Regulatory structures are, and should remain, the primary constraints on behavior in the nonprofit sector, but we should not have to rely more heavily on them than we do now.

A second set of constraints in the nonprofit world consists of those captured by phrases such as "media scrutiny" and "bad publicity." Like for-profit board members, trustees of nonprofits care deeply about both their own reputations and how the organizations with which they are associated are perceived. The changes in leadership, and in board governance, that occurred at the Getty Trust were, without question, provoked by the unrelenting media coverage of management practices, by the *Los Angeles Times* in particular. In the world of major museums, the Museum of Modern Art (MoMA) in New York City has surely suffered from the unfavorable publicity associated with the revelation of a largely secret fund used to supplement the salary of its director, Glenn D. Lowry.[28]

This "glass bowl" character of governance in many nonprofit settings, especially in higher education and the health care field, assures one kind of accountability that, if acted on in time, can be a protection against serious blunders. Or, if it comes after the fact, it can inform the need for changes in both staffing and governance. To be sure, intense media coverage can focus attention on the wrong issues and divert energy from questions that are more fundamental, but in general I am persuaded that the relatively high degree of scrutiny characteristic of colleges and universities is beneficial.

Both nonprofits and for-profits are also subject to internally constructed process constraints. Such constraints are especially important in colleges and universities. Long-established internal decision-making processes, including delegation to faculty of the responsibility for many curricular matters, as well as for academic requirements and academic appointments, constrain what trustees can and should do. By-laws and articles of incorporation serve similar purposes elsewhere in the nonprofit world and among for-profits.[29]

Regulation, media scrutiny, and internal process requirements are not, however, the most significant constraints on either nonprofit organizations or for-profit companies. Markets and quasi markets are almost always more powerful constraining mechanisms (except in the case of grant-making foundations, which I discuss at the end of the chapter), although they operate quite differently in the two sectors.

MARKET CONSTRAINTS AND "OWNERS"

The best-known companies operate in public markets, and dissatisfied shareholders can register displeasure simply by disposing of their stock (the "Wall Street Rule"). Share prices are quoted constantly, and rapid adjustments in prices and valuations tell their own stories—which of course financial analysts and media spin in one way or another. Shifts in market valuations represent more or less instantaneous votes of confidence (or no confidence) in corporate action or inaction. It was the marketplace that eventually shut off commercial paper financing for Enron, and short sellers played a major role in putting pressure on Enron's stock price and thus on the company itself.[30]

For-profit organizations may have their futures altered dramatically by external buyers or sellers, as anyone who has participated in a corporate merger or takeover will attest. In such situations, the ultimate sanction is a proxy vote by shareholders to unseat recalcitrant directors. Having been unseated myself (along with the other members of my "class" of directors, in the final stages of the AT&T takeover of NCR), I can attest to the reality of this ultimate source of shareholder power. Large institutional investors are hardly bashful in letting companies know what they think about potential takeovers.

This story illustrates an important point: we should not glorify mergers or assume that the market always knows best. For reasons that were never clear, AT&T decided that moving actively into the computer field by acquiring NCR was "a strategic imperative" (in the words of Robert Allen, the CEO and chairman of AT&T at the time). After a hard-fought proxy battle, AT&T was able to use its financial muscle to gain control of NCR—a takeover that ended up costing AT&T and its shareholders billions of dollars. The NCR of that time was essentially destroyed, although it has since been born again after having been spun off by AT&T. As Exley put it, one lesson of this sad experience is that "a sick elephant can kill a healthy dog by just falling on it" (a phrase he attributes to the legendary head of the Burroughs Corporation, Ray W. MacDonald).

Technological changes can also compel boards of for profits to shift directions. In the 1970s and 1980s, IBM was forced to shift from heavy reliance on mainframes to distributed processing. As Charles Exley, then CEO and chairman of NCR, explains what happened,

> IBM . . . was the victim of a technology revolution which spelled big trouble for the company no matter what they did. When you make the best milk bottle in town [mainframe computers] and someone discovers milk cartons [distributed processing], you confront one huge problem to which there are no easy solutions.

More generally and less dramatically, capital markets are constantly regulating the behavior of for-profit companies—especially those that cannot rely solely on retained earnings to finance themselves. In many situations, corporate strategies and their implementation are applauded or dismissed via third-party decisions to provide or withhold capital. Specialists in industrial organization and corporate finance will continue to debate just how efficient capital markets really are, whether "short-termism" is a serious malady in America today, and if complaints of underinvestment in certain fields are justified.[31] No one doubts, however, that markets in general influence and ultimately constrain board decisions.

This is hardly to say that we are living in an "Adam Smith age" in which atomistic units respond automatically to the signals provided by impersonal, unseen market forces. There are plenty of opportunities for boards to make big mistakes, just as there are opportunities to find the right new direction before others do.

In the nonprofit world, certain constraints also mimic market forces and resemble those present in the for-profit sector. For example, the leaders of performing-arts organizations remind us regularly that market demand matters greatly to the health of their organizations, as it does to museums and many historical societies that rely on paying visitors for revenues. Such entities and many other nonprofits that provide services also have to pass what are, in effect, market tests of another kind when they recruit volunteers and appeal to donors to raise funds. We are reminded every day that educational institutions compete vigorously with each other for students and faculty, as well as for charitable contributions and government funding. As their stepped-up advertising attests, nonprofit hospitals and health care providers compete for patients as well as for private and public funding.

Important as they are, the market and pseudomarket constraints faced by nonprofits tend to be less circumscribing than those encountered by directors of for-profit entities. Nonprofits can choose among a wider variety of objectives, and they can assign a wider variety of weights to different objectives, than can for-profit entities, which are presumed by their shareholders and others to have earnings and profits always in mind. In the nonprofit world, outputs and outcomes are harder to measure, and constituencies harder to define. Normally, no single measure of success is analogous to the proverbial bottom line for a business.

One of our commentators with experience on both nonprofit and for-profit boards (Nicholas Donatiello) argues that "owners" provide clear guideposts in the for-profit sector that are just not available to nonprofit boards. In his words,

> Directors of for-profit companies have an absolute obligation to act in the best interest of shareholders. While there is much judgment involved, including choosing the right [time] horizon and respecting employees and customers who are critical to the long-term success of the enterprise, there is no uncertainty about the

objective. In nonprofits, determining what should guide decisions is a more complex calculus. The mission of the organization is seldom a sufficient navigational beacon. Often the interests of the constituencies being served must be balanced against those of donors, members, and volunteers.[32]

Nonprofit boards enjoy more freedom from market constraints than do their for-profit cousins for another reason. As a general rule, fundamental choices can be made by nonprofit institutions without the worry that these decisions may be subject to abrupt reversal by market forces. After all, nonprofit entities are not routinely for sale, and mergers and closings in this sector tend to occur only rarely, when nonprofit institutions are in deep trouble. One would not find an NCR–AT&T takeover example in this sector. The lack of regular buy-and-sell markets for nonprofit organizations, and the almost complete absence of takeovers, is a major difference between the two sectors. It helps explain why, as we noted earlier, companies are much less likely to have long lives than, say, any of the numerous colleges and other nonprofit organizations that have been in existence since the eighteenth century.

I think it is fair to say that, overall, nonprofits as a group are far less closely constrained by external forces than are for-profit organizations. The combination of global competition, daily market checks, aggressive institutional investors ("owners"), and highly engaged business media is powerful. Nonprofits, in sharp contrast, have no well-defined owners or external overseers (apart from the board itself), and in fact, only rather poor substitutes for them exist. In rare cases, the attorney general of the state in which the nonprofit entity operates (or is chartered), or the courts in that state, will become involved—but only in extreme circumstances.[33] These politically chosen representatives of the public interest are, ultimately, the nonprofit world's owners of the underlying assets, but they exercise far less oversight than do owners and their surrogates in the for-profit world.

There are, however, some quasi owners in the nonprofit sector who are likely to exert influence well before the attorney general or the courts are aware of a problem. In the case of membership organizations, the members themselves serve this function. Individual directors and trustees are a second broad class of potential watchdogs. Although the law is not as clear as it might be concerning "standing" in the nonprofit sector, both members and directors plainly have the right to bring suits in court. Beyond these groups, however, accountability is hard to pinpoint. In the usual case, no constituency has legal power to elect trustees or directors; most nonprofit boards are self-perpetuating.

Large donors may be thought to constitute another set of quasi owners, since their largesse is critical to the long-term well-being of many organizations. Understandably, nonprofits are reluctant to offend generous patrons. This is partly a matter of feelings of obligation and of good faith—respecting wishes and intentions. Trustees of foundations may well hark back to the interests of a principal donor when considering directions and priorities, but this is generally more a matter of respect than of obligation. In other contexts, concern for the views of donors can be a matter of prudence—especially if the donors are still alive and might make additional gifts! Boards of colleges and universities are often sensitive to the likely response of alumni to decisions they might make, as are boards of organizations of all kinds that have established donor bases. Public universities must be alert to the views of key legislators. The Smithsonian, a unique institution that nonetheless is in some ways similar to large public universities, is subject to scrutiny by Congress, which has demonstrated that it can exert influence by refusing to approve appropriations or by simply embarrassing those charged with the governance of the institution.[34]

More generally, accountability is usually related to dependence, and any nonprofit that is dependent on a particular individual, corporation, government funder, or constituency will pay more than passing attention to the views of the individual, entity, or group in question. This is a major reason why the boards of nonprofits that value their independence attach such importance to achieving a diversity of funding sources. Of course, most nonprofits are dependent on far more than donors, and the same principles apply to audiences, clients, and other potential purchasers of services. Nonprofits that lack a well-established base of donors or that must rely on their ability to attract substantial earned income can be nearly as likely to go out of business as a family restaurant or small shop, though exits are heavily concentrated among new, and small, entities.

The wide range of circumstances notwithstanding, the fact remains that significant numbers of nonprofits function for years, sometimes struggling along, without attracting the attention of powerful outsiders. Because of the lack of access to most of the mechanisms for radical transformation that markets represent, some nonprofits may survive too long. The questions of when and how to transform, or even to dissolve, a nonprofit entity are both major challenges to boards and of great significance as issues of public policy. But they attract attention only when a combination of the press and political interests alerts the general public to the travails of a venerable organization such as the New-York Historical Society (which, in the late 1980s and early 1990s, was in danger of being unable to continue to support its outstanding library).[35] Generally speaking, by the time an alert of this kind has been sounded, a number of perhaps promising options will have been closed off altogether or made much more expensive.

Finally, a special note is in order about constraints, "ownership," and accountability in the sector in which I worked for eighteen years: the world of the large grant-making foundation. This subsector is more insulated from external constraints than are either for-profits or other nonprofits. Few constituencies can be relied on to challenge the leadership of a foundation or the directions it is taking. In contrast to the university world, there are no faculty members, students, parents, or alumni to function as counterweights—and no student newspapers! In addition, grantees are usually reluctant to criticize or complain. A leader of one foundation is reputed to have said to someone who was about to assume a similar role, "You will never again have a bad lunch—or hear the truth!"

As noted earlier, foundations are, of course, subject to the terms of deeds of gifts and the charters that established them, and they are likely to feel an obligation to respect the wishes of their donors. Foundations are subject to some degree of public scrutiny, as well as to myriad government regulations, and, on occasion, to review, if not discipline, by membership organizations such as the Council on Foundations. Nonetheless, trustees retain a great deal of leeway within which to set directions and make choices. *In my view, the trustees of foundations have more opportunity to affect institutional performance than do the directors of any other set of entities in either the for-profit or nonprofit sector.*

This is not at all a bad thing, assuming that proper oversight is provided by responsible boards of trustees. Considerable freedom of action is one of the great strengths of independent foundations, and a major justification for the tax privileges that they enjoy. Such freedom is especially important in a society in which it is often hard to generate support for programs that serve broad public purposes. In my view, our society needs private initiatives able to overcome bureaucratic impediments to change, as well as other forces of inertia, and to test out ideas. I would much prefer to live in a world in which freedom of action leads to some poor decisions (as will inevitably be the case) than in a world in which foundations are fearful to strike out in new directions or to support unpopular causes. The challenge is to find ways of preserving freedom of action while simultaneously meeting proper standards of accountability. It is in reconciling these objectives that trustees of foundations have a decisive role to play.

* * * * *

IN THIS CHAPTER I have outlined the roles and responsibilities of boards in both the for-profit and the nonprofit sectors, as well as described the contexts and constraints that inescapably influence the decisions made by directors and trustees. Board members in both sectors have the obligation to steer their organizations as best they can, given the choices that their settings present to them. It is not, however, for boards alone to define strategies, never mind execute on them. Boards can be effective only if they develop a strong partnership with the day-to-day leadership of the organizations for which they are responsible. In the next chapter I will discuss the evolving relationship between boards and their CEOs/presidents. Getting this key relationship right is arguably the most important challenge faced by boards of directors and trustees.

2

Board Leadership

ONE OF THE MOST hotly debated issues in corporate governance is how best to define the relationship between the board and the CEO. Commentator after commentator told me that this is *the key question*. Some argue passionately for separating the roles of chairman and CEO, which has long been the practice in the nonprofit sector and is the norm today in the United Kingdom and in Canada. Others believe that giving one person both roles is the most effective way to provide leadership for the company and the board. Still others believe that the right answer to this question, as to most interesting questions, is, "It all depends."

I am convinced that there is much to be said for taking a practical, "situational" perspective. But that does not mean that we should be agnostic about what arrangement would be best in a perfect world, and I begin the chapter by assessing the conceptual arguments in favor of both separating and combining the roles. My conclusion, let me say up front, is that the arguments in favor of the separate chairman model are persuasive at the level of first principles. Certain practical considerations, however, argue in favor of the single CEO-chairman model in particular situations. Taking into account these situational considerations leads to an examination of the increasingly popular lead director model, whether seen as a long-term organizational solution or as a transitional stage in the evolution of the relationship between boards and their CEOs.

My own intuition is that the lead director model may indeed prove to be transitional and that we will see a slow-paced movement toward a separation of the roles of chief executive officer and chairman. The chapter concludes with a postscript in which I discuss the reasons for the persistent differences that we observe in the typical board–CEO relationship when we compare the for-profit and nonprofit sectors.

A Separate Chairman?
The Conceptual Arguments for and against Splitting the Roles

Splitting the roles of chairman and CEO in the for-profit sector has two major advantages. A separate chairman

(1) Positions the board to exercise properly its key oversight responsibility vis-à-vis the CEO, reduces the risk of autocratic rule by creating a regime of checks and balances, and promotes a healthy dynamic in board deliberations

(2) Divides a heavy workload by allowing the CEO to concentrate on managing the business while the chairman concentrates on managing board affairs

The fact that the CEO works for the board, which represents the shareholders, is a prima facie case for separating the board's oversight function and the CEO's management function. As a writer for the *Financial Times* argues, "There is a clear conflict of interest between leading a board that oversees a company's management and being the senior manager."[1] Worries about excessive concentration of power in the hands of one person are widely shared. In the words of John Whitehead, "One man rule is a bad idea. A single CEO-chairman can do great damage before being reined in—often when it is too late, or almost too late." Separating the roles of chairman and CEO is the most obvious way of addressing this concern. Paul Volcker agrees. He writes, in his characteristically direct way, "The board's inescapable and prime responsibility is hiring and firing the CEO. The firing part is hard, often botched, and typically delayed. A chairman will have a greater sense of authority and responsibility in his own eyes, in the eyes of the board and the CEO."[2]

Following this checks-and-balances line of argument, some management specialists have claimed that "corporate disasters can be traced to concentrating power at the top."[3] Dick Debs, one of the "eight grumpy old men" who led the revolt at Morgan Stanley resulting in the ouster of Philip Purcell as CEO and chairman, is quoted as concluding: "Our struggle showed the fault lines in the US system of corporate governance. Here we had one man who was the boss, the CEO and the chairman, who was able to stack his board with friends and allies, keeping them happy with rich compensation and extensive perks, isolated from the people who worked for the firm."[4]

It is certainly true that decisions to split the chairman and CEO roles have often followed scandals or near-scandals. Conversations with a number of experienced directors have led me to the not surprising conclusion that board members who have been through an excruciating crisis involving the performance of a CEO are the most likely to be strong advocates of splitting the roles. Several people with whom I spoke emphasized that in earlier days they did not favor separating the roles, but they certainly do now—and at least one went on to describe his "conversion" in passionate language that had almost a theological tinge. Having "been there" obviously helps people see what can happen when power is concentrated in a single CEO-chairman.[5]

It is tempting to cite WorldCom and Enron as examples of disasters that occurred in spite of a separation of the roles of chairman and CEO, but in both cases the chairman was the former CEO and was deeply implicated in the problems that led to the collapse of the company. These cases hardly illustrate how a separate chairman can be an effective counterweight to a wrong-headed CEO. In fact, I believe that having a former CEO serve as non-executive chairman can have a decidedly negative effect: such an arrangement can interfere with the often necessary task of reexamining directions taken in the past and reaiming the organization.

One telling piece of evidence in favor of separate roles comes from the insurance companies that must assess the risk they accept in writing policies covering directors' and officers' liability. Lou Ann Layton, managing director in charge of national directors' and officers' liability insurance at Marsh, has been quoted as saying, "We always ask, 'Are you considering dividing the titles, and if not, why don't you?'"[6] Peter Tulupman, a spokesman for AIG, has observed that companies that split the roles are starting to ask for discounts. The Council of Institutional Investors, whose members include most large pension funds, favors having independent directors as board chairs.

A related argument concerns the effect of splitting the roles on board dynamics. In explaining why he has come to believe so strongly in separating the positions of chairman and CEO, one highly experienced director said simply, "Having a separate non-executive chairman just changes the entire dynamic; it is a way to avoid cronyism, and it both encourages more open discussion among board members and allows management people below the CEO level to feel freer to talk with the chairman." In explaining why he favors having a non-executive chairman, Ezra Zilkha stresses a related need: "for board members to have a legitimate place to go if they have concerns or questions."

Nicholas Katzenbach, former attorney general and undersecretary of state, as well as a onetime general counsel at IBM and later chairman of the WorldCom board after it was reconstituted, also favors a separate non-executive chair. Katzenbach worked closely with Robert Kennedy, and he told me that Kennedy was very, very good at getting each participant in a discussion to say exactly what the participant believed. In the Cuban Missile Crisis, Katzenbach recalls that Bobby Kennedy did not want the president to be part of the discussions because he knew that the president's presence would be intimidating and that the others would not speak up. Katzenbach's analogy in the corporate context is that having the CEO chair board meetings can inhibit a candid exchange of views. The dynamics will be better with someone else presiding, Katzenbach opined, and this is also why executive sessions, without the CEO even in attendance, are so valuable.

The second main reason for splitting the roles of chairman and CEO emphasizes the need to achieve a sensible division of labor in the governance of large and complex organizations. As Larry Bossidy has observed, "The CEO job is much more challenging today. Worldwide competition is more intense; because of the Internet, required speed of response is much faster; constituents demand more attention, and more attention now. In short, the CEO needs more help."

If the right people can be found for what should be two highly complementary roles, and *if* the right relationship can be established between them (and these are two big ifs), there is much to be said for dividing the work. The CEO's focus should be on running the business, and it can be very helpful if the CEO has a competent colleague who can manage board matters. An effective non-executive chairman will facilitate constructive interactions within the board and between the board and management—without competing with the CEO or interfering in the management of the business itself. A non-executive chairman can also be a helpful point of contact with large institutional investors, giving them, as outsiders, a recognized place to go to raise questions and voice concerns. Increasingly, large institutional investors expect to have access to the board, as well as to the CEO, and it is in everyone's interest to have such interactions channeled appropriately.[7]

In certain contexts the presence of a non-executive chairman can also protect both the CEO and the board from what the late Alan Pifer, president of the Carnegie Corporation, referred to as "the occasional bully who can appear on any board." Controlling such behavior is necessary, if other board members and senior staff members are not to be intimidated. A separate chairman may be more effective than a CEO in curbing such tendencies and, if necessary, in seeking the resignation of the offender. The CEO, after all, works for the board—and, therefore, for any bullies who may be on it. The chief executive should not have to deal personally with the inappropriate behavior of cantankerous board members.

Furthermore, as Louise Parent, general counsel of American Express, has pointed out, the law and regulatory requirements make it clear that the CEO simply should not (and cannot) do certain things: lead the process of nominating and selecting new board members; evaluate the work of the board collectively, as well as the performance of individual directors; orchestrate the work of an independent audit committee; and organize a responsible process for evaluating the CEO and setting the CEO's own compensation. To be sure, these tasks can be handled collectively by independent directors through appropriate committee structures, but a non-executive chairman can ensure that they are carried out in an orderly, well-coordinated way.

It is instructive that Mark Hurd, CEO of Hewlett-Packard, when asked why he had not paid more attention to the board's investigation of board leaks, acknowledged that he was at two meetings where the investigation was discussed, but said that he did not pay attention because the investigation was not as high a priority as running the company. "I pick my spots where I dive for details," he is reported to have said.[8] Having been made CEO in the aftermath of the firing of Carly Fiorina and in the context of a heated debate over the direction of the company, it was entirely understandable—and sensible—for Hurd to want to focus on getting his hands around the core business/strategic/management issues at HP.

Unfortunately, however, the non-executive chairman, Patricia Dunn, did not handle the investigation of board leaks well. Because neither of the two big ifs was satisfied, this effort to take advantage of the principle of division of labor, as well as to provide proper oversight of a new CEO, failed. But the lesson here is not that splitting the roles is inadvisable; the CEO should not be expected to do everything, especially in early days at the helm of a ship that needs strong steering. Rather, the lesson is that it is critically important to have the right combination of highly competent players in place, and to have a board that functions well in general (is the opposite of dysfunctional, as various commentators have described the HP board). An even broader lesson of the bizarre HP experience is that a well-conceived formal leadership structure is, in and of itself, no guarantee of good governance.[9]

The Merck board's 2005 decision to elect an insider, Richard Clark, as CEO—but not to ask Clark to start out by serving as chairman too—has had a much happier history. Like Hurd, Clark needed to concentrate on core business issues. At the time, the entire pharmaceutical industry was being challenged, Merck was embroiled in the VIOXX litigation, and major organizational and strategic issues inside the company needed to be addressed. For reasons peculiar to the Merck situation, an unusual organizational structure was put in place for a limited time. A small executive committee was created, consisting of three independent directors: Larry Bossidy, former chairman and CEO of AlliedSignal, who chaired Merck's Compensation Committee; Samuel Thier, former head of the Institute of Medicine in Washington and most recently CEO of Partners HealthCare in Boston, who chaired the Public Policy Committee; and me, as the chairman of Merck's Governance Committee and the special committee investigating the development and marketing of VIOXX. This executive committee, chaired by Bossidy, was asked to discharge the chairman's role in a collaborative fashion, on the explicit understanding that this was to be a transitional arrangement.

Outside observers questioned whether this seemingly unwieldy beast could walk at all, never mind run. In fact, however, the arrangement worked well—in large part because the three of us had complementary skills, were comfortable working together, and had a high regard for Dick Clark, who performed superbly as CEO. The arrangement was helpful to Clark, he said, in part because he gained assistance, feedback, and support from three directors, each of whom had something to contribute in the areas that each of us knew best. Relatively minor aspects of this arrangement might have been improved upon, but overall, Clark and the Merck board judged the experiment a success.

In addressing the larger question of whether separation of the roles of chairman and CEO can serve corporate goals effectively in a large number of situations and over a considerable period of time, it is helpful to consider the extensive experience in the United Kingdom and Canada. Splitting the roles is the norm in these countries, and testimony from, among others, David Kimbell, co-leader of Spencer Stuart's board services in Europe and worldwide chairman of Spencer Stuart from 1987 to 1999, is instructive. Kimbell writes, "Most observers, as well as chairmen and CEOs themselves, would agree that separating the roles has been good for British business."[10]

A Booz Allen Hamilton study of CEO turnover and various succession models found that, in 2005, shareholder returns were higher in situations in which the CEO and chairman positions were separate and the chairman was not the previous CEO. These results held for both Europe and North America. A later Booz Allen Hamilton study found that "in 2006, *all* of the underperforming North American CEOs with long tenure had either held the additional title of company chairman or served under a chairman who was the former CEO."[11] In both 2006 and the nine-year period ending in 2006, the study found, investors earned appreciably lower returns if the CEO was also the chairman of the company or served under a chairman who used to be the CEO.[12]

The conceptual arguments for separating the roles of the chairman and CEO are powerful. What are the main offsetting arguments? As several commentators have noted, the strongest points in favor of combining the roles focus on practical reasons why a division of responsibilities either will have bad consequences or simply is not needed, and I examine these propositions in the next section. In addition, however, there is one conceptual argument in favor of having the same person serve as CEO and chairman that needs to be considered:

> *The one-person CEO-chairman model avoids the risk of confused signals, or disharmony, at the top of the organization.*

There is the risk of ending up with, in the words of one observer, "ambiguous leadership, split allegiances . . . , and an incoherent vision for the company's future."[13] Such an arrangement can create the potential for rivalry between the chairman and the CEO, leading to ineffectual compromise rather than crisp decisiveness. In short, it may be more efficient to have a single individual responsible for everything.

There are two rejoinders to this line of argument:

(1) Although it is certainly possible to have individuals in these positions who are so at odds that the company will be damaged by the latent if not actual conflict, there is absolutely no reason to create (or tolerate) such a situation. Great care must be taken to define the roles clearly and to be sure that the chairman will not undermine the CEO—who has to be, without question, the individual responsible for leading the company. The chairman, in turn, should be responsible for leading the board, but quietly and in ways that underscore the partnership between the chairman and the CEO. Except in unusual circumstances, there is no reason for the chairman to speak on behalf of the company to the press or to others outside the boardroom (meeting with large institutional shareholders at their request, and with the approval of the CEO, can be one such circumstance). The CEO should run the annual meetings and handle conference calls with analysts.

(2) Efficiency is not the objective; maximizing outcomes for shareholders is. Autocracies sometimes make for efficient governments—with "the trains running on time"—but they are not good models for providing responsible oversight, stimulating productive debate, or achieving complex objectives that often require balancing a number of competing interests.

I do not believe that the conceptual arguments for and against separating the roles of CEO and chairman are anything close to even. In my view, the conceptual case for separation is extremely powerful—close to compelling. Why, then, do so many American companies continue to combine the roles? The answer is that practical considerations can overwhelm conceptual arguments and rebut any general presumption in favor of having a separate chairman.

Practical Considerations: The Need to Take a Situational Perspective

In any given situation, directors may conclude that the CEO and chairman roles should be combined for three practical reasons:

(1) In corporate America today, most CEOs want both titles (for status and other reasons), and it can be dangerous to offend them. Insisting on separating the roles can also make it harder to recruit an outstanding CEO.
(2) The right candidate for chairman may not be available.
(3) Splitting the roles of chairman and CEO is an unnecessarily contentious way of meeting the need for checks and balances and achieving a good division of labor. Effective use of the lead director model is an attractive alternative that avoids, in particular, the status issue associated with depriving the CEO of the chairman title.

To begin with the status issue, it is widely understood that most CEOs want to be seen as fully in charge, and it continues to be true in the United States, though apparently not elsewhere, that CEOs who are *only* CEOs sometimes feel that they have been given half the job and are not trusted with full responsibility. A British commentator suggested that this is the "alpha male (or female)" syndrome at work and that "a combination of crowd psychology and vanity is probably to blame. No one wants to turn up at the golf club as a mere chief executive, no matter how well-rewarded his job and big his company, to be surrounded by two-title guys."[14]

This comment may overstate the status aspect of the question, but status does matter to people and separating the roles can raise questions concerning the authority of the CEO. At Merck, when Dick Clark was named CEO but not chairman, some questioned whether Clark was really in charge, and occasionally made snide comments such as "Dick Clark riding on training wheels." Fortunately, these questions were put to rest through a combination of effective leadership by Larry Bossidy (as chairman of the three-person executive committee), and the outstanding job that Clark did as a CEO who was clearly in charge.

In any event, the bald fact remains that most corporate CEOs in the United States are opposed to having someone else serve as chairman. If a CEO-chairman is doing well, the board is highly unlikely to risk aggravating its key leader by even raising the question. If the board is seeking a new CEO from outside the company, separating the roles can make it harder to recruit an outstanding candidate, especially if the individual already has both titles in another company. Finally, if the two positions have been separated during a transition and the new CEO then performs exceptionally well, there can be a strong inclination to reward good leadership by giving the CEO the additional title of chairman.

Boards in the United States are thus forced to confront a rather deep-seated cultural issue when considering the separate chairman model, and the right decision at a particular moment in time may be to allow custom to prevail. In electing new CEOs, however, I believe that boards should be more aggressive than they have been in trying out the idea of a separate chairman. Some highly qualified individuals have been willing to accept CEO jobs without the chairman title. If the separate model has been established, boards should resist the temptation to use the chairman title as a reward for good performance—even as we recognize that, as a practical matter, recombining the roles is sometimes the right thing to do.

The second practical reason for concluding that the roles of CEO and chairman should be combined (or recombined) is far more important than many people suspect. I am referring to what I call the "availability problem": it may be anything but easy to find just the right person to serve as non-executive chairman at just the right time. It is tempting to assume that any prominent organization will have a ready claim on several worthy candidates, but my own experience and my reading of the experiences of other organizations, suggests that this is a wildly optimistic and even dangerous assumption.[15]

To appreciate the seriousness of this concern, it is helpful to ask what attributes make a person well qualified to serve as non-executive chairman. Here is a provisional list (in no particular order) that may be helpful in its own right and that may also underscore the difficulties involved in finding a good candidate to be non-executive chairman:

- Unquestioned integrity and high ethical standards

- Intelligence, a good listening capacity, an abundance of common sense, and an ability to build consensus

- A full quiver of interpersonal and communication skills

- A constrained ego, since, in the words of one commentator, "no egomaniac can energize colleagues"

- The promise of an excellent, mutually respectful relationship with the CEO

- Knowledge of the business in sufficient depth to understand well the key strategic issues, and a strong belief in the value of what the organization is doing

- Experience as a CEO of a reasonably complex organization that allows the prospective chairman to appreciate the tasks of the CEO and the pressures under which the CEO works

- Ideally, previous service on the board of the company in question, so that other board members are comfortable with the person in charge

- Willingness to commit the time necessary to stay in touch with "the campus" and to be available for regular consultations with (in particular) other board members and the CEO

It will almost always be difficult to find an individual with a large majority of these attributes, never mind all of them. In light of this daunting list, it is hardly surprising that even companies that have had good experiences with the separate chairman model may feel that they have to recombine the roles at some juncture. In the case of Merck, at the time of the search for a successor to Ray Gilmartin as CEO, the board looked energetically outside the company as well as inside it for someone who could serve as non-executive chairman, at least for a time. It turned out to be exceedingly difficult to identify promising candidates. One highly qualified member of the Merck board, Larry Bossidy, eventually agreed to share the role of chairman with two other board members, but Bossidy was adamant in declining to serve as chairman by himself.

The Hewlett-Packard case is also instructive. Some commentators were highly critical of the decision by the HP board to recombine the roles of CEO and chairman following the resignation of the chairwoman, Patricia Dunn, in the wake of the extraordinary controversy over board leaks and spying at HP. A British commentator, John Gapper, wrote that "the board of Hewlett-Packard has behaved pretty eccentrically of late, but its decision last week to make Mark Hurd chairman of the board of directors as well as chief executive takes the biscuit. Hello? If any company has proof that chairing a board is an important job in itself and not merely a nice additional title for a chief executive, it is HP."[16] I am in no position to evaluate the qualifications of other board members at HP to assume the chairmanship, but I would not be quick to assume that it would have been easy to identify someone able and willing to serve at such a highly contentious time. In addition, getting the board and the CEO back together, solidifying relationships, had to be a high priority. This could well be a prime example of an instance in which situational considerations dictated the decision to recombine the roles.

Focusing attention on the importance of pools of candidates able and willing to serve in these leadership roles also helps us understand why the British experience with separation of the CEO and chairman roles is so different from the American experience. Executives in the United Kingdom, where mandatory retirement at age sixty was only recently abolished, tend to retire earlier than they do in the United States. These retired CEOs form a sizable pool of strong candidates for the non-executive chairman positions that are common in Britain.[17]

The third and final argument for continuing to combine the roles of CEO and chairman is that the real benefits of separation can be achieved through other governance mechanisms—in particular by adoption of the lead director model. Much has changed in recent years, and there are undoubtedly more effective checks and balances in place now than there were even five years ago. Board members are in fact, as well as in appearance, more independent; board recruitment has become far more professionalized and less dependent on the CEO; executive sessions without the

CEO are now the norm; and boards have demonstrated an increasing willingness to challenge and replace underperforming CEOs. Lead directors have become very important in achieving a better sharing of responsibilities between the CEO and the board. Indeed, the institutionalization of the role of lead director is the single most important governance reform of recent years in the for-profit sector. This organizational development is so important that it merits a section of its own, before I comment on how the different organizational models are likely to sort themselves out over time—and how I believe they should sort themselves out.

The Lead Director Model

This is one idea whose time certainly appears to have come. Spencer Stuart reports that as of mid-2006, 96 percent of all S&P 500 boards had designated a lead or presiding director, up from 36 percent in mid-2003 and an infinitesimal percentage a dozen years ago.[18] In some cases, no doubt, companies adopted this model simply because they knew that the New York Stock Exchange and rating agencies expected them to "tick this box." But I am persuaded that the support for this concept is much more substantive than that. It reflects a recognition that a well-conceived lead director structure can provide many of the advantages offered by the separate chairman model—but with much less of an apparent departure from past practice.

If the combined CEO-chairman model is the starting point, adoption of the lead director model is clearly considered a more modest step than the election of a separate chairman. Some argue that the combined CEO-chairman model has produced good results for American companies and that drastic change is not required. Tom Neff of Spencer Stuart emphasizes both the record of generally ethical behavior of companies led by CEO-chairmen and what he regards as the lack of compelling evidence of economic gain associated with splitting the roles. My personal experience supports the argument that combining the roles in one person can work well, but the widespread adoption of the lead director model is evidence that many companies have come to see the need to move beyond sole reliance on one person to lead both the company and the board.[19]

As various surveys indicate, the specific responsibilities assigned to a lead director in the United States vary from company to company. However, they almost always include the following:

- Chairing meetings of all independent, "outside" directors

- Acting as the principal liaison between the independent directors and the chairman/CEO

- Helping to develop agendas for board meetings

- Monitoring the flow of information to the board

- In general, coordinating all aspects of the work of the board itself, including the work of the nominating/governance committee

More generally, the lead director serves as the point person to whom members of various constituencies can turn if they have a worry or a suggestion that they prefer not to take to the CEO in the first instance. If real trouble develops, the lead director can facilitate a thoughtful review of the performance of the CEO (if that is the issue) or can do whatever else seems appropriate to address a vexing issue or head off an impending problem. There is much to be said for having an authorized person within the organizational structure to whom directors can go to register concerns and check impressions. Appropriate use of the lead director model also can provide "ballast in turbulent times."[20]

Serving all of these functions obviously requires judgment and tact. The lead director must be careful not to suggest, by word or deed, that he or she is competing with the CEO for authority, is functioning in a managerial role, or is authorized to make decisions. One role that the lead director does not perform (that the separate chairman does) is to preside at meetings of the full board. This is a limitation of the lead director model; as the Katzenbach comment quoted earlier indicates, there can be real advantages to having someone other than the CEO chair board meetings. In any case, the lead director must have a quintessentially correct understanding of the difference between board oversight and day-to-day management. The CEO and the lead director need to work closely and comfortably together. They need to help each other, respecting their complementary roles.[21]

The potential consequences of failing to have either a separate chairman or a lead director are not good ones: suppressed concerns, sub-rosa grumbling, or the formation of informal cabals outside of regular channels. As I can attest from painful experience, the unstructured, informal way of dealing with contentious issues can entail high costs. In addition to aggravating people and encouraging divisions within a board, it also operates slowly and depends on the more or less accidental emergence of a director prepared to take the lead on a given issue. Counting on a spontaneously generated, ad hoc process to solve major problems is not sensible. A major responsibility, then, of a lead director is to function on standby, to be ready to provide leadership if the need arises. The lead director provides, as it were, an insurance policy on which the board prefers never to collect. A great virtue of this particular insurance policy is that it is cheap—precisely because such a person may also be helpful in quieter times, and may in fact assist in preventing the most serious kinds of crises from ever arising.

Five open questions about the lead director model remain to be discussed. The first is whether the person should be called "lead director" or "presiding director." I think that the term "lead director" is preferable, for the simple reason that the person in this position needs to do much more than simply preside at meetings of the independent directors. The phrase "presiding director" suggests too passive a role. To be sure, some worry that the term "lead director" may signify that the person in question is a superdirector, superior to all of his or her colleagues on the board, who might be tempted to regard themselves as merely rank-and-file members.[22]

My own thinking about anti-egalitarian connotations of the "lead director" terminology has changed over time. In earlier days, and especially in the context of my service on both the American Express and the Merck boards, I shared the view that it would be a mistake even to suggest distinctions among directors by using a title such as "lead director." I now believe that both practices and attitudes have evolved sufficiently to reduce whatever discomfort the use of such a title may once have caused. There is more and more recognition that *boards really need someone to function as "lead" director*, and I think it is wise to have language reflect reality.

If the lead director is to substitute in at least some respects for a non-executive chairman, the role that the individual is being asked to play needs to be recognized explicitly. There is no reason to insist that all members of a board view themselves as the same in every way. Directors are the same in many respects (rights, fiduciary obligations, and standing), but they need not be the same in what they are asked to do—and often they will not be the same in what they are able to do. In any complex organization, some allocation of duties among individuals, taking account of differences in interests, experiences, and, yes, abilities, is entirely appropriate. As one commentator put it, if somewhat indelicately, "The good of the whole is more important than the tender feelings of the less able and most insecure." I also believe that boards are now more able to accept whatever structure they believe is necessary to function effectively because board service is now less "club-like" than it used to be.

A second question is whether it is better to have many lead directors rather than a single lead director—the notion being that the particular individual acting as lead director can vary depending on the task at hand, whether it is nominating new directors, discharging the audit function, or setting compensation. Why not expect the director who chairs the relevant board committee to function as lead director? There is little doubt that the director who chairs a committee responsible for a specific topic should lead the discussion on that topic, but this does not obviate the need for an all-purpose lead director who can be called on no matter what the issue, and who can function as a kind of quarterback, distributing the "ball" to appropriate board colleagues in specific situations.

A third question is whether the responsibility of lead director should rotate among the directors. In principle, there is much to be said for some rotation. It is desirable that more than one board member have the opportunity to serve in this role, and it is also wise to avoid the risk that a long-time lead director (*the* lead director) and the CEO may, in the words of one commentator, "become too cozy." Still, I think it would be a mistake to insist on a mechanical principle of rotation or to rotate assignments too frequently. Lead directors who serve for some reasonable period of time gain experience that is helpful, and both the CEO and the board are likely to be more comfortable if there is some continuity in the lead director position. Habits and styles naturally vary, and the CEO and the board should not have to cope with the "flavor of the month" too often.

A fourth question is whether a board committee, such as a committee on governance, acting through its chairman, can serve the functions of a lead director and obviate the need to name any individual specifically to this role. I used to believe that this committee approach was viable, and this model was in fact used reasonably successfully at Merck for some years. I am now persuaded that, for the same reasons that a lead director is preferable to a presiding director or to having many lead directors, having an individual explicitly assigned the role of lead director is superior to expecting the chairman of any single standing committee to attend to the duties of the lead director. The tasks to be performed inevitably extend beyond the mandate of even a broadly charged committee on governance.

The fifth and last question is the most difficult to answer: Will the lead director model become the established answer to the question of how the relationship between the board and its CEO should be structured, or will there be a further evolution in the direction of the split model, with a separate chairman?

Summing Up:
Prospects for Organizational Change in the For-Profit Sector

My intuitive response to the last question is that the role of the lead director, now institutionalized, will become more and more consequential and that, in some number of instances, it will morph into the position of non-executive chairman. Whether or not this intuition is correct, I see absolutely no reason to believe that there will be any reversion to the old CEO-centric model. *The day of the imperial CEO is, and should be, over.* However well the model of a combined CEO-chairman with no lead director or other identified board leader worked at times in the past, it is inappropriate now.

My proposition is not that a pure CEO-centric model can never work—a statement clearly at variance with reality. Rather, the point is that the CEO-centric model is unnecessarily risky and suboptimal in other respects. In sum, it deprives the board, and the shareholders, of an important protection against abuses of power. In addition, it decreases the likelihood that the CEO (and all board members, for that matter) will hear the kinds of authentic second opinions that should be expressed freely in meetings of a truly engaged, independent board that knows it is accountable and feels comfortable debating key issues.

Companies need to have appropriate checks and balances in place in advance of difficulties. As already noted, this widely shared understanding has led to the near unanimous adoption by S&P 500 companies of a variant of the lead director or presiding director model. But this current "resting place" in the search for the best organizational structure need not be an end point. The conceptual arguments in favor of separating the roles of chairman and CEO when circumstances allow are powerful and create a strong presumption in favor of the separate chairman model.

With this presumption in mind, we need to ask whether, over time, the practical objections to splitting the roles can be overcome. These are my thoughts.

- The status issue is real, and great care should be taken not to offend the leader on whom the board and the shareholders must rely. But it should be possible to lean against the prevailing culture by seeking to separate the roles when the timing is right—especially when a new person is being made CEO.[23] Experience in other countries suggests that the status/culture problem need not be insurmountable. In addition, experience in the nonprofit sector in the United States suggests that competent leaders of complex organizations can be highly regarded, even if they are not expected to chair their boards. It will take time, perhaps a great deal of time, for assumptions about what is normal and expected in corporate America to erode, but boards should be willing to test the waters and, in the words of one commentator, "to chip away at the culture."

- The limited availability of talented individuals able and willing to serve as non-executive chairmen is an unfortunate reality. Boards should be more proactive in working to develop pools of candidates for the chairman role. I also suspect that some of those now serving as lead directors will become more comfortable, over time, with the idea of chairing their boards.

- Lead directors can make a great deal of difference in improving governance, but in my view it is a mistake to assume that having a lead director meets the company's full need for board leadership apart from that provided by the CEO. There is always a risk that a lead director will lapse into too passive a role. The very title of "chairman" carries an authority that, as several commentators have emphasized, just changes the board dynamic.[21]

There has been some movement, albeit modest, in the direction of the separate chairman model. The *Spencer Stuart Board Index* for 2006 reports that the number of S&P 500 companies with a combined chairman and CEO has come down to 67 percent from 74 percent in 2001, although in the majority of situations where the roles are split, the chairman was formerly the CEO. The report goes on to note that "158 companies have separated the role, compared with 140 last year. Of these, . . . 48 have an independent chair [a chair who was not the former CEO or otherwise connected with management of the company], compared with 43 last year."[25] A 2007 Booz Allen Hamilton study reports that, over the last nine years, boards have been "increasingly splitting the roles of CEO and chairman."[26]

It would hardly be surprising if, among the ranks of the considerable number of companies that currently have a former CEO serving as chairman, there was some movement toward replacing former CEOs with more truly independent chairmen. If there is a greater willingness on the part of some corporations to try out the separate chairman model, a number of others might follow. The direction of change certainly seems clear.

What will happen, though, if inertia prevails? One commentator has suggested that there is at least some risk of rigid, mandated changes being imposed from outside the board—either by shareholder action or even by regulators or legislators who have concluded that the combined CEO-chairman model is fatally flawed.[27] "Once-and-forever" solutions are to be avoided because they deprive a board of the flexibility needed to respond to practical issues and implement whatever structure seems best suited to their specific situation.

This is precisely the thinking that led the Merck directors in 2005 to oppose a shareholder resolution that would have committed the board to separating the chairman and CEO roles on a permanent basis. The board's position was that it should have the freedom to ask the CEO to serve as chairman (supported by a lead director), to ask someone else to be chairman, or to find a third way—as, at this juncture, Merck did when it named a three-person executive committee to discharge what otherwise might have been a separate chairman's responsibilities.[28] Several years later (January 2007), when a new judgment had to be made about the leadership of the Merck board, the board decided that the CEO, Dick Clark, should be asked to serve as chairman as well as CEO, with the understanding that both the CEO and the board would benefit from the active involvement of an able lead director (Samuel Thier). This decision to recombine the CEO and chairman roles, while simultaneously establishing formally the position of lead director, was prompted by both the board's high degree of confidence in the abilities of Dick Clark, who has been outstanding as CEO, and the board's awareness that Clark's temperament and values reduced dramatically any risk that he would ever contemplate trying to function as an "imperial CEO." Circumstances vary, and providing some flexibility in settling on arrangements makes a great deal of sense.

Another significant question unaddressed thus far is why structural relationships between boards and their CEOs in the for-profit and non-profit sectors have been so different in the United States for so long. The postscript that follows addresses this question. Reflecting on it may not only be of independent interest, but may also provide a sharper sense of how likely it is that the separate chairman model so prevalent in the non-profit world will insinuate itself into more and more for-profit settings.

Postscript:
Characteristic Differences in Board Structure between Nonprofits and For-Profits

In the nonprofit sector, a paid executive most often functions as CEO alongside a part-time, usually unpaid chairman, who is the leading "lay" trustee. An informal study of nonprofit organizations receiving grants from the Mellon Foundation revealed that the CEO was also the chairman in less than 10 percent of the cases. Most of the exceptions were foreign organizations, entities still led by their founders, or literary presses—which may have evolved only recently from for-profit status. Other exceptions are the National Academy of Sciences and the Institute of Medicine, as well as Princeton and Yale universities, where the president presides at board meetings.

Although nonprofit boards have numerous shortcomings, this is one respect in which customary arrangements work reasonably well most of the time. Before turning to the larger philosophical and historical forces responsible for the differences in typical leadership structures, however, we should recognize two problems that are at least somewhat peculiar to the nonprofit world.

First, the danger that a board chairman will act like management is appreciably greater in the nonprofit sector than in the for-profit sector. In his widely quoted 1985 speech on governance, Ken Dayton remarked, "I regret to tell you that I have known volunteer chairmen of the [non-profit] board who clearly think that they are the CEO. And, even more I regret to tell you, I have known paid executives who ought to be the CEO but who are not, and who are perfectly willing to let the board and/or its chairman call the shots."[29]

Part of the explanation for such behavior is, I suspect, the sometime tendency for boards of nonprofits—lacking shareholders and freer from some of the other external constraints that operate in the for-profit world—to believe that they are accountable only to themselves. The solution to such problems lies in the recruitment of stronger executive leadership and an insistence on having boards that understand the boundaries implicit in their oversight roles. But there are also situations in which the chairman is just too intrusive and too inclined to function in a managerial role. One experienced nonprofit trustee, Barbara Robinson, has observed that the worst offenders tend to be current or former CEO-chairmen from the for-profit world, who bring typical for-profit behavior with them to the nonprofit world.

An additional problem is that nonprofits sometimes do not pay enough attention to the selection of the chairman and to ensuring that the chairman and the CEO are compatible. Let me cite two examples based on my personal experiences:

- Years ago, Fred Friendly of the Ford Foundation founded the TV program Public Broadcasting Laboratory (PBL). In the process, he appointed separately an executive director (Av Westin) and a board (chaired by Edward Barrett, former dean of the Journalism School at Columbia), on which I also served. The board was not given the opportunity to decide if it thought Westin was the right leader for this pioneering enterprise, and Westin was not given the opportunity to think about whether he could work effectively with the board that Friendly chose. As it turned out, there were real differences of philosophy and working styles between the executive director and the board, and the result was confusion and wasted effort. Eventually the board sent a delegation to see Mac Bundy, president of the Ford Foundation, to explain that the situation was unworkable and that either the executive director or the board had to be changed. Shortly thereafter, a new executive director was named. Although it may be easy, in retrospect, to understand why Friendly's enthusiasm for his project caused him to move ahead without thinking about the relationship between the CEO and the board, the lesson is obvious: there needs to be reasonably clear agreement between the board and the CEO as to mission and operating philosophy. The two should never be chosen independently.

• When I was elected president of the Andrew W. Mellon Foundation in 1988, the chairman at the time, William O. Baker, with whom I had a splendid working relationship, informed me that he was about to retire. The senior member of the board of trustees told me that he expected to succeed Baker. Although the trustee in question was a fine person, it was evident that we would have difficulty working effectively together. I spoke with one or two other trustees and then decided, with their encouragement, to take a major risk: to go out on my own initiative and identify from outside the board a person who, if elected by the trustees, would make a superb chairman and with whom I was confident I could work well. Fortune smiled on me, and I was able—with the help of Paul Mellon—to persuade John C. Whitehead, who was just stepping down as deputy secretary of state, to stand for election as chairman of the board of the foundation. Whitehead's status, professional qualifications, and personal qualities made his election a foregone conclusion.[30] It would have been easy for me to simply let nature take its course in the selection of a chairman following the retirement of Baker—and it would have been a huge mistake.

The much larger and more fundamental question is what explains the basic differences in how the nonprofit and for-profit sectors in the United States typically structure relationships between the CEO and the board. More specifically, given the prevalence of the combined CEO-chairman model in the for-profit world, why do the CEOs of nonprofits so rarely chair their boards?

First, leadership structures in much of the nonprofit world owe a good deal to the long-recognized needs of most of these organizations for generous external patrons. Managements of nonprofits simply could not survive on their own—as most managements of businesses did prior to the separation of ownership and management. The existence of lay boards of trustees for colleges, museums, and hospitals has a venerable history, which is tied to the American traditions of voluntarism and strong private-sector support of such activities. Unpaid volunteers often founded nonprofit entities, and it is hardly surprising that they have continued to play major roles in governance.

Second, the public in general may be more than mildly skeptical about the capacity of nonprofits to govern themselves. Many nonprofits reflect the interests of individuals who are idealistic, committed to a set of nonmonetary goals, and generally less experienced in some kinds of practical work than are those who live principally in the business world. These are stereotypes to be sure, but to the extent that the generalizations hold, nonprofits need both the help and the stamp of approval that can be provided by the active presence on their boards of prominent business leaders, investors, lawyers, and statesmen—with one such person usually serving as chairman. Potential donors may want assurances that boards are led by responsible, well-respected outsiders, who can be counted on to be sure that funds are invested wisely, that proper accounting practices are followed, and, in general, that the enterprise is conducted in predictable, certifiable ways.

Third, the distinctive missions of nonprofits have strong implications for organizational structure. In the case of colleges and universities, for example, the central importance of academic freedom and of academic judgments constrain the roles played by the president, other officers, and trustees. In such a setting, it is easy to see why a regularized, highly structured, CEO-centric model of governance has little relevance. More generally, the broadly collegial character of many nonprofits implies the need for a strong external presence on boards. In most nonprofit organizations, it is assumed that many of the professionals on the staff (the faculty at a university, the curators at a museum, the doctors at a hospital) owe allegiance to their professions as well as to the particular institution for which they work.[31]

These considerations help explain why the key actors in a nonprofit enterprise are usually comfortable with a strong outside chairman and why it makes sense to rely on the board itself and the institution overall, not on the CEO, to provide continuity. Heads of nonprofits such as universities and hospitals are accustomed to working with faculties and groups of doctors; they are used to sharing power and to operating within complex decision-making structures where there is much sharing of authority.

For-profit entities, in sharp contrast, often originated as creatures of either entrepreneurs or strong-willed managers and investors, and many evolved from family businesses. Internal "directors" were natural, since they were the ones who understood the business and had to run it. Their money and their futures were at stake. One can see why there would have been less of a sense of public accountability associated with business enterprises—and less reason to engage outsiders in overseeing their affairs.

Times have changed, and we forget too easily that today's emphasis on the outside director is relatively new. It reflects major shifts in patterns of ownership, and especially the rise of the large institutional shareholder. As we see from the current debate over how to nominate and elect directors (discussed in Chapter 6), we are still trying to find the best ways to reflect legitimate shareholder interests in the oversight of large companies. Some practices already common in the nonprofit world could prove useful to businesses as they seek to cope with this evolutionary process, and to find the right balance between the need for crisp decision making and the need for oversight.

My expectation is that businesses will continue to learn from their nonprofit cousins, even as we recognize that the precise organizational forms that have worked in the nonprofit sector will not be carried over, without modification, to the corporate sector. As I will say again at the conclusion of this book, differences in mission between the sectors are both profound and consequential.

3

Compensating the CEO

WHATEVER DECISIONS are made concerning the structural relationship between the board and the CEO, there is near-universal agreement that the board's primary responsibility in both the for-profit and nonprofit sectors is to evaluate the performance of the CEO. Evaluations are necessary, first, to decide how much the CEO should be paid—a task that is to be taken anything but lightly. Approving "perks" is also part of determining compensation, as is monitoring the use of perks and overseeing the CEO's expenses. In recent years these responsibilities have been every bit as demanding in the nonprofit sector as they have been in the for-profit realm. This chapter addresses compensation issues in both sectors.

A Hot-Button Issue in the For-Profit Sector

It is hard to find anyone who will own up to believing that boards have CEO compensation right in the corporate world, though there is considerable disagreement about both the severity of the problem and what to do about it.[1] Judging by the decibel level of the numerous angry voices reported in the press, outrage over what is frequently perceived to be excessive CEO pay, often *not* linked to performance, is pervasive.

A *Los Angeles Times*/Bloomberg survey in February 2006 found that "about 81 percent of Americans . . . think that the chief executives of large companies are overpaid, a percentage that changes very little with income level or political party affiliation."[2] A "new movement" is said to have "turned executive-pay activism into a potent mainstream force, and not just the redoubt of gadflies." Participants include a Harvard law professor, a mutual-fund trustee, foreign institutional investors, union leaders, and politicians.[3] According to Institutional Shareholder Services (ISS), investors had submitted 266 shareholder proposals related to executive pay through March 9, 2007—almost double the number in the same period of the preceding year. Critics direct their ire not only at illegal practices such as backdating of stock options, but at perks of all kinds, at what is perceived to be "pay for failure," and, most fundamentally, at the very sizes of many pay packages.

To start with the most obvious problem, no one can defend the backdating of options, a practice whereby executives are given options to buy their company's stock at the low price that prevailed during an interval of time prior to the issuance of the grant rather than at the price prevailing when the options were granted. The result is options that are immediately "in the money." This practice began with small Silicon Valley start-up companies in the 1990s (and was also used by Microsoft during part of that decade), and then spread to some larger companies. United-Healthcare was the first big-time, well-established company outside Silicon Valley to be implicated; and William McGuire, its chairman and CEO, was forced to resign and give back a portion of the $1.1 billion that he held in "harshly criticized stock options."[4] Although the extent of the practice is still being investigated, it would be wrong to suggest that the manipulation of option prices is commonplace among mainstream companies. But just a few instances of wrongdoing encourage a cynicism about executive compensation that hurts even those companies that are adhering to strict standards of compliance with applicable regulations.

Outsized perks of all kinds, and improper use of expense accounts, are other aggravating abuses that have received considerable attention through court cases, as well as reporting in the press. Tyco and World-Com are prominent examples. In addition, the highly publicized retirement benefits given to Jack Welch of GE, though in no way illegal, were sufficiently troubling to many people that Welch decided to relinquish many of them.[5] Perks not directly related to the duties of the CEO, even when modest in size, have been severely criticized. One simple example is company payments covering personal financial counseling expenses for very well paid CEOs who presumably could pay these bills themselves. Boards, and especially their compensation committees, have a clear obligation to ensure that expense accounts are not misused and that what is really compensation is treated (and reported) as compensation and not as a business expense.

Something is also very wrong when huge payments are made to executives who have been asked to resign in the face of complaints about company performance, skepticism about strategic directions, and criticism of CEO compensation itself. The compensation of Hank McKinnell at Pfizer is a commonly cited example. During his time as CEO, McKinnell is reported to have received $65 million in pay, a pension worth $83 million, and a total exit package said to be worth nearly $200 million. Pfizer shares plummeted 43 percent during his tenure. Robert Nardelli at Home Depot was fired in the wake of arguments over strategy, dismay at his handling of a now infamous annual meeting at which outside directors did not appear and shareholders were muzzled, and embarrassment over compensation arrangements. Nardelli left with a package valued at $210 million. Purcell left Morgan Stanley with a total package of $113.7 million, which included a "departure bonus" of $42.7 million. The *New York Times*, in an editorial entitled "The Wages of Failure on Wall Street," decried not only this award to a blatantly unsuccessful CEO but also the payment of $32 million to Stephen Crawford, a person who had served only three months as co-president and was described by the *Times* as "Mr. Purcell's attentive protégé."[6] To cite one lower-profile case, Bruce Rohde, former chairman and CEO of ConAgra Foods, is said to have received more than $45 million during his eight-year tenure and a $20 million retirement package—even though ConAgra "routinely missed earnings targets, underperformed its peers, . . . and saw its share price fall 28 percent."[7]

"Paying for failure," as many have dubbed such cases, generally has its roots in initial employment agreements. The problem is not that boards suddenly started handing out big sums of money; it is that they agreed to up-front arrangements that proved to be much too generous when things went bad. The desire to recruit a big-name executive can cause directors to overlook possible downsides of severance agreements. It is also far from clear that in some situations (such as McKinnell at Pfizer), directors really understood the fine print in the agreements that they had approved. There may also be some tendency, as one commentator suggested, for boards to cover up their mistakes by giving CEOs large sums to leave quietly, without a public fight. In the private-equity world, there is rarely, if ever, pay for failure. On the contrary, managers are required to have substantial capital of their own at risk, and, as one person put it, "you lose out if you don't perform."[8]

It is not only the highly publicized cases that have driven the widespread dissatisfaction with executive pay: it is the sheer size of many pay packages. The complex, even arcane, character of many executive compensation programs, with their mix of base salaries, annual bonuses, long-term incentive grants, and equity features (including stock options, "performance units," and restricted stock), make it devilishly difficult to describe levels of total compensation and rates of increase in any readily comprehensible manner. Carola Frydman (MIT Sloan School of Management) and Raven Saks (Federal Reserve) have made a herculean effort to compare executive compensation with the pay of the average worker between the 1930s and 2003. They find that in 1940 the median compensation for top executives of large companies was 56 times the average worker's pay—a ratio that actually declined during the 1950s, 1960s, and 1970s, before rising dramatically in the 1990s. The ratio is approximately 100 to 1 today.[9]

A study by economists Xavier Gabaix and Augustin Landier of the increase in CEO pay since 1980 finds that it can be attributed in large measure to trends in average firm size (market capitalization). As one of the authors says, "If all companies increase in size, the amount people are willing to pay for the same talent goes up." Being even a little better CEO than your competitor matters more when the scale of the entire enterprise is larger. The authors find, however, that CEO pay does not have much to do with motivating CEOs to work harder, and that little economic harm would be done by taxing them more heavily. In attempting to answer the question of why, if this model is correct, increases in CEO pay were sluggish from the 1940s through the 1970s, economist Frank Levy at MIT has suggested that, in those years, many people were afraid of labor unrest. The

Wall Street Journal story on the Gabaix–Landier research concludes, "For a while, fear topped greed. But fear of unions and government restraints on market forces faded around 1980. Greed took over."[10]

Absolute dollar levels are easiest for most people to understand. According to a survey by Equilar of 150 of the biggest companies (ranked by revenue), the typical chief executive at one of these companies earned $10.1 million in 2006. A survey by Mercer Human Resource Consulting found that direct total compensation of CEOs at 350 big corporations was about $6.5 million.[11] At the top end of the distribution, Ray R. Irani, Occidental Petroleum's chief executive, earned $52 million, and the heads of Wall Street's big investment banks all appear to have been in the $40 to $50+ million range.

Attitudes toward these compensation levels vary widely among knowledgeable observers. One of my friends, who never hesitates to be critical of business practices, says that big absolute pay numbers do not bother him — provided that they are performance driven. After all, he says, look at the extraordinary earnings of rock stars and even mediocre professional athletes. Others who are sympathetic to high pay levels call attention to instances in which inspired leadership (for example, by Steve Jobs at Apple) has driven shareholder values way up, and ask what is wrong with rewarding the CEOs who have guided companies to such outstanding results.

Sympathy for high pay is not, however, the norm. Some top executives, as well as leading investors, have joined the chorus of those complaining about executive compensation. Edgar S. Woolard Jr., former CEO of DuPont, has spoken out strongly on this subject, as have John Bogle, founder and former chairman of the Vanguard Group ("We need to bring some reality back"), Charlie Munger of Berkshire Hathaway ("About half of American industry has grossly unfair compensation systems where the top executives are paid too much"), and others. At one private gathering reported on at length by *Fortune*, Jeff Immelt of GE is quoted as saying, "There's a right amount for CEOs to get paid, and it could well be lower than it is today." He then added, "I wish the debate would end . . . It's crowding out important debates on education, innovation, technology, globalization, competitiveness."[12] Immelt is right. Whatever one's position on compensation levels is, the debate over executive pay has become a major distraction at a time when other topics deserve more attention than they sometimes receive.

There is also a broader dimension to the debate. As Henry Schacht, now at Warburg Pincus and former CEO of Cummins Engine Company and of Lucent Technologies, has argued ever since the late 1990s, excessive executive pay is part of the problem of "staggering income disparities" both within and between countries—a problem that has grown more serious rather than less serious each year.[13] One reason for being concerned about executive pay is the image that it conveys of American business—and of capitalism. As Woolard puts it, "I honestly don't understand why more CEOs aren't concerned about the image of business leaders in general."[14]

Public dissatisfaction with CEO pay is sufficient today to invite a new form of government regulation if boards themselves don't tackle the problem. "Restrain CEO pay" is listed right behind "Raise minimum wage" on one list of proposals for addressing widening economic inequality.[15] To the surprise of many, President Bush joined this debate when he gave a talk on Wall Street urging companies to "rethink pay practices." President Bush said, "America's corporate boardrooms must step up to their responsibilities. You need to pay attention to the executive compensation packages that you approve." According to the *New York Times*, "White House officials said that Mr. Bush decided to raise the issue out of his own sense of outrage over deals in which executives have left flagging or failed companies with huge compensation packages, as workers and lower-level executives have been left far behind."[16] In April 2007, the US House of Representatives approved "say on pay" legislation that would give shareholders the right to nonbinding votes on executive pay—a bill that passed amid "rising concerns over income inequality."[17]

A final reason for concern is nothing more complicated than a gut feeling on the part of many that current levels of compensation are simply inappropriate; the word "obscene" is used surprisingly often. More than twenty years ago, Irving Shapiro, former chairman and CEO of DuPont, uttered a by now classic warning that "feathered nests" are destructive to morale inside a company and to confidence outside:

> One of the most destructive mistakes a board can make, destructive to morale inside and confidence outside, is to leave the impression that top management lives in a feathered nest and will

stay warm and dry regardless of stormy weather. There have been cases where large companies have been devastated by adversity, even to the point of collapse, while the management took excellent care of itself through some sort of self-managed protection network. Meanwhile employees have been tossed out and stockholders left to pick over the corporate carcass for whatever scraps remained. To avoid such instances, you need not only an alert board (how did the patient get so sick before the doctors knew of it?) but one with a hard-boiled, independent compensation committee. There is a further prerequisite here, though, and that is good judgment as to what constitutes performance. If a company is rolling on momentum, a do-little management may turn in pleasant-looking numbers for several years while in fact the company's future prospects and internal organization are falling apart. A company battered by hard times may continue for a time to show losses, even though a brilliant management team is taking all the right steps to rebuild and will in future years be recognized as the corporate savior. It takes some wisdom in a compensation committee to know what to compensate.[18]

Actions to Consider

It has taken some time, but compensation committees today are clearly feeling the heat. The reputations of members of these committees, and especially their chairmen, are at risk. Dan Ryterband, president of the compensation consulting firm Frederic W. Cook & Co., says that, when it comes to being a director, "there are two things you stand to lose—your wallet and, more important, your reputation."[19] Ryterband notes much more of a risk avoidance posture on the part of directors these days, and my own experience supports the proposition that members of compensation committees, and especially their chairmen, have become highly sensitive to the need to think carefully when setting CEO pay. Ira Millstein, among others, has been emphatic in stating that "no one but the board can bring compensation under control."[20]

I agree entirely with Millstein's assessment of where responsibility rests. I believe that boards, and their compensation committees, should[21]

- Be diligent in preventing any madness such as backdating of options.

- Reject any seemingly trivial perks that do not support the business purposes of the organization. I do, however, support expenditures such as those that protect the security of the CEO and that allow enormously hard-pressed people to work effectively on corporate business when traveling; these are not perks, but entirely justifiable business expenditures.

- Be careful, in recruiting new CEOs, not to enter into separation agreements that could create problems down the road. Boards should negotiate hard with potential CEOs so that they will be rewarded for delivering value, not protected unduly from the consequences of failures.

- Restrain overly enthusiastic sponsors of high CEO pay on compensation committees—a phenomenon that one commentator dubbed "the Langone" problem, referring to Ken Langone's strong support of what many considered excessive compensation for Richard Grasso at the New York Stock Exchange.

More generally, one step that compensation committees can take is to ensure that compensation consultants are truly independent. As one highly knowledgeable compensation consultant puts it, "Historically the head of HR hired a compensation consultant that worked for management and made recommendations to the compensation committee, but the board wasn't engaged in the hiring process."[22] Furthermore, sometimes little attention was paid to the fact that the same firm that provided advice on compensation also provided other services to the management of the company. It is now widely understood that directors on the compensation committee, not management, must hire the consultant, provide direction and guidance, and be sure that protections against conflicts of interest are in place. Public identification of the compensation consultant (now required by the SEC) is also a useful protection for all parties.

Even if all proper standards of independence are respected, committees must monitor closely the principles and techniques used by compensation consultants. A number of commentators lay the blame for what seem to be never-ending pressures to raise compensation on the tendency to justify high pay for CEO A on the basis of what CEO B gets, after B's pay was based at least in part on a comparison with A's pay, and on and on. Trying to get everyone to the 75th percentile implies an upward spiral that is all too easily understood. Sometimes there is a temptation to act as if we live at Lake Wobegon, of Garrison Keillor fame, where all the children (and all the CEOs?) are above average. Aiming at the 50th percentile makes more sense, but the fundamental point is not to be obsessed with comparisons. They should be seen as reference points only. As one commentator observed, "The trouble today—and it is exacerbated by executive compensation consultants—is that mediocre talent is trying to keep up with the highly talented, who can write their own ticket."

Warren Buffett, in one of his widely read annual reports, had this to say about "Ratchet, Ratchet, & Bingo":

> Too often, executive compensation in the US is ridiculously out of line with performance. The upshot is that a mediocre-or-worse CEO—aided by his handpicked VP of human relations and a consultant from the ever-accommodating firm of Ratchet, Ratchet, and Bingo—all too often receives gobs of money from an ill-defined compensation arrangement.[23]

Ways out of the peer group horse race must be found, especially if the "peers" are not all that well chosen. It can be tempting to define a company's peer group in what might be called an "aspirational" manner, including as peers the high-performing companies that one wants to emulate. James Robinson, former CEO of American Express, states the problem this way:

> Too often, CEOs game the system. You pick the highest-paying company as part of the competitive set, and then you put forth the concept, based on testosterone, that, "Clearly, we see ourselves as a leadership company. Therefore, we should target our compensation at the 75th percentile. We don't want to be just average."[24]

It is fine to have high aspirations, but it is not fine, in defining benchmarks, to give too great a weight to the rewards enjoyed by the leaders of the most successful companies.

There is widespread agreement that a large part of the solution is to base compensation on well-conceived measures of performance. Finding the right metrics is a challenging but essential task. I am a strong believer in giving industry benchmarks considerable weight rather than overemphasizing success at achieving internally devised business plans. Close attention should be paid to long-term increases in earnings and to returns on invested capital—not just to growth in revenues or short-term movements in earnings per share. At Merck, substantial progress has been made in quantifying measures of performance other than just increases in earnings per share—such as operating efficiencies, research productivity, and success in retaining and motivating key staff. These other factors make a great deal of difference in how the company performs in the long run—and thus in determining long-term shareholder values—even if they have limited impact on next quarter's earnings.

With regard to forms of compensation, there is increased skepticism about heavy reliance on stock options, whose value depends on stock price movements that can be erratic—the product of rising tides that lift all boats—and sometimes even manipulated. Some use of standard stock options is fine, but there should also be room for other equity components of compensation packages, such as performance-based stock units, especially for the CEO and senior management. I agree with those who argue that grants of restricted stock that vest over time, once in disfavor, can be a useful part of compensation packages when accompanied by a requirement that the CEO hold the stock for an extended period. CEOs should, I believe, have a substantial share of their own net worth directly dependent on the success of the business they lead.[25]

In the private-equity world, the problem of proper incentives largely takes care of itself, because CEO compensation depends directly on the ultimate value of the stock held by the CEO. As Steven Kaplan of the University of Chicago Graduate School of Business puts it, "Private-equity owners *really* pay for performance, and the CEOs won't be criticized for making a lot of money [by gaming stock options or other gimmickry]." Private-equity companies offer more upside at the same time that they avoid "CEO-can't lose compensation."[26] According to Scott Sperling, co-president of Thomas H. Lee Partners, a large leveraged buyout firm, "Around 90% of the compensation the management teams get at our companies is driven by the performance of the equity value."[27] There are clearly lessons here for publicly traded companies.

In addition to basing pay on performance and agreeing on a sensible mix of compensation elements, full discussion with the entire board of *all* elements of the CEO's compensation is essential. Even before new SEC disclosure requirements for publicly traded companies took effect, a number of companies employed tally sheets to be sure that the directors understood the current and prospective value of CEO compensation in all its forms. Adding it all up can be sobering and has caused tally sheets to be nicknamed "Holy Cow" sheets. In at least some instances, effective use of tally sheets has led boards to change both the amounts and the forms of executive compensation.[28]

In a ruling in the fall of 2006, Judge Charles E. Ramos concluded that Richard Grasso, former CEO of the New York Stock Exchange, had failed in his fiduciary duty to keep his board informed of his mushrooming compensation and that he must return as much as $100 million. The implication of this ruling in New York State Supreme Court, which Grasso has appealed, is that a chief executive cannot defend his pay by saying simply, "They [the compensation committee] gave it to me." I agree with the thrust of this ruling, but I think that individuals other than the CEO should be responsible for communicating the essential facts about compensation. Specifically, the compensation committee needs to insist that the head of HR, and independent consultants reporting directly to the committee, act on their shared obligation to make sure that the sizes and characteristics of pay packages are understood by all members of the committee. Directors should not allow themselves to be surprised by what they have done in approving complex executive compensation packages.

What was at least semi-voluntary has now become obligatory, as the SEC has imposed new and far-reaching disclosure requirements. Among other things, all public companies now have to provide a bottom-line number for total annual compensation of the CEO and other key executives that includes all components, including deferred pay, pensions, and perks, as well as long-term incentive awards. Compensation committees also have to explain in some detail how they reached the compensation decisions reflected in the required table(s), list the firms that were included in their peer group analysis, and identify their independent compensation consultant. Larry Bossidy has made the useful suggestion that compensation committees give shareholders more of a sense of how they are thinking, perhaps by suggesting reasonable "bands" of salaries, bonuses, and long-term incentive pay.

Now that there has been some experience with the new disclosure requirements (following the filing of proxy statements detailing 2006 compensation), it is clear that . . . not all is clear! Even heroic efforts to achieve comparability do not always succeed, at least immediately, and the sheer volume of paper used to disclose elements of compensation and describe compensation principles can be overwhelming. One specific complication is that, although the new disclosure rules are more consistent with current accounting requirements, values for volatile components such as stock options, dependent on markets, can now be very different from what they were when the awards were first made. "Weird" numbers can result.[29]

A number of commentators have expressed the hope that, following the dictum of early-twentieth-century Supreme Court Justice Louis Brandeis, sunlight will prove to be the best disinfectant. Given this newly mandated transparency, fear of public embarrassment may well restrain pay packages and perks that are hard to justify in terms of their relationship to performance. Disclosure requirements also are bound to discourage complex mechanisms for concealing pay and seeking to avoid proper tax payments. At the same time, some skeptics question whether disclosure will have any real effect. ("[It] is like aspirin: it can make you feel a little better, but it can't even cure the common cold.") Still others have suggested that disclosure could accelerate increases in compensation by making visible what others are getting. There is, nonetheless, agreement that more extensive disclosure rules will, at the minimum, stimulate fuller discussion of compensation issues.[30]

More self-restraint on the part of CEOs would also help, though it is hard to know how realistic it is to expect much assistance from this quarter. As Derek Bok warns, "I fear that this is a case where the inevitable excesses of the minority create an all but irresistible pressure for other CEOs to follow suit." The controversy over Henry McKinnell's compensation at Pfizer is instructive. Frederick E. Rowe Jr., the head of the Investors for Director Accountability Foundation, met with McKinnell and asked him to give back some of his $83 million pension. Here is Rowe's argument: "He [McKinnell] is the head of the world's largest drug company and head of the Business Roundtable, and he could have set an example for the entire business world." McKinnell rejected the idea and thereby, in the words of one columnist, "squandered a leadership opportunity."[31]

In trying to understand why leading executives require such outsized pay packages, it is useful to move beyond speculations about pure greed. My own view is that status, and the desire to be perceived as the best, are often more powerful motivators. As I know from experience in several corporate settings, it can be difficult for directors to resist arguments that, if their truly superb CEO is not paid at least as well as "Jones," he will feel unappreciated. As someone who believes both in recognizing outstanding performance and in adhering to a standard of reasonableness, I have felt conflicted in such situations. I should add that I have also witnessed cases in which strong self-perceptions of one's own value, and personal priorities, have eased any felt need for boards to yield to the pressures of the moment. I remember well the failure of AT&T to induce Charles Exley, then head of NCR, to agree to their propositions regarding a takeover of NCR, despite offers to Exley of substantial additional compensation. Exley's response was, "I have a boat. What would I do with two boats?" It is not overly romantic, I think, to believe that frank conversations between chairs of compensation committees and their CEOs can at least weaken the perceived link between pay and status.

A final question is whether boards should resist shareholder pressures to be allowed to cast nonbinding votes on compensation of CEOs. I am torn. The purist in me says that the "say on pay" idea is wrongheaded, since shareholders are never likely to know enough to cast informed votes on such questions. But my political sense says that nonbinding votes might be useful in sending messages to boards as to what shareholders regard as excessive compensation. The proverbial bottom line is that, whether or not there are advisory votes, compensation committees have to make much tougher decisions than many have been prepared to make. There are, I am told, few known cases in which corporate CEOs either rejected job offers or left their jobs because they felt undercompensated.

Analogous Issues in the Nonprofit Sector

Boards of trustees in the nonprofit sector must wrestle with many of the same compensation issues that face the directors of for-profit companies, and many (but not all) of the same considerations apply. Certainly careful oversight of expense accounts and perks is every bit as important in the nonprofit sector—and perhaps even more important, given the tendency to use perks and expense allowances to offset what can be low levels of base pay—a practice, let me say emphatically, that I consider very unwise. The long-running examination of the improper expenditure of charitable funds by Barry Munitz, former president of the Getty Trust, and his eventual dismissal, is one case in point. In retrospect, it is clear that the trustees did not oversee properly the expenses charged to the Getty Trust, including payments for the travel of Munitz's wife.[32] Similarly, it is clear that the regents of the Smithsonian failed to oversee adequately the expenses that Secretary Small charged to the institution.[33]

There is no need to cite other examples. The basic points are clear enough. Boards of nonprofits must be diligent in establishing sensible guidelines for the perks and expenses of their presidents and executive directors, equally diligent in monitoring actual practice, and then careful to report on these oversight activities to *all* trustees. I emphasize "all" because I keep hearing of situations in which some trustees are kept in the dark about compensation deals struck by board chairs or executive committees. This is simply wrong practice. All trustees have the same fiduciary duties, which they can discharge only if they are informed. I would go further and suggest that nonprofit boards (and especially their chairs) should accept an affirmative obligation to provide guidance and advice to presidents and executive directors, and especially to those new to their posts, on sensitive matters that can cause difficulties if not handled well. Costly renovations to presidential residences are usually at the top of this list.[34]

The highly publicized controversy over payments to a number of individuals throughout the ten-campus University of California system illustrates powerfully the need for processes that will guarantee careful monitoring and full disclosure. The president of the California system, Robert Dynes, tried hard to recruit top talent in a fiercely competitive market while having to work within a total compensation framework that was less generous than were compensation systems at many other universities. Operating in this environment, Dynes tried to make the most of the resources at his disposal by tailoring compensation and perks to the needs of particular individuals—but unfortunately the process and its somewhat complicated outcomes were not always consistent with university policies and were not disclosed fully to the regents. Dynes then committed himself and his administration to doing a better job of providing "full disclosure of full compensation." Subsequently, Dynes resigned. It is evident that expectations concerning both transparency and disclosure have risen dramatically—which is probably all to the good, within reason.[35]

Until recently, overall levels of pay in the nonprofit sector have not received nearly the attention given to executive compensation in the corporate sector. By the standards of the corporate world, the compensation of university presidents and heads of most other nonprofit organizations remains modest. But this landscape has also changed rather dramatically. A 2006 survey found a total of 112 presidents of traditional four-year colleges and universities, public and private, who had compensation packages of at least $500,000—more than a 50 percent increase in the number in this category from the previous year. Especially noteworthy is the spread of high compensation from well-endowed private universities to public universities.[36] Gordon Gee's sudden and surprising move from Vanderbilt back to the presidency of Ohio State has refocused discussion on the pay of the presidents of public universities. Apparently his compensation at Ohio State, including deferred compensation, will be $1 million. Whatever one thinks about this level of remuneration, I agree with Gee that there is no reason that public university presidents should be paid less than their private counterparts.[37]

Compensation of presidents of major grant-making foundations is roughly comparable to that of presidents of research universities. In other parts of the nonprofit world, compensation of heads of hospitals and medical schools has always been relatively high for this sector (with, for example, Harold Varmus at Memorial Sloan-Kettering Cancer Center earning about $2.5 million), a long-standing pattern that reflects compensation paid to leading doctors and members of medical school faculties. Leaders of major art centers and museums also tend to be compensated above $500,000 (sometimes substantially above). Music directors of symphonies are also well compensated.

Many presidents and executive directors of less visible nonprofits, however, are paid very modestly. *In my view, the generic problem with compensation in the nonprofit sector—in sharp contrast with the for-profit sector—is that it is too low, not too high.*[38] These are often demanding positions, and the individuals holding them frequently work long hours, enjoy limited staff support, and face withering criticism whenever anything goes wrong. Leaders of complex nonprofit organizations, including presidents of colleges and universities, certainly should not have to apologize for earning compensation in the mid-six-figure range. And of course many earn much less.

Highly paid outliers are, however, a different matter. It is easy to see why members of Congress and others were troubled by the level of compensation provided to Secretary Small at the Smithsonian (over $900,000 when he left office), as well as by the aggressive role that the secretary played in raising his compensation (insisting that it be at the 75th percentile of what Smithsonian management had chosen as comparable institutions). The situation was made still worse by the inclusion of a compensation component that was styled as a housing allowance to conceal the true size of Small's total pay package, and by the fact that the terms of the package were not fully disclosed to the board of regents.[39]

It is, I believe, always a mistake to conceal either the level of pay or the means used to deliver compensation. It was reported in February 2007 that the director of the Museum of Modern Art in New York, Glenn Lowry, had been paid considerably more than the museum reported on its tax forms (though Lowry paid tax on all the money he received), thanks to the use made of a little-known trust created by several major donors. This practice was stopped in 2004, and in retrospect it seems unwise to have gone to such lengths to complicate, and even obscure, elements of compensation.[40] Whenever payments are made from special sources, they should be fully disclosed.

The disclosure problem is real and needs to be taken seriously by nonprofits. The Executive Compensation Compliance Initiative, launched by the IRS in 2004, found that, where there was missing information on Form 990s (used to report compensation), a substantial number of the affected public charities and private foundations had to file amended returns to reflect accurately executive compensation. It is noteworthy, however, that these were disclosure problems, *not* problems with the level of compensation itself. Although "high" compensation amounts (in the context of the nonprofit sector) were found in many cases, the survey noted that "generally they were substantiated based on appropriate comparability data."[41]

From my perspective, it is encouraging that the rate of increase in compensation for chief executives of nonprofits, including lesser-known ones, is increasing. Students of this upward trend believe that it results in part from a shift in the basic relationship between supply and demand. The number of nonprofits—and thus the number of openings for executive directors of nonprofits—continues to grow at a time when, largely for demographic reasons, there are atypically large numbers of retirements.[42] Boards of trustees are learning that they have to be more competitive to attract top talent. In the university world, there has been much discussion of the consequences of paying presidents too little. The University of Iowa has lost four presidents to higher-paying jobs at other universities, including three private universities, since 1987.

A variety of factors have led to much more regularized methods for setting the compensation of presidents and other chief executives in the nonprofit sector. These include spillover effects from developments in the for-profit sector, more regulatory oversight, and simply greater recognition of the critical importance of discharging this major board responsibility properly. One major change is the increasing frequency of systematic annual reviews of the performance of the president or executive director at the time when adjustments to compensation are considered. (The appendix to this chapter contains a detailed explanation of how one major nonprofit, television station KQED in San Francisco, carries out systematic reviews.)

For too long, such reviews were often thought to be awkward, and something that high-minded institutions like colleges and universities just did not do. That attitude has changed. The Association of Governing Boards of Universities and Colleges (AGB) today argues vigorously for two general principles:[43]

(1) Linking a president's compensation to achievement of agreed-upon performance goals to be measured through a regular process of evaluation

(2) Setting compensation with reference to appropriate benchmarks within and without the institution, including of course the compensation provided by peer institutions

Mention of performance goals leads directly to the topic of "incentive pay," a phrase that I prefer to "bonuses." Incentive compensation in one form or another is, of course, commonplace in the for-profit world, and it is not surprising that the concept has now migrated to the nonprofit sector. This migration is in large part a result of the tendency for trustees with high-level business experience to bring business concepts with them when they serve on nonprofit boards. In addition, it can be easier for boards to justify paying more if the president or executive director has met what may be regarded as "stretch" goals—and if it is clearly understood that incentive compensation will not be paid otherwise.

The use of an incentive pay system has the advantage of compelling the leader of the organization, and his or her board, to develop a set of goals against which the leader is to be measured. This can be a very difficult and demanding exercise, and great care has to be taken to establish goals that reflect appropriately the true mission of the organization. For instance, I think it is a mistake to tie incentive compensation in the university world to raising an institution's *US News* ranking, as Arizona State is said to have done as part of a new compensation contract with its president, Michael Crow.[44] It is also easy to overuse, or misuse, fund-raising goals in designing incentive compensation plans. Meeting such goals may depend heavily on the work of trustees or others not under the president's direction. Use of such incentives can also lead to bad practices. I have been told of one situation in which senior staff of a college were unable to resist the temptation to cook the numbers so that they would appear to have met fund-raising targets when in fact they had not.

Incentive pay systems work best, I believe, when a nonprofit organization is somewhat entrepreneurial and can set quantifiable goals that are related directly to its mission. JSTOR (an electronic repository of the back files of leading scholarly journals) is a good example. The success of this organization in delivering valuable scholarly content to users all over the world has depended on signing up journals that would agree to contribute content, digitizing efficiently the content obtained from the publishers, designing an effective platform and other features that deliver the content in a user-friendly way, and then encouraging libraries to sign up for licenses.

Many metrics related to the satisfaction of these requirements were readily identified, and the trustees decided to base part of the executive director's total compensation on hitting ambitious targets (including some bottom-line financial goals). But even in this case, those of us on the board took care not to be overly rigid or mechanical in coming to final judgments concerning the appropriate level of compensation. Performance grids, defining what the chief executive is expected to accomplish along various dimensions, can help inform decision making; but they are never a substitute for the inevitably somewhat subjective exercise of judgment needed if all aspects of the performance of the president or executive director are to be assessed fairly.

It is far harder to envision a sensible set of quantifiable goals at many other nonprofits. More generally, I do not think that nonprofits will ever want to make as much use of incentive pay as for-profit companies do. It is very difficult for much of the nonprofit world to measure "return on mission" reliably—and in ways that do not end up distorting the mission itself.

There is one final difference between the nonprofit and for-profit sectors in how presidents and chief executives think about their compensation. Presidents of many nonprofits, including the presidents of many colleges and universities, exercise more self-imposed restraint in limiting their own compensation than do CEOs in the for-profit sector. An example is Lawrence Bacow, president of Tufts University, who receives reasonable compensation (in the $500,000 range) but who has insisted that Tufts pay him less than its board wants to pay him. Why does he do this? Because he recognizes, as do a number of other presidents, that his institution is highly collegial and that it is unproductive to allow too big a gap between the salary of the president and the salaries of other key officers and faculty members.

An important consideration for many of us who served as presidents of universities and of similarly collegial nonprofits was that the organization needed to recruit and motivate the colleagues on which our success depended. Our colleagues had to know that we thought they were vital to the success of the enterprise—a message that would have been much harder to convey if presidential compensation exceeded what colleagues were paid by too large an amount. Making money is, almost by definition, much more closely aligned with the missions of for-profit companies than it is with the missions of nonprofits, and this is another reason why the compensation of the president or chief executive can be viewed very differently in the two sectors.

Appendix to Chapter 3

BOARD EVALUATION OF CEOs IN A NONPROFIT SETTING

By Nicholas Donatiello, chairman of the board of Northern California Public Broadcasting (NCPB), which operates KQED, the large public television station in San Francisco, and four other public radio and television stations in northern California, March 2007

Roughly five years ago the board of KQED, recognizing that hiring, evaluating the performance of, and if necessary replacing the CEO are perhaps the most important roles that the board performs, decided it was unwilling to leave this critical task to any subgroup of the board. However right-minded this decision might have been, it presented more than a few practical challenges for a board with twenty-seven members.

Since then, a process has evolved that, although somewhat time-consuming, works very well and has given rise to unforeseen benefits. The process begins at the outset of the year with the CEO drafting his own goals and objectives for the year, using the five-year strategic plan as a guide. The board reviews the draft in closed session (without the CEO) and a designee (or designees) provides the board's feedback and works with the CEO to refine the document, which the executive committee reviews and the board ultimately approves. This document also establishes the basis for the CEO's bonus eligibility.

At the conclusion of the year, the chairman of the board (or sometimes the chairman-elect) circulates to all board members a questionnaire, together with the final goals and objectives from the beginning of the year, as well as information and commentary from the CEO regarding the extent to which each goal has been accomplished. The questionnaire—meant only to stimulate thinking—is brief and very general. Board members are encouraged to provide commentary on any topic they believe to be of importance. Both commendations and suggestions of areas where improvement is required are solicited. Board members provide written responses to the chairman via e-mail. At the same time, a separate questionnaire is circulated to each person (approximately eight people in total) who reports directly to the CEO. The anonymous written feedback to this questionnaire is mailed back to the chairman in unidentified return envelopes. Both board and staff responses are anonymous, but not confidential; that is, the substance, and sometimes the exact words, may be shared with the CEO, but never for attribution.

The chairman reviews all responses in search of patterns and themes. He then creates a draft CEO review that incorporates those themes both laudatory and critical—and includes quotes from the responses to support the theme. (With an engaged and thoughtful board, this process is actually much easier than it sounds.) The review includes an evaluation of the CEO's performance against the goals set at the beginning of the year, along with a draft bonus amount and salary adjustment. The draft is circulated to the board and discussed in closed session, and to the extent necessary, the chairman is charged with making changes and finalizing the document. The goal is a document that reflects the consensus view of the board. The final document is provided to the CEO; and after he has had some time to review it, the chairman and another board member (usually a vice-chairman or chairman-elect) sit down with the CEO to review and discuss the document and answer any questions. The CEO then drafts goals and objectives for the coming year, and the process begins again.

The process runs quite smoothly and entails only a reasonable amount of concentrated effort. It requires each board member to spend about an hour (many spend less) providing written feedback and to participate in two executive sessions—one of which lasts about an hour, and the other about half that time.

This process has yielded many unanticipated benefits. First, the CEO has confidence that the feedback represents the whole board, not just the leadership. Second, the discussion of the draft review is a unique opportunity for board members to hear detailed and candid comments from their fellow board members on the CEO's performance. This open forum is particularly important in a large board where much of the work is done though committees. The views of the CEO's performance with respect to a given committee's purview can differ radically between those who serve on the committee and those who do not. The discussion leads to a shared sense of how the board as a whole feels. Third, the CEO's bonus and salary adjustment are "owned" by every member of the board, not just a subcommittee. This consensus-driven approach to CEO pay seems especially important in a nonprofit of substantial scale where the CEO is necessarily highly compensated relative to many other nonprofits and where executive staff compensation is a matter of public record. Finally, all board members are involved in setting the CEO's goals and objectives for the coming year and therefore are both invested in and intimately familiar with them.

Some board members have now taken this process—with adjustments appropriate to the situation—to other nonprofits on whose boards they serve, and they report equally good success.

4

Evaluating and Replacing the CEO

A s IMPORTANT AS IT is to evaluate the CEO or president annually to set appropriate compensation, it is even more important—much, much more important—for boards to know when to replace a CEO and, when they know, to act.

The Obligation to Decide When New Leadership Is Needed

Ezra Zilkha, a wise man who has served as director/trustee of innumerable for-profit and nonprofit organizations (including Revlon, Wesleyan University, and the Brookings Institution), says simply, "The main job of a trustee/director is to make sure the management is right, and if it is not right, to fix it." This straightforward admonition is hardly new, but the willingness of boards in both sectors to take it to heart and to act on it is much more evident now than it was in pre-Enron days.

According to *Bloomberg News*, one corporate CEO departs every 6 hours. US companies were said to be on track to fire or lose a record 1,400 chiefs in 2006, up from 1,322 in 2005, and 663 in 2004. The *Wall Street Journal* tells us that, in 2005, about 40% of CEOs worldwide were at retirement age—sixty-two or older—when they left office, a figure that is down from about 66% in 1995. According to Booz Allen Hamilton, one in seven of the world's largest companies made a change in leadership in 2005, up from one in eleven in 1995; almost one-third of CEOs leaving a US company in 2006 were forced out, up from 12% in 1995. The CEO turnover rate does, however, now appear to have leveled off, albeit at a high plateau.[1]

No comparable data are available for the nonprofit sector overall, and the 2006 survey of colleges and universities indicates that, in this sector, presidents are, on average, staying longer (8.5 years, up from 6.3 years in 1986).[2] But such averages can conceal more than they show, and there is ample anecdotal evidence, cited later in the chapter, to suggest that "life at the top" is harder in this sector too. Scrutiny of the performance of the leaders of nonprofit organizations, as well as of the CEOs of for-profit companies, has increased.

Compiling a list of publicly discussed terminations/resignations is easy to do, but such an exercise is not terribly instructive. In the comments that follow, my objective is to see if there are lessons to be derived from recent terminations that can provide some insight for board members faced with the inescapable need to decide when new leadership is needed.

As the data just cited indicate, there has been a sea change in the willingness of for-profit boards to come to hard judgments about CEO leadership. The tendency in earlier days for directors to look the other way and hope that conditions would improve is clearly out of favor. Pressures from three sources—regulators and courts, increasingly aggressive institutional investors, and internal constituencies—have without question changed assumptions as to what boards should be prepared to do. In addition, the greater independence of board members today—a result of the stronger role of independent nominating committees in selecting directors and the correspondingly reduced role of CEOs (see Chapters 5 and 6)—has been important in diminishing the likelihood that hand-picked "friends" of the CEO will overlook faults and discourage corrective actions.

A review of the factors that, according to press reports, have led to most terminations/resignations in the for-profit sector suggests that many of the issues that boards have had to address can be grouped into five broad categories:

(1) *Corruption/accounting issues.* In some situations, resignations were required de facto (and maybe de jure too) by "regulators," generally in the aftermath of questionable accounting practices or another violation of widely accepted norms—even when the CEO was not involved personally and there was no legal wrongdoing. The resignation of Frank Raines at Fannie Mae is one example. Hank Greenberg at AIG left his position in the aftermath of controversies with regulators. Klaus Kleinfeld, CEO at Siemens, departed in 2007 as "the latest casualty in a widening corruption scandal that has shaken corporate Germany."[3]

(2) *Personal problems.* Sometimes personal health issues such as alcoholism have required boards to act, even if (as has happened in at least one high profile case known to me) they would have preferred not to see what was evident to many others and had managed to cover their eyes for a long time.

(3) *Differences in vision and bottom-line performance.* Disagreements over strategic directions and issues of bottom-line performance have led to the terminations/resignations of a number of CEOs. Carly Fiorina at Hewlett-Packard is said by many to belong in this category.[1] Kai-Uwe Ricke resigned as CEO of Deutsche Telekom "amid an ailing share price and growing pressure from discontented investors."[5] Bill Ford resigned as CEO (but remained as chairman) of the Ford Motor Company so that an outsider, Alan Mulally from Boeing, could come in as CEO and lead a restructuring effort. Stan O'Neal at Merrill Lynch and Charles "Chuck" Prince at Citigroup left in the aftermath of huge write-offs driven by the subprime loan debacle.

(4) *Compensation.* Terminations have also resulted from controversies over executive compensation, including evidence of practices such as backdating of options, misuse of perks, and criticism of pensions. In addition to examples from Chapter 3—the dismissal of William McGuire at UnitedHealthcare and the removal of Hank McKinnell by the Pfizer board—Robert J. O'Connell at Massachusetts Mutual Life Insurance Company was fired by his board for alleged expense account irregularities and misuse of corporate aircraft, as well as for improper relations with employees.[6]

(5) *Fit.* A broader issue is "fit," by which I mean the match (or mis-

match) between the characteristics of a CEO, especially management style, and the needs of the organization for which the CEO is responsible. One consequence of a poor fit can be major morale problems, as the tenure of Phillip Purcell as CEO of Morgan Stanley illustrates so well. After dismissing complaints about Purcell's management style, including a lack of collegiality, for a considerable period of time, the Morgan Stanley board eventually acknowledged that it could not continue to countenance the "alarming exodus of talent" at the company. "The troops were in disarray," and the board finally concluded that management had to be held accountable for the firm's lack of cohesion.[7]

In a perceptive column, Joe Nocera of the *New York Times* argued that this case reflects a broader change in corporate culture—a movement away from the tough-guy model of CEO leadership to an emphasis on openness, helping colleagues to feel good about themselves, and being the kind of colleague with whom others want to work (the late Richard Fisher, former chairman of Morgan Stanley, was a prototype of this model). Purcell's board was widely perceived as consisting mainly of his own people, but not even "his board" could save him as criticism mounted.[8]

In the nonprofit sector, notable examples of terminations or resignations fall into some of the same categories just discussed in the context of for-profit companies. Certainly the question of fit loomed large in perhaps the most widely discussed case in the university world: the resignation of Larry Summers as president of Harvard University after protracted controversies with faculty members, dramatized by the no-confidence vote by the Faculty of Arts and Sciences. To this day, no one doubts Summers' capabilities, and many, including a number of his detractors, acknowledge that his sense of strategic directions for Harvard was well considered. Nonetheless, it became clearer and clearer to the Harvard Corporation (the governing body at Harvard with ultimate responsibility for evaluating the performance of the president) that Summers simply could not get along well enough with significant numbers of the Harvard faculty to lead effectively.

This was not, in my judgment, a question of differences in ideology or a controversy over "academic freedom," as some argued.[9] Rather, it was a question of Summers' ability to work constructively with highly talented colleagues holding a variety of views on educational matters. In almost all academic settings, a high degree of collegiality and a talent for building consensus are important if a president is to succeed. In other settings these attributes may be less important than, say, sheer intelligence and decisiveness, which is why the Summers situation seems to me such a clear case of lack of fit.

The tenure of Larry Small as secretary of the Smithsonian represents an equally clear example of lack of fit. In the words of the report of the Independent Review Committee established by the regents, "Mr. Small's disposition was ill-suited for the position of Secretary." The report goes on to argue that Small's "attitude and disposition were ill-suited to public service and to an institution that relies so heavily . . . on federal government support." The report is especially critical of Small's "desire to maximize his personal income and have the Smithsonian pay his expenses."[10]

The board of Gallaudet University, the nation's leading university for the deaf, faced a somewhat different problem: protests by students, faculty, and alumni opposed to the appointment of Provost Jane Fernandez as president-elect became so intense that they forced the temporary closing of the university. Although there were, as always, many reasons for the opposition to Fernandez (including complaints about her personality and management style, which led some of her critics to describe her as "stiff" and "humorless"), the most fundamental issue was whether Fernandez was "deaf enough." Would she speak out forcefully against audism—the assumption that hearing is superior to deafness—and lead the deaf community to a new understanding of the role of Gallaudet?

In short, deep-seated issues that were at least partially ideological combined with other considerations to create a situation in which the board of trustees concluded that it had no choice but to terminate the appointment of Fernandez. This controversy illustrates again that a university president has to have more than a modicum of support from the faculty and the academic community to be able to lead effectively.[11] Boards need to support presidents whom they have chosen (as the governing boards of both Harvard and Gallaudet did, for considerable periods of time), but board support alone cannot make a president effective or keep a president in office.

A less dramatic but more common occurrence than the shutdown of a campus is a termination or resignation that stems simply from a growing sense of dissatisfaction with the leadership that a president is providing. The decision by William E. Cooper to resign as president of the University of Richmond a year before the expiration of his contract was attributed by the press to a growing number of complaints related to his leadership style—with the "trigger" an ill-advised comment by Cooper that Richmond needed to attract better students if it was going to "transform bright minds into great achievers instead of transforming mush into mush." The "mush into mush" reference became a rallying cry for Cooper's detractors.[12] But in this case the president himself elected to resign in the face of mounting criticism, and it is fair to ask if the board should have been more proactive in dealing with what appears to have been a deteriorating situation.

Other terminations in the nonprofit sector can be attributed directly to controversies over compensation and perks that were similar to cases in the for-profit sector (although there were, of course, no options to backdate in the nonprofit sector!). The example of the Getty Trust has already been mentioned, and the termination of Benjamin Ladner as president of American University was a direct consequence of his improperly charging the university for personal and other expenses.[13]

One source of terminations that is peculiar to the college and university world is difficulties associated with athletic programs. The resignation of Elizabeth Hoffman, president of the University of Colorado, was caused in no small part by a football scandal involving allegations of sexual assaults. Auburn University is an example of a public university plagued by governance problems related directly to athletics, including micromanagement by members of the board of trustees. The usual rules for good governance cannot be set aside because of the wishes of zealous football devotees.[14]

Trustees also need to recognize the often uncomfortable position of college and university presidents caught betwixt and between, with faculty members complaining about compromises in academic standards at the same time that sports fanatics among the alumni (and sometimes on the board) demand better and better won–lost records. As President Graham Spanier of Penn State wryly observed in a discussion of these tensions, presidents—unlike both their faculty critics and alumni supporters of athletics—can be fired.

I know that President Spanier would agree that no president should have tenure—or even a presumptive, indefinite hold on a leadership position. But there has been one important change in the formalities associated with presidential appointments in the college–university world. Today, employment contracts are expected and almost required—as, of course, they have been in the for-profit sector for a very long time. In my time as a university president, handshakes sufficed, and I recall vividly my inability to answer a question asked by the *New York Times* reporter covering my election as president of Princeton: "What is your salary?" I said that I didn't know, but that I was sure the trustees would be fair—as they certainly were.

The trust model has much to be said for it, but I have concluded—albeit reluctantly—that everyone's interests are protected best by at least a simple set of written understandings concerning not just compensation but other matters too, especially severance arrangements. Because terminations have become more common—in both the for-profit and the nonprofit worlds—it is important that individuals and boards understand the commitments that have been made so that they can abide by them. Fear of the need to honor contractual provisions can make boards reluctant to dismiss a president, but the absence of such provisions can cause no end of controversy. Of course, many departures are entirely amicable, and apparently a well-crafted employment contract was helpful in allowing Robert Gates, in late 2006, to move smoothly from the presidency of Texas A&M to the position of secretary of defense.[15] It is also important that departing leaders of organizations understand what they are, and are not, entitled to in their post-retirement years.

The Role of a Careful Evaluation Process

The dramatic character of many of the terminations described in the preceding discussion reminds us that events sometimes overtake normal processes—and that boards have to be prepared to act promptly when circumstances dictate. Still, there is increasingly widespread agreement that careful adherence to a well-designed and well-understood evaluation process is highly desirable. The details of an effective process will, of course, vary from situation to situation, and today there are many how-to guides and manuals available for organizations to use, as well as many consulting firms ready to offer their services. All I can do here is suggest some general principles.

First, the purpose of the CEO evaluation should be broader than making a simple assessment of how well previously established goals and metrics have been met and what annual compensation is appropriate. In-depth evaluations (which, in the nonprofit sector, may be conducted on something like a 3- to 5-year cycle, in addition to annual evaluations focused on compensation) should have a clear developmental aspect. Presidents and CEOs can benefit greatly from candid feedback that identifies areas for improvement.

Second, those carrying out the evaluation should consult closely on a confidential basis with senior managers/staff, with key customers or clients (grantees in the case of foundations), and with peers in the same industry or field. Simply assuming that you, as a board member, know what others think can be a huge mistake.

Third, the entire board, and not just the compensation or nominating committee, should be involved in reviewing past performance and speci-fying near-term and longer-term goals. Board members should exchange impressions and debate differences in interpretations of what has been learned.

Fourth, as important as bottom-line results are in a for-profit setting, they should not be the sole focus of an evaluation. It is important to judge not just what results were achieved, but *how* they were achieved. Are the fundamentals of the company's business getting better? How is employee morale, and is the workplace environment one in which a diverse staff can feel comfortable? Is the CEO doing a good job of developing other leaders within the organization? Is the ethical tone at the top what it should be? How successful has the chief executive been in strengthening the organization's reputation for integrity, as well as for outstanding performance?

Historically some nonprofits have been reluctant to carry out formal reviews of the performance of the president/executive director, perhaps feeling that such a process is either unnecessary ("we already know how 'Jones' is doing") or that it could actually harm the affirmative relation-ships between the board and the president or executive director that are desired by all parties. One good effect of Sarbanes-Oxley has been to change these assumptions. At Princeton University a board review of governance practices stimulated in part by SOX highlighted the value to the president, as well as to the board, of systematic reviews of how the president is doing. No such process existed when I was in the president's office at Princeton in the 1970s and 1980s, and I am sure I would have benefited from the insights that such a process can yield. When conducted in the right way, with the right balance between quantitative and qualitative measures, reviews can strengthen rather than weaken relationships between the president and the board. Too much informality can lead to mistaken impressions of how things are going, and to inadequate guidance as to what aspects of presidential performance need to be improved.

There is, however, always a danger that the way in which a review is carried out will exacerbate stresses and strains rather than alleviate them. Nancy Dye's announcement in September 2006 that she would retire as president of Oberlin took place amid some evident faculty dissatisfaction with her leadership, in spite of a ten-year tour of duty widely regarded as highly successful. A controversy over the handling of her final performance review, which centered on who was to have access to the detailed findings produced by an outside consultant, did not help the situation.[16] It is important that the ground rules for such reviews be clear and well understood at the outset of the process.

The outcome of a careful evaluation need not be a simple dichotomous choice between either reaffirming the board's support for the chief executive or deciding that an immediate change in leadership is required. An evaluation may give the board a sense of how long the incumbent should be expected to serve and what kind of search process will be needed to choose the right successor when the time comes. A well-conceived evaluation should connect fairly directly with succession planning and, ultimately, with a good search process.

The Proper Length of the Leash: Different in the Two Sectors?

The increased willingness of boards to terminate CEOs whose performance disappoints leads naturally to the question of time horizons. There is an active debate over how rapidly CEOs should be expected to achieve turnarounds or fix mistakes, and the proper time frame surely differs by situation. Achieving the right degree of patience requires high-level judgment and an astute reading of signs of progress or the lack thereof. Boards of for-profit companies should take a longer-term view of performance than many seem to do today, and there has been valid criticism of the near-obsessive focus by some CEOs and their boards on quarter-by-quarter results. But at least one respected columnist has written in defense of "short-termism."[17] Similarly, Alan Murray of the *Wall Street Journal*, in an article appropriately titled "Leash Gets Shorter for Beleaguered CEOs," observes, "We know from past experience that CEOs on long leashes can get in trouble. The experiment with CEOs on short leashes is just beginning."[18]

Whatever the correct answer is in a for-profit context, there is a strong argument against assuming that the same guideline should apply in nonprofit settings, especially educational institutions. The presumed perpetual nature of colleges and universities suggests the need for a long time horizon, and a key role of trustees is to make sure that the pressures of the moment do not lead to decisions that harm future prospects. The attitude toward the harvesting of earnings on the endowment is one example of this proposition. When total returns are high, presidents or chief financial officers may be tempted to channel an appreciably higher fraction of earnings into the operating budget. This can be a short-sighted and dangerous policy. When returns decline, as they almost assuredly will, it can be very hard to reduce expenditures to a commensurate degree. A steady-as-you-go approach, based usually on a spending formula, is a better way to ensure the long-term health of the college or university.

Highly successful presidents of colleges sometimes accomplish even more during the latter stages of their presidencies than they did in their early days. Certainly the success of Freeman Hrabowski at the University of Maryland, Baltimore County (UMBC) in raising academic standards and the overall reputation of his university illustrates well what an exceptional leader, with a commitment to his institution and its values, can achieve if given a reasonably long time in office. At the same time, there are countless stories of highly competent leaders who failed to understand the importance of leaving when there was still some semblance of a band playing.

The altogether proper recognition that many nonprofits should operate on the basis of long time horizons can lead to complacency and a reluctance to address pressing issues. In my experience, nonprofits are often too slow in facing up to leadership problems and, if anything, too patient with mediocre performance by chief executives. A major source of this problem is the difficulty of measuring success in the nonprofit sector. Market guidance, while hardly nonexistent (note trends in donations and attendance, for example), is less clear-cut than a dramatic drop in a company's stock price. In any case, this "patient" attitude on the part of many nonprofit boards may have changed—perhaps too much—at least in part as a result of the increasing presence of high-powered business executives on boards of trustees.

Of course, time horizons within the nonprofit sector differ depending on the type of organization. For example, service delivery organizations that are not "delivering" should be held immediately accountable. There is, however, a difficult issue here that Derek Bok brought to my attention: If you are on the board of a nonprofit that is living hand to mouth, your evaluation of the executive director is constrained by the knowledge that, if you were to seek a new leader, the process would take at least six months, and then the person chosen would need another six months to settle in—by which time the organization could be dead. So, the temptation can be great to just muddle along.

In the past I argued that business members of nonprofits often fail to insist on the same kind of discipline and concern for the bottom line that defines their lives in their day jobs. Too often, I argued, they joined nonprofit boards to "enjoy a vacation from the bottom line."[19] There may have been truth to that perception in the early to mid-1990s, but I doubt seriously if it is nearly so true today. In fact, the pendulum may have swung too far the other way, with trustees failing to recognize appropriate differences in time horizons and failing to consider the consequences of abrupt responses to economic setbacks.

The dismissal of Judith Bailey as president of Western Michigan University has been cited as an example of the tendency to treat educational institutions as if they were "just businesses," where the performance of the president should be judged on the basis of quarterly results. In December 2005, the board of Western Michigan was so pleased with the job Bailey was doing that it granted her a raise and a bonus and extended her contract from 2008 to 2009. In March 2006, the chairman of the Western Michigan board, James P. Holden, a former CEO of DaimlerChrysler, reiterated his support for her as she faced faculty disaffection associated with cost cutting. Five months later, in advance of the normal December evaluation, the chairman notified Bailey that five of the eight members of the board had voted to fire her.

I have no independent knowledge of the specifics of this situation, but I do agree with Raymond Cotton, a Washington lawyer who specializes in presidential contracts and compensation matters, that abrupt terminations in the college and university world can have far more serious consequences than many board members may recognize. Cotton emphasizes that college and university presidents are expected to raise money from governmental sources and private donors on the basis of personal relationships that can take years to develop. Moreover, the collegial nature of these institutions means that a sudden change at the top can have destabilizing personnel consequences that percolate throughout the organization. In addition, an abrupt termination of a president could well make it much harder to recruit a new one with the desired credentials. Cotton suggests a number of ways in which boards can handle such situations, and his guidelines—including proper review, withholding public announcements until termination arrangements have been settled, being sensitive to the needs of the departing president, and appointing a transition committee—are wise reference points.

My conclusion is that the leash should be at least somewhat longer in most nonprofit settings than it needs to be in much of the for-profit world. The role played by boards with respect to removing a leader should be conditioned—strongly conditioned—by the characteristics, cultures, and time horizons of the organizations for which the boards are responsible.

Establishing a Set Retirement Date

A different but related question that leads directly to our discussion of management succession in the next chapter is whether a set retirement date is helpful, and whether retirement should be mandatory at a specified age. In the for-profit world, this topic received extensive coverage in the British press in connection with the public announcement that Lord John Browne, the chief executive of BP, would retire at the end of 2008, having reached the company's mandatory retirement age of sixty in February of that year. As one would expect, some commentators initially decried this policy, given Lord Browne's accomplishments. Others applauded the company's decision to stick with an established departure date, thereby eliminating the uncertainty that otherwise would prevail.[20]

The central point is that a board cannot allow the current CEO or president to control the timing of his own retirement and the election of a successor. This can be a highly sensitive matter, since boards are understandably reluctant to appear to force what may feel like a premature retirement on someone who has done well. Given how difficult it is to find outstanding leadership, however, boards can ill afford to let top inside candidates be enticed away because they feel they are being asked to wait too long to lead the company. Furthermore, as Barbara Robinson of Debevoise & Plimpton has emphasized, too long a tenure gives rise to another problem: it prevents organizations from learning how to cope with change and makes them too comfortable in assuming that all is well.

The departure of Louis Gerstner from American Express, where he was the heir apparent, for RJR Nabisco and then IBM, is a classic example of this damaging scenario.[21] But the American Express board did learn from this experience, and when it had another high-achieving CEO aspirant in the number two position (Ken Chenault), it did not hesitate to work with the CEO at the time, Harvey Golub, to schedule his retirement appropriately. Golub performed superbly as CEO and no doubt would have continued to do well for several more years, but it would have been folly for the board to allow Chenault to pursue any other opportunity because of a relatively small difference in the length of Golub's tenure. Chenault's subsequent performance as CEO of American Express has certainly vindicated this key judgment, and both Golub and the board of American Express deserve credit for having understood that the future is now.

I will have more to say about the general subject of retirement, especially mandatory retirement, in the context of the discussion of the tenure of directors and trustees in Chapter 7. Here I want simply to recognize that the board is better able to discharge its twin tasks of succession planning and the recruitment of a new leader when it controls the timing of retirement decisions. Needless to say, in some situations the board will want the CEO to stay longer than the CEO might like to stay, so this is not entirely a discussion about how to shorten tenures. CEOs who care greatly about their organizations may make big contributions by carrying on in the interest of a smooth transition. The central point is that, in deciding how long a person should serve, and when an individual should step aside, the needs of the organization have to dominate.

5

CEO Transitions

A COMPARISON OF the literature on succession planning and press accounts of perceived successes and failures reveals an interesting contrast. Everyone agrees, in the abstract, that the number one responsibility of boards in both the for-profit and nonprofit sectors is to identify and recruit an excellent CEO or president when the time is at hand. One commentator modified an oft-used real estate adage to make this point. As he put it, the three top jobs of the board are to "pick the right CEO, pick the right CEO, pick the right CEO." At the same time, an astonishing number of organizations have no succession-planning process in place, and boards themselves confess that they are more dissatisfied with this aspect of their work than with any other.

Slightly less than half of the corporate directors surveyed by Price-waterhouseCoopers in 2006 were satisfied with the succession plans in place at their companies; 20 percent of directors reported that their companies have no succession plan in place. The *Spencer Stuart Board Index* for 2006 states, "In an alarming finding, 31% of boards surveyed said that they do not have an emergency succession plan." Ram Charan says bluntly, "The CEO succession process is broken in North America. Almost half of companies with revenue greater than $500 million have no meaningful CEO succession plan, according to the National

Association of Corporate Directors, [and] even those that have plans aren't happy with them."[1] The recent (fall 2007) lack of succession plans at both Merrill Lynch and Citigroup illustrates dramatically the seriousness of this problem.

It is safe to say that—lack of comparable data notwithstanding—succession-planning problems are even more pronounced in the non-profit sector. Nonprofits are much less likely even to claim to think systematically about succession planning until the need for new leadership is upon them. At one level, it is easy to understand why this is the case. These organizations are less hierarchical and less likely to promote from within. Identifying and attracting outstanding leadership is just as important to nonprofits as it is to for-profit organizations, but the next president or executive director of a nonprofit is very often recruited from outside the organization. In higher education, for example, 80 percent of presidents come from outside.[2]

When a non-profit board undertakes the search for a new president or executive director, it almost always devotes considerable time to the task. Traditionally, discharging this responsibility has been an episodic activity that failed to justify adopting the regularized succession-planning apparatus common to corporations. This thinking may have to change, at least to some degree, given the greater willingness of the boards of nonprofits to terminate their leaders. Within the nonprofit sector writ large, there is certainly an argument to be made for investing much more heavily in leadership development.[3]

Within the corporate sector an obvious question is, What accounts for the odd disjunction between the accepted need for an effective succession-planning process and the lack of in-place machinery? There are basically two explanations. First, boards may not want to create nervousness or upset sitting CEOs by even raising the succession question, absent an obvious imperative to do so. Second, organizing and managing an effective process is just plain hard work. Some boards have excused their lack of attention to this task by citing overwhelming pressures to focus on compliance and Sarbanes-Oxley issues, but I find this argument resoundingly unconvincing.

Before I discuss the succession process in greater depth, I want to share a finding based not on statistics, but on my own experience with searches in both the for-profit and nonprofit sectors: *search committees almost always believe that they will have a much easier time finding a pool of well-qualified candidates than in fact they have.* While participating in efforts to find new leadership at the Smithsonian, at Denison University, at Princeton, at TIAA-CREF, and most recently at Merck, I have been struck by the inordinate optimism among board members that typically marks the onset of a search. Near the end of the process, almost all admit to a sobering realization: "Yes, we are very lucky to have found one— repeat, one—good candidate." And, as the sharp rise in early terminations of newly chosen CEOs/presidents demonstrates, the "one good candidate" does not always turn out to be the right person for the job.

Improving the Succession-Planning Process

Given the widespread dissatisfaction with the succession-planning processes in place now, what can be done to improve them? First, boards need to acknowledge their failure to deal with this problem. In both sectors, but in the nonprofit sector especially, simple demographics make clear that a crisis is at hand. Demands for new leadership in the nonprofit sector far exceed projected increases in the supply of candidates. To fail to see the significance of this potential leadership deficit amounts to a failure of vision on the part of boards. In the for-profit sector the same demographics are relevant: baby boomers are retiring, and the demand for new leaders is accelerating.

One sensible response is to modify board structures to put more emphasis on succession planning. Morgan Stanley has amended the charter of its compensation committee to include responsibility for management development and succession planning. The committee has been renamed the Compensation, Management Development, and Succession Committee. This is a healthy change, provided everyone understands that the entire board, not just one committee, needs to focus on management development and succession.

Surely no one believes that merely renaming a committee solves the problem. Companies have to work harder to create a strong pool of internal candidates for advancement, to provide nurturing opportunities for them, and to monitor progress. It is increasingly common for boards of for-profit companies to review, at least once a year, the "depth of the bench" and to ask specifically, within each functional area, who has the greatest leadership potential, who is ready now for new responsibilities, and who needs a different kind of assignment. Thoughtful movements of individuals from one role to another facilitate their development and give the board more information about the potential of younger executives. Companies also need to take reasonable risks to prepare new leaders: individuals have to be given the opportunity to fail.

Increased specialization in all fields makes conscious attention to providing a range of experiences all the more important. As the late Richard Fisher, chairman of Morgan Stanley, observed, many capable people are "kept in small boxes" for a long time, and some of them are never given an opportunity to test themselves in larger arenas until it is too late. In addition to fashioning a well-crafted development process that will position their organizations for the steady infusion of new leadership, boards need to have an emergency management succession plan in place so that they won't be taken by surprise in the event of a calamity, including the death of the CEO.

Recruiting a New Leader: Job Specifications

When the time comes to move from thinking about succession to the hard work of conducting an effective search, boards must understand what is involved, what expectations they should have, how the search is to be managed, and what attributes they should be seeking in a new leader.

The process should start with a full discussion within the board of job specifications. What skill sets are most needed at this juncture in the organization's history, what kinds of experiences are likely to prove especially valuable, and what personal qualities should be given heaviest weight? Deciding on the final job specifications requires a delicate balance. Too much vagueness up front is a sure recipe for trouble later on, but at the same time it can be dangerous to be highly specific. If a board is too demanding when it sets specifications, it will establish an unattainable standard for prospective candidates. Insisting on transformational leadership is not always realistic.

In the nonprofit world, it is at least as important for boards to think through key institutional issues before launching a full-fledged search. Such ruminating can be done informally (though not casually), and it is important in part because a new leader can be recruited more easily if, in the words of one of my former colleagues, "the institution knows what it is about and is ready to be led." There can be a tendency to think that succession is a personal rather than institutional issue. It is both. In fact, it is surprising how often the search process leads nonprofit boards to reexamine what they are doing. If the board contemplates a radical change in mission during an executive transition—a phenomenon more likely in the nonprofit sector than in business—it should hash out any disagreements about direction so as not to confuse potential candidates with lack of clarity. To be sure, learning from the ideas and perspectives of prospective candidates is healthy, but it is highly desirable that the trustees have their own priorities reasonably clear before seeking a new leader. Otherwise, the risks of wasting time and misleading good people increase dramatically.

The Search Process

Every search process is unique, but certain guidelines deserve consideration.

- *Searches need to be guided by a board committee that is small enough to be able to function effectively and that understands its obligation to keep all members of the board, who share equally in final responsibility for the selection of a new leader, appropriately informed of progress.* The intensive nature of a well-run search requires that the board establish efficient machinery for carrying it out, and having too many people involved complicates excessively the scheduling of meetings and managing of the process. The board members who assume primary responsibility for guiding a search must be prepared to devote the necessary time and attention to the task, but this practical fact of life does not in any way relieve the search committee of the responsibility for communicating regularly and effectively with other board members. At the end of the day, the decision to elect a new leader is a collective one for which all board members are responsible.

- *In setting up a search, allow enough time to make a well-considered decision, but make sure the search committee moves expeditiously.*

Wasting time can lead to the loss of promising candidates. Searches carried out under intense time pressure run real risks of going astray. Orderly processes are important, and there needs to be ample time to examine both internal and external candidates, to consult widely, and to conduct extensive due diligence. But, once the search is launched, there is everything to be said for keeping the process moving.

Competition for top talent is increasingly keen in every sector, and boards must recognize the constraints imposed by the realities of the marketplace. Search-firm professionals and others testify that this is no less true in the nonprofit world than in the for-profit world. In the words of a story in the *Chronicle of Higher Education*, "Like it or not, your institution's list of potential leaders is dictated by the laws of supply and demand . . . Your institution is part of a national market and its presidential options are dictated by that market, your reputation, the challenges of the position, and the relative compensation for the opportunity to lead your organization."[4] Often different institutions are conducting searches simultaneously, and, as the member of one presidential search committee put it, "We seem to talk, talk, talk while comparable colleges are moving ahead and interviewing the people we should be pursuing."

• *To the extent possible, committees should respect the legitimate interest of potential candidates in confidentiality; otherwise, potentially promising candidates may not agree to be considered.* This is not normally a problem in the for-profit sector, but it can be a serious problem for nonprofits. Public universities in particular may be compelled by law or regulations to have an "open" or "public" search. Private colleges and universities can encounter difficulties as a result of aggressive reporting by student newspapers. There is no full solution to this problem, since at some stage it is necessary for various constituencies to be in the loop, but those involved should take great care to prevent premature, and unauthorized, disclosures of lists. Such disclosures can be unfair to all parties and damaging— especially if potential candidates high on the list who already hold positions elsewhere are pressured by their home institutions to withdraw their names.

• *Search committees should have realistic expectations concerning the depth of the pool of well qualified candidates.* As I noted at the start of the chapter, exaggerated notions of how easy it will be to assemble a list of promising candidates are common, even when the open position is CEO or president of an exceptionally well regarded institution. Over and over, search committees begin their work convinced that their opening is so enticing that they will surely end up with five or ten top candidates. This almost never happens. Winnowing invariably leads to an often painful recognition that the committee has, if it is lucky, two or (luckier still) three strong candidates. Often only one person looks truly right for the job. When this situation arises, for reasons that may well be idiosyncratic, it is necessary to accept reality and press on.[5] Searching for top people is challenging, and to end up with even one truly outstanding candidate should be grounds for celebration, not self-castigation.

• *The retiring CEO/president should be consulted closely throughout the search process, but it should be absolutely clear that the responsibility for making a decision rests with the outside directors on the board.* The CEO will have, one hopes, an especially astute understanding of both the qualities that a successor needs to lead the organization and the strengths and weaknesses of internal candidates. It would be foolish in the extreme to fail to take advantage of this knowledge base. Outside directors are unlikely to have a nuanced sense of the qualities and capabilities of managers below the level of the CEO— who presumably knows the pluses and minuses of his immediate co-workers better than anyone else. It is entirely possible for the CEO to be helpful without presuming to have the last word, but the days should be gone when boards rely on the CEO to choose a successor. It is the board, looking ahead, that has to exercise this responsibility.

Relying too heavily on the current CEO can inhibit independence of judgment, stifle fresh thinking, and perhaps obscure the need to establish new strategic directions. As one commentator observed, boards have to be wary of the "stealth candidate," advanced and promoted too aggressively by the retiring CEO. Of course, recognizing that the board is responsible for choosing the next CEO in no way relieves the current CEO of responsibility for nurturing a new generation of leadership within the organization.

In the nonprofit sector, the responsibility of the board itself to search for a new president or executive director has been understood for some time. In fact, in this sector the greater danger is that the current president will be kept at too great a distance from the search process. As one highly experienced leader of nonprofit boards observed, "It makes no sense not to consult with the retiring leader, who should know best what is required for successful leadership of the organization." The objective, then, should be to consult closely with the current president/CEO, but to be clear from the outset where final decision-making responsibility rests.

- *In both sectors, the search committee should also consult closely with senior executives—and, in the case of colleges and universities, with faculty members and staff.* These consultations are important, first, because the members of the senior leadership team will have thoughts about the needs of the organization that should be taken into account. Second, if some members of the team, though not themselves prime candidates to become CEO, are nonetheless especially important to the future of the organization, the search committee needs to reassure them that it appreciates their importance and will give careful consideration to their views when making its decision. In the course of the search for a new CEO at Merck, these propositions turned out to be critically important. The members of the search committee learned a great deal from the interviews that we conducted with each member of the senior management team; and we were able, at the same time, to assure managers that we understood their value to the company. In the college/university context, it is generally understood that, for similar reasons, the faculty leadership must be closely involved throughout the search process.

- *It is wise to "take it from the top" when reviewing lists of candidates.* In too many instances, search committees seem to feel an obligation to rank twenty or thirty candidates—and to spend a great deal of time deciding, for example, who is fourteenth and who is fifteenth. This approach has never made sense to me. Searches are not about trying to field a football team; the objective is to identify a small number of outstanding individuals and then sign up the most promising candidate. Because candidates will have different backgrounds, it may help to group them into categories—such as insiders and outsiders, scientists and humanists (in the case of colleges and universities), experienced leaders and promising younger people—and then select the top candidates from each group before making comparisons across groups. Concentrating the search committee's limited time and energy on the best prospects is the wise approach.

• *Search firms can be helpful, but their role needs to be clearly defined.* Boards generally recognize that finding a new CEO is likely to be time-consuming and, quite probably, controversial. As a result, some are tempted (especially in the nonprofit sector) to delegate too much authority to the firm chosen to assist in the search. In some cases with which I am familiar, board chairs essentially turned over the process to search-firm executives who, however well intentioned, could not be expected to understand the needs of the organization as well as the board members. There is also the unavoidable danger that a search firm operating with too little guidance will want to impose not only its own job description but even some of its favorite candidates.

In my experience, search firms are especially helpful in (1) producing lists of possible candidates, including some truly fresh names; and (2) managing the paper and the logistics of the search process—a function that is especially important if the organization looking for new leadership has limited staff resources of its own. Opinions differ as to whether search firms should also contact candidates to determine their interest/availability. In some cases, senior members of a search firm may be in a good position to open doors and to learn if an individual has an interest in the position. But I prefer that board members take direct responsibility for conducting important conversations of this kind. A strong candidate often requires considerable persuasion even to agree to participate in a preliminary discussion of the opportunity. In such circumstances, it is often best if a member of the search committee, or the chairman of the board, calls the prospective candidate.

In one specific situation in which I was asked to help, a highly promising candidate for a college presidency was contacted initially by a search-firm representative. The candidate, who already held an important position at another institution, flatly declined to become part of the process. The search committee accepted this apparent rejection of its overture at face value. However, further informal checking revealed that there could be an excellent fit between the needs of the college and the interests of the individual. A leading member of the board agreed to call the candidate personally, and the rest is, as they say, history. The individual was elected, and there is every reason to believe that he will be successful.

- *Boards must do their own due diligence, and do it very carefully.* In this critically important part of the search process, it will not suffice for boards to hear only what friends of a candidate, or others with special interests in the outcome, have to say. Hard work is required to check references, and to contact people in a position to provide helpful information, even though they may not have been listed as references. Thus, it may be tempting to hand these tasks over to the search firm. However, as a search reaches its final phase, it can be dangerous for board members to assign these responsibilities to anyone else. The search firm may not be well positioned to make all the critical contacts that need to be made; moreover, the firm has an understandable interest in concluding the process.

  Unfortunately, it has become harder and harder to obtain candid, honest references, in part because of legal commitments by former supervisors and colleagues to "speak no evil" about individuals who have signed severance agreements—and the attendant fear of lawsuits. Severance agreements may prohibit senior management and members of the board from disparaging a person who has been let go, and the agreements sometimes even provide "scripts" that suggest positive comments that should be made in response to queries. I regret this development because it increases the risks that the wrong people will be appointed to positions.

  Legal issues aside, individuals may simply be reluctant to say anything negative about anyone. In one high-profile search, I was told that a person whom I happened to know well had a good opinion of a particular candidate. That assessment puzzled me because it was at odds with my own impression of what the person thought about the candidate. I placed a call to the reference and received an entirely different report from the one the search firm had presented. The representative of the search firm was not reporting inaccurately; rather, the reference explained to me that he simply did not know the search firm or the individual who called him, and that he was uncomfortable being forthcoming with a stranger. In other searches, near mistakes have been made because of a failure to verify the past performance of a candidate through channels other than those proposed by the candidate. Finally, I am painfully aware of a situation in which a wrong appointment was made because the search committee members already knew what they wanted to hear, and thus did not think it necessary even to contact a person well positioned to provide extremely relevant information.

As the end of a search nears, there is just no substitute for carrying out an all-encompassing, Soviet-style, "KGB" probe of a candidate's actual performance in other settings: to learn as best one can how the candidate has handled setbacks and pressure, what hard evidence there is of a spark of creativity, how successfully the candidate has recruited good colleagues and inspired others, whether there are any warning flags about integrity, and how hard the person can and will work. The objective is to create as fine-grained a picture as possible of the candidate's strengths and weaknesses. Of course, no candidate is without flaws, and the goal should be to understand a person's limitations and to assess how detrimental those limitations are likely to be in the setting at hand. In some situations, key members of a search committee have traveled many hours to have a long face-to-face discussion with the individual being considered. And no one has said that this was time wasted.

- *There is much to be said for self-selection, and for letting prospective candidates help the board make its final decision.* Candidates know more about themselves than a search committee will ever know about them. Accordingly, candidates should be encouraged to think seriously—and openly—about whether a particular opportunity is right for them. Board members must listen carefully to what a prospective candidate says and avoid the temptation to over-persuade. Some of the worst mistakes I have made in filling key positions have resulted from a foolish belief that I understood what would work for an individual, and what would make him or her happy, better than the individual did. Reluctant dragons are rarely, if ever, good choices. If a candidate seems genuinely reluctant, it is almost always best to thank the individual for his honesty and to move on.

• *Not every search will succeed, and it is better to acknowledge that a search has failed than to elect a mediocre candidate.* One commentator put it this way: "Mediocrity is like the Roach Motel; once it checks in, you can't get it out." No one likes to admit that a search did not produce the desired result, but it does happen sometimes. It is almost always better to seek an interim solution than to start down a path that seems unlikely to lead the organization where it needs to go, even if this means persuading the incumbent to stay in office a little longer or naming an acting president or interim CEO.

Personal/Professional Qualifications of Candidates

Next I would like to list some propositions concerning the review of candidates that I believe deserve careful consideration.

• *Settle for nothing less than unquestioned integrity.* As obvious as it may seem, this key quality is sometimes overlooked, misperceived, or undervalued. The scandals and mishaps of the 1990s and thereafter illustrate dramatically the consequences of recruiting a CEO or president with fatal flaws. It is hard to avoid the conclusion that it was the lack of integrity—combined with a lack of humility[6]— in the top ranks of Enron that led to its demise. If the Enron board is to be faulted for a single failing, it is that it did not see this key shortcoming of its top management. If there is reason to doubt the integrity of the person leading an organization, there is every reason to question the organization's prospects.

A challenging question, raised by Herbert ("Pug") Winokur on the basis of his experience on the Enron board, is how, in fact, a board can judge integrity, and do so before the fact, as it were. I doubt that there is a facile answer. The obvious things to do are to check the background of the individual with the greatest care, and to take testimony from people who have watched the person function in other settings, perhaps under some stress and strain. As my longtime colleague Neil Rudenstine suggests, there is no real substitute for long personal conversations, for watching body language, and for respecting one's intuition—at least to some extent. A starting point, in any case, is to recognize the centrality of this question, to observe actions meticulously, to demand full reports of business processes as well as decisions, and to keep asking hard questions.[7]

There is also a powerfully positive side to the integrity question. It was tremendously comforting to me as a Merck director to know that successive CEOs/chairmen of that company—John Horan, Roy Vagelos, Ray Gilmartin, and now Dick Clark—are individuals of impeccable integrity. When data became available from a clinical trial that showed an increased cardiovascular risk associated with the long term use of the painkiller VIOXX, the CEO at the time, Ray Gilmartin, gave scientists and others at Merck an unambiguous instruction: "Do what is right for patients." The drug was voluntarily withdrawn, and a subsequent independent report on the development and marketing of VIOXX by Judge John Martin and his colleagues at Debevoise & Plimpton confirmed in exhaustive detail that at no time did the senior management behave with a lack of integrity. Would Mr. Gilmartin and his colleagues have liked the clinical trials to yield different results? Of course. But clinical trials are conducted to produce the results that they produce, whatever they may be.[8]

- *Avoid putting too much emphasis on charm and charisma.* Careful due diligence provides an effective offset to becoming overly impressed by interview skills. Sometimes board members can be so charmed by a candidate, so taken with the candidate's presumed "vision," that they insist on electing that individual in the absence of real evidence that the person can get the job done. No one understands this point better than Larry Bossidy, who has written about the importance of choosing "doers":

> Boards of directors, CEOs, and senior executives are too often seduced by the educational and intellectual qualities of the candidates they interview. They don't ask the most important question: How good is this person at getting things done? In my experience, there's very little correlation between those who talk a good game and those who get things done come hell or high water. Too often the second kind are given short shrift. But if you want to build a company that has excellent discipline of execution, you have to select the doer.[9]

The other side of this coin is that, as Bossidy's statement implies, search committees can overlook outstanding candidates who may be more reserved and thus seem insufficiently flamboyant, or those who lack a high public profile. One of the country's most outstanding educational leaders, Yale president Richard Levin, is a case in point. During the selection process, the Yale search committee became convinced that Levin, then a forty-six-year-old professor of economics and dean of the Graduate School at Yale, who was highly regarded within Yale for his intelligence, wisdom, and interpersonal skills, would be a strong leader. Although at the time of the search Levin was not well known to the public at large, the committee concluded that Levin would gain, through his accomplishments, the national stature that it thought its president should possess. The committee, and then the Yale board, made an inspired choice.

- *Do not focus overly on fixing the last mistake.* When a search is conducted in the aftermath of problems of one kind or another, there is a natural tendency to focus on not letting the same bad thing happen again. This is understandable and even appropriate, but only up to a point. I recall all too clearly errors I made in attempting to fix first one mistake and then another (in the context of appointing, I have to confess, athletic coaches). I finally realized, somewhat belatedly, that we had to find an individual who had *all* the necessary qualities—not just someone who lacked the predecessor's limitations.

- *Consider strong candidates from all backgrounds, and look carefully at minority candidates and at women. Do not simply go through the motions, as this is both patronizing and demeaning.* There should be absolutely no presumption in favor of "traditional" candidates. At the same time, it is insulting to the process, and to the individuals caught up in it, to bring before the committee women and minority candidates who are not within range. No one deserves to be a token candidate, included only so that the process will seem legitimate in the minds of some people. Being straightforward and honest in both assessing qualifications and talking with potential candidates is essential.

- *Do not be formulaic in ranking insiders and outsiders.* The only way to resolve the insider-versus-outsider debate is case by case. In large companies, there is a natural desire to see if an outstanding person already on the scene can become the next CEO. The advantages are obvious: because the individual is better known to other managers and to the board than is any outsider, the risk of making a big mistake is reduced, including failing to perceive a consequential character flaw. In addition, contrary to what is sometimes assumed, an insider may actually have a better chance of bringing about significant change, because the right insider will enjoy the support of key colleagues.

  In the search for a new CEO at Merck, we gave considerable attention to outside candidates because we believed that major changes were needed in the entire pharmaceutical industry and that an outsider's fresh perspective could be a significant plus. After considering carefully a number of outside candidates, none of whom seemed exactly right, we went back to our list of insiders and chose Richard Clark, president of the manufacturing division of Merck, who had previously served as CEO of Medco (a leading pharmaceutical benefits manager).

  Clark has been a tremendous success; he has led major changes in the company's organization and business model that would have been much harder for an outsider to bring about. In retrospect, the question my colleagues on the search committee and I have asked ourselves is, Why did it take us so long to make such an obvious choice? The answer is not entirely clear, but at least we (and Clark, following his election as CEO) had the satisfaction of knowing that we considered all the options.

In nonprofits, the tendency to appoint outsiders is much more pronounced than it is within large for-profits because nonprofits are less likely to have a large pool of suitable talent in the organization. In colleges and universities, for example, disciplinary boundaries make it difficult to move a promising person from one area to another. Would it be as easy to move a person from the deanship of law to the deanship of medicine as it would be to move someone in charge of international equities to CFO? Hardly. This reality must be recognized, although I do think that nonprofits in general, including colleges and universities, should think anew about steps that they can take to develop larger pools of internal candidates.

One serious risk, especially in colleges and universities, is inherent in appointing someone from outside the institution: if things go badly, as they undoubtedly will at some juncture, a new president must be able to be forgiven at least some mistakes. It is much more likely that someone who has spent a fair part of his or her life at the institution will be able to command the personal loyalty—the affection—needed to survive stormy weather. During the tense time of the Vietnam War, I witnessed a specific instance in which an outsider president of a liberal arts college lacked the capacity to be forgiven that would have been so helpful—to the institution as well as to the individual. In contrast, I was fortunate to have been at Princeton as a faculty member for a number of years before being elected provost and then president, and to have made enough friends that I could count on some reservoir of goodwill during difficult days—when there was much they had to forgive!

- *Established mind-sets can be hard to change, and it is important to get the fit right between an individual's accustomed way of working and the needs of the institution.* In considering the appointment of a leader who has done well in a quite different organization, it is necessary to remember how difficult it can be for even the best-intentioned person to change a style of leadership that worked well in one setting but that may work less well in another. Differences in scale, and in the appropriate degree of delegation, can be important in this regard. In the educational world, for example, the skills required to lead a large public university are rather different from the skills needed to lead a small liberal arts college. It is certainly possible for talented people to adjust to a new environment, but the adjustment process may not be entirely smooth or comfortable for either the new president or the new institution.

- *Experience counts, especially experience in overcoming adversity.* It is important to be able to make a considered judgment as to how a candidate will perform when under stress and when faced with adversity. The only reliable way to make such judgments, at least in my experience, is by seeing how the individual has responded to difficult problems in the past. For this reason, committees may want to give some "edge" to individuals who have a track record of showing resilience in adverse situations.

- *Do not discount the benefits of freshness and new energy.* This consideration must be weighed against experience. Being the new leader of either a for-profit or a nonprofit organization generally requires fresh thinking, a sense of new possibilities, and a great deal of energy. My own preference has always been for people on the way up, who appear to be on a steep trajectory, and who have a capacity to be excited by aspects of the job that might bore those who have been doing similar things for some time. It can be hard to rekindle fires.

Graceful Transitions: What Should Be the Ongoing Role of the Former CEO/President?

In the process of choosing a new leader, boards have to decide not only who should lead the organization going forward, but also what will be the future role of the retiring CEO/president. Because this question is almost certain to come up in conversations with potential new leaders, the board needs to be prepared to answer it, and to be sure that the incumbent knows the board's intentions.

For some years, boards in the for-profit sector were accustomed to inviting a retiring CEO to stay on as a board member. As we saw in Chapter 2, in one governance model the retiring CEO is asked to chair the board. But both this "apprenticeship" approach to governance and the continuing presence of the former CEO on the board are much less common today. Although practice continues to vary, there appears to be an emerging consensus that the outgoing CEO/president should leave both the executive suite and the boardroom—and right away. I agree.

A clean break makes clear to one and all that the new CEO is, in fact, in charge and fully accountable. It can be impossible, especially in contentious situations, to make that fundamental point as long as the former CEO continues to serve on the board. In addition, the former CEO's presence makes it difficult to review past decisions and earlier practices openly and candidly. Even with the best will in the world, it is hard for any former CEO to be entirely objective about decisions made on his watch. Moreover, friends of the former CEO, and others who do not want to hurt feelings or give offense, will inevitably find it more difficult to raise questions if the architect of past decisions, for whom one has both affection and respect, is sitting across the table. Furthermore, some chairmen who were CEOs protect their protégés, when boards should assess on the merits how the new CEO is doing.[10]

Michael Blumenthal, former CEO and chairman of Unisys, as well as former secretary of the treasury, has observed,

> I absolutely agree that a former CEO should not be on the board. Such a person, even a very good one, can be in an impossible bind. If he criticizes the new incumbent, he is suspect. If he has real reservations and doesn't speak out, he is not doing his job. Save him that dilemma. Also, the new CEO is bound to be a bit embarrassed to reverse policies in front of his old boss, particularly if they remain good friends.

John Horan, former CEO and chairman of Merck, told me,

> I made a big mistake in staying on the board after stepping down as CEO . . . The discussions were painful, I never knew when I should comment or when I should stay quiet, and it was just not a good idea to stay there. If people wanted my views, they could obtain them in other ways.

Larry Bossidy said that when he became CEO/chairman of AlliedSignal, his predecessor (Edward Hennessy) wanted to stay on the board. Bossidy encouraged the nominating committee to ask him to step down, which they did—and Hennessy did step down. Bossidy explained his reasoning this way:

> In most instances, a departing CEO should not stay on a board. His or her presence can do two damaging things. First, it can create some discomfort for the succeeding CEO. Second, it's frustrating for the departing CEO. He may have to listen to things that are contrary to what he believes in and has done, and yet [he must] hold back from explaining or defending his choices.[11]

My personal experience with this question spans almost thirty years. When I first became president of Princeton, in 1972, I could not understand why it made sense to deprive the board, and me, of the wisdom of my accomplished predecessor, Robert Goheen. He would have been a fine board member and a source of help rather than difficulty for me, but he did not want to stay on. I now believe that the members of the Princeton board who, in company with President Goheen, thought it better for me to start out on my own were absolutely right. Years later, when I retired from the presidency of the Mellon Foundation, in June 2006, I made it clear to one and all that I believed that when you leave the position of president or CEO, you should leave. As I have said on many occasions, "One president at a time is enough—maybe more than enough!"

I am opposed to leaving the decision as to whether a CEO should or should not continue to serve on the board in that individual's hands. Although I agree that an exceptional person may be able to handle, with style as well as judgment, the inevitable ambiguities of such a shift in roles, opening the door for any exceptions may invite the wrong individual to step through it. A wise friend (Arjay Miller, former Ford Motor Company executive and then dean of the Stanford University Graduate School of Business) observed that a perverse pattern may develop: "The CEOs who would be okay as continuing members of the board do not usually want to stay, whereas the CEOs who want to stay on the board after their retirement are the very ones who should leave."

A prime example, from my experience, is the role played by George

Grune at the Reader's Digest Association (RDA). Grune believed passionately in what the *Digest* stood for (all to his credit), but he had great difficulty accepting that times had changed, that the *Digest*'s customer base was—literally—dying off, and that the company needed a dramatic shift in directions. No real consideration could be given to a major repositioning of the business (or to the option of selling the company) with Grune at the table following his retirement as CEO. All of this was very sad because Grune wanted only the best for the *Digest*—but the best was unattainable, I believed, as long as he was the dominant presence in the room. It was this conclusion that led me, in 1997, to leave the boards of the RDA and of the Wallace Funds, which held a controlling interest in the company.

As several commentators have testified, the advice and help of the retired CEO can be obtained absent a formal board relationship. In the case of the Mellon Foundation, my predecessor, Jack Sawyer, never hesitated to provide helpful advice, while being scrupulously careful to give me full freedom of action. Similarly, Bob Goheen was always ready to do anything I asked him to do at Princeton. In corporate contexts, I have seen the same willingness on the part of former CEOs to offer help—but only if asked. Indeed, former CEOs can have their feelings hurt if they are not asked informally—at least on occasion—for their views.

In short, the arguments for leaving the board when a person's time has come, following service as CEO or president, are compelling in both the for-profit and nonprofit sectors. Having stated this strong position, I must acknowledge that it is dangerous to say "never." In some unusual situations, a CEO with special chemistry can help a successor CEO become accustomed to the board and comfortable in a new role. But I think—with all due respect to those who have served admirably during such transitions—that this is rarely the right model.

*　　*　　*　　*　　*

THE SUCCESS OF A board in choosing the right CEO, at the right time, depends greatly on the board itself—on its members and how well they work together. Building the board is a critically important activity in its own right, and in the next chapter I will discuss the recruitment of outstanding board members and the sensitive but essential task of renewing the board on an ongoing basis.

6

Building the Board

Having focused in the last three chapters on the evolving relationships between boards and their CEOs (or presidents), including the recruitment of new leaders and the importance of graceful transitions, we now turn to the board itself, how it is comprised, how it is structured, and how it functions.

One of the major changes in governance over the last ten years is the much greater attention that directors and trustees are now paying to the building of the board itself. No longer is it assumed, even in the best-run organizations, that board development will simply take care of itself. Careful attention has to be given to the size of the board and its composition; the process whereby new directors are chosen; the criteria relevant to identifying and recruiting new board members; the emphasis to be given to diversity; and the definition of director "independence." These aspects of the ongoing process of building a board are the subject of this chapter. In Chapter 7 we will consider key aspects of how boards work, including the internal "machinery" that boards need to function effectively and to renew themselves.

The Size of the Board

There is widespread agreement that a board's capacity to perform its functions is critically dependent on its size. Although there is nothing magical about any particular number, it seems clear that boards can be both too small and too large. The severity of problems associated with size can be mitigated by skillful leadership and careful management of board affairs, but there is no escaping the fact that size itself matters.

At the bottom end of the usual ranges, a board with fewer than eight to ten members runs the risk of being insufficiently diverse in the range of backgrounds, experiences, skill sets, and perspectives that it encompasses. Very small boards can be overly dependent on one or two people to contribute certain talents, a particular perspective, or a distinctive style. Even exceptionally dedicated board members miss an occasional meeting because of illness or conflicts, and such absences can be debilitating if the board is so small that it contains no backups. Finally, small boards naturally provide fewer candidates to serve in leadership positions—to chair committees, if not the board itself, and, in the case of nonprofits, to lead fund-raising campaigns. Boards need at least enough members to populate key committees and carry out essential tasks.

Boards of for-profit companies controlled by private-equity funds or venture capitalists may be an exception to worries about the pitfalls of small size. These boards often consist of five to seven members, and their small size seems to fit well within cultures that stress informality, hands-on oversight, the lack of committee structures, and relative freedom from the concern about external relationships that is characteristic of both publicly traded for-profits and nonprofits. Still, the risks of being too dependent on one or two people remain. Apparently the sizes of some of these boards are increasing at least modestly as more firms are involved in some of the largest deals (with each firm wanting representation on the board) and as the need for a mix of capabilities is recognized.

At the other end of the spectrum, it is undeniable that boards can be too large. As one experienced CEO (Michael Blumenthal) observed, "Certainly at 18–24, real group cohesion, interaction, debate and collegiality become impossible." Quite apart from effects on the quality of discussion and interchange of ideas, boards can be too large for individual accountability to survive. Beyond some limit, it becomes easy for individual members to be anonymous—to defer, de facto, to everyone else. When all members of a large group are thought to be equally responsible, no one may feel really responsible. John Whitehead, who has served on more boards than almost anyone else, offered this candid observation about himself: "I find that there is an inverse correlation between the size of a board and my sense of responsibility to it."

In recent years, especially in the for-profit sector, boards have converged in size, and fewer now are very small or very large.[1] After shrinking for a number of years, average board size among S&P 500 companies now appears to be stable at about eleven directors. In this sector at least, the question of optimal size appears to be resolved.

Not so in the nonprofit sector. Nonprofit boards tend to be larger than their for-profit cousins—much larger in some cases. Although it is hard to find a systematic survey of board size for charitable nonprofits, a combination of the surveys that are available, reports by entities such as the Association of Governing Boards of Universities and Colleges, an informal analysis that we have made of Mellon Foundation grantees, and personal knowledge leaves no doubt as to the general picture. The average size of these nonprofit boards appears to be roughly twenty. And some nonprofit boards are appreciably larger—thirty, on average, for private colleges and universities. According to the American Symphony Orchestra League, the orchestras with the largest budgets have boards that average sixty-five members.[2]

There are two reasons why nonprofit boards are often larger than may be desirable purely from a decision-making standpoint:

(1) Many have to satisfy a wider range of constituents than do for-profit boards; therefore, they are likely to have a greater need for diversity measured along many dimensions. College boards are a good example. As is true of other types of boards, they need a broad range of professional perspectives, as well as individuals who have experience with educational issues. In addition, these boards need to reflect the diversity of their student and alumni populations in terms of age, geography, gender, and race.

(2) Many organizations also need to include major donors and those able to solicit contributions.[3] Clear trade-offs are made. Some

boards knowingly become larger than they believe they should be because of the high priority given to fund-raising. In an attempt to satisfy fund-raising needs without enlarging their boards too much, nonprofits often make use of development councils, advisory boards, and similar mechanisms. Though such parallel structures can definitely help, they are rarely a full solution. Some people will be satisfied with nothing less than a seat on the one organizational entity that has power—or, perhaps more important yet, prestige.[4] In addition, coordinating the activities of two complementary instrumentalities is no easy task, as presidents of Harvard University will attest on the basis of their experience working with both the Harvard Corporation and the Board of Overseers.[5]

The active use of an executive committee is a common way of addressing the problem of size. I am told that this approach has worked well in a number of situations, including the American Academy in Rome and the International Rescue Committee. There is, however, always the danger that some trustees not on the executive committee will feel that they have been consigned to the second tier of a two-tiered board. Skillful board leadership, candor, and good humor can go a long way toward easing such sensitivities, but it may not be possible to eliminate them altogether.

The Memorial Sloan-Kettering Cancer Center has developed an even more subtle approach. Its annual report contains a list of fifty to sixty "members of the Boards of Overseers and Managers."[6] No distinction is made between these two groups. Thus, all of these individuals can say, and believe, that they serve on "the board." At the same time, real decision-making authority rests with the board of managers, which consists of not more than thirty individuals who meet four times a year. The board of overseers meets concurrently with the board of managers and serves in an advisory capacity. The board of managers has a committee structure, and overseers are asked occasionally to serve on various committees of the board of managers.

Grant-making foundations are a revealing exception to the conventional wisdom about the characteristically large size of nonprofit boards. According to the Council on Foundations, the average size of foundation boards is now 12.5.[7] One reason for their smaller size is that the boards of grant-making foundations do not normally solicit contributions and therefore do not need to make room on their boards for potential donors or fund-raisers. Nor do foundations have to recruit students, attract audiences, or seek clients.

The truly serious problems, in any case, involve nonprofit boards that are so large that their size compromises their ability to govern effectively. My favorite quotation underscoring this danger was contributed by a Mellon Foundation trustee with much experience as a board member in the nonprofit sector, Taylor Reveley: "As a rule, if there are more than 30 members, the sheer size of the board erodes its effectiveness. *Members can shelter poor attendance, lack of preparation, avoidance of difficult issues and failing to do anything significant amid the heaving mass of the board*" (my emphasis).

It is noteworthy, and troubling, that some nonprofits that encountered difficulties in the early 1990s *increased*, rather than decreased, the size of already large boards. In the wake of complaints about both inefficiency and lax oversight, the United Way, for example, increased its board from thirty-seven to forty-five. This board added new members in an effort to meet evident needs. But the obvious question is whether the better solution would have been to create places for new members by retiring some current members. The Red Cross, troubled by myriad problems (with the board having been too intrusive in some respects), offers a more encouraging picture in its decision to gradually reduce the size of its board from fifty to a maximum of twenty, with complementary changes in the method of choosing board members. A study of the difficulties experienced by the Red Cross makes it abundantly clear that the size of the board, and other failures of board structure, were major obstacles to good governance.[8]

Recruiting Board Members: The Context and Process

In the for-profit world it has become increasingly difficult to recruit new directors, even though reductions in the average size of boards mean that there are fewer places to fill. There are several reasons:

- Time commitments for board members have increased substantially as service on major for-profit boards has become more demanding.

- Greater scrutiny of board behavior by activist investors, investigative reporters, and regulatory agencies has increased the risk of embarrassment and damage to reputations, even in situations in which a particular director has behaved in an exemplary fashion. As Martin Lipton of Wachtell, Lipton, Rosen & Katz has put it, "Media critics and governance watchdogs simplify scandals and assume that all directors are at fault when something goes wrong. Thus, directors risk public embarrassment for any misbehavior at their companies, however diligent the directors may have been."[9] Relevant, too, is the growth of shareholder litigation against directors.

- Active business CEOs—traditionally a favored group of candidates—are now limiting the number of outside boards on which they will serve, in part because of the factors just cited, and because their own boards don't want them to be distracted by outside responsibilities. Whereas the average number of outside boards for a sitting CEO used to be two, it is now less than one; approximately one quarter of active CEOs of S&P 500 companies serve on *no* outside boards. Of independent directors newly elected in 2006, 29 percent were active CEOs, compared with 48 percent in 2001.[10]

This more difficult recruitment environment in the case of for-profit boards means that they need to consider groups of candidates who might have been overlooked when it was easier to fill vacancies with sitting CEOs. Recently retired CEOs are one such group. Another is promising executives on the way up, even though their own CEOs may be reluctant to "expose" these people, lest they be recruited away—a particularly serious problem, I am told, in the case of promising women executives. Chief financial officers are now receiving considerable attention as board candidates, in part because financial expertise is increasingly valued on the board, especially on the audit committee. There are also other highly qualified professionals—lawyers, accountants, scientists, experts on government processes and international affairs—who deserve more consideration than they have often received in the past. One puzzle is why the growing number of eminent women attorneys, many of whom hold leadership positions in their firms and on nonprofit boards, are so poorly represented on business boards.[11]

To be sure, recruiting outstanding trustees to serve on nonprofit boards can be difficult too. As in the for profit sector, increased scrutiny—by media, Congress, and regulators—may make some candidates leery of serving. More generally, as board chairs and leaders of nominating committees can attest, the best candidates always seem overcommitted. Still, I do not believe that it is more difficult now than before to recruit strong candidates for service on nonprofit boards. In these days of both "venture philanthropy" and the shift of responsibility for many activities from government to the nonprofit sector, it is widely assumed that civic leaders, including business CEOs, should contribute to nonprofit causes, often by serving on boards.

One danger, in fact, is that it may be *too* easy to recruit trustees—by which I mean simply that individuals may agree to join nonprofit boards without having really thought through the commitment that board membership should entail (beware of reflexive acceptances!). It is incumbent on those invited to join boards to think hard about whether they can satisfy the obligations of board membership. Several commentators noted the sometime tendency for people to join boards for "the honor of it," or simply to pad their résumés. This proposition applies to the for-profit sector as well, and it is important for companies to guard against electing candidates who want to serve on the board of a for-profit just for the prestige. As one commentator who has served on the boards of both publicly traded companies and privately held for-profits notes, it is refreshing to know that in the private-equity sphere, board members are there for business reasons (to enhance the value of their investment as owners), not just to be seen.

Probably the most important change in board governance in recent years is that primary responsibility for identifying and recruiting independent directors in the for-profit sector is increasingly understood to rest with the board itself, not with the CEO. As Joan Warner, managing editor of *Directorship* and a former senior editor for *BusinessWeek*, puts it, "Twenty years ago, most directors were handpicked by the chief executive, largely on the basis of their people skills . . . Today, canvassing the golf course just doesn't cut it anymore."[12] Steve Norman, longtime secretary of the American Express board and an active observer of corporate boards in general, was emphatic in stressing the importance of this fundamental change in governance. Of course, the CEO needs to be an integral part of the process—in Norman's words, "you can't just parachute a stranger into the boardroom"—but the CEO should not do the choosing. At Morgan Stanley, Purcell, as CEO/chairman, vetted candidates for board positions before deciding whether to send them on to his handpicked chairman of the nominating committee, Michael Miles.[13] SEC proxy rules now require companies to state how each candidate was nominated.[14]

In practice, if there is goodwill and a shared sense of what needs to be accomplished, the appropriate board committee and the CEO can work together quite successfully to build an effective board. In keeping with this collaborative spirit, the needs of the CEO/president must be understood and taken into account, along with the needs of the board itself. I am a firm believer in giving the CEO/president a de facto veto in the selection process, but this is a privilege that should be used sparingly and not abused. When I was at Princeton, I remember vividly exercising such a veto once, when someone proposed a high-profile candidate who I thought would be problematic because of a history of arrogant, noncollegial behavior. In my view, it is never wise to force the election of a new director or trustee on a CEO/president who has serious doubts about the candidate in question.

The gracious granting of veto power is very different, however, from allowing the president/CEO to dictate who *should* be elected. Thought-ful business CEOs understand that, in today's world, it will not do for board members to feel beholden to the CEO for their seats on the board. This has never been a big problem in the nonprofit sector, since nonprofit boards have long taken a more active role in recruiting new trustees. Of course, presidents of nonprofits and CEOs in the for-profit sector should not hesitate to bring the names of promising candidates for board seats to the attention of nominating committees, as I often did, but always with the understanding that the board, not the president or the CEO, would decide whether the candidate should be elected. This is an instance in which well-established practices in the nonprofit world have spilled over—appropriately—to the for-profit sector.

The question of who chooses is also posed by the current debate in corporate America over how much support nominees should have to receive in order to be elected to the board. Activist investors and dissi-dent shareholders have voiced increasing dissatisfaction with the com-mon plurality voting policies under which a board-nominated candidate for an uncontested seat is elected if the individual gets just one shareholder vote. Such policies make it impossible for shareholders to remove directors by withholding support at the annual meeting. John Connolly, head of the proxy advisory firm Institutional Shareholder Services (ISS), expects 450 resolutions calling for majority voting to come before US companies in 2007—up from 140 in 2006, 89 in 2005, and just 12 in 2004. Gavin Anderson, who heads the rating firm GovernanceMetrics International (GMI), called the majority voting movement an "unstoppable train."[15] Many corporate executives agree and see no grounds for fighting these provisions. Thus, it seems highly likely that within a few years there will be majority voting provisions everywhere—which means simply that, to be elected, a director will have to receive more votes in support of his or her election than the number of votes withheld. In a positive development, companies such as Wal-Mart, Intel, Home Depot, and Merck have already adopted majority voting policies, sometimes embedding them in the company's charter.

There is much less agreement on a variety of proposals that would make it easier for shareholders to nominate candidates for board membership. Of course, any shareholder can propose a candidate to the company's nominating committee; and if the shareholder owns enough stock, presumably the board will take such a nomination seriously. Just before the May 2007 annual meeting of Home Depot, Richard Ferlauto, the director of pension investment policy at a major union pension fund, led a delegation of shareholder activists to a private meeting with the board's nominating committee. If such informal efforts to influence nominations fail, proxy fights remain the main vehicle through which shareholders can elect their own directors. Increasingly, proxy fights are ending in settlements that involve awarding at least one board seat to the dissident group. There is a delicate balance to be struck here. It should be possible for shareholders to challenge an entrenched board to consider new directions, but if challenges can be mounted too often or too easily, orderly board processes can be disrupted by the arrival on the scene (or even the impending arrival) of "single-issue candidates."

In the nonprofit world these issues take other forms, if they arise at all. Many private colleges and universities allow alumni to play a role in nominating and electing a limited number of trustees. In most situations, these efforts to incorporate some form of democracy into the selection process work smoothly and give alumni a sense that they matter. However, the heated debates at Dartmouth, where alumni have succeeded in electing some trustees who were nominated by petition, demonstrate that machinery of this kind can engender controversy.[16] Colleges and universities should want to have individuals with a variety of perspectives on their boards, but they are also understandably wary about electing trustees who will feel obligated to represent a particular constituency. Many colleges and universities take a different tack and arrange for informal consultation with campus groups, as well as with alumni, in the course of the nominating process.

However decisions are reached concerning ways in which potential candidates are nominated, it is encouraging that there is a growing understanding, in both the for-profit and nonprofit sectors, that building a strong board is a multiyear process. This process should include a systematic assessment of the needs of the board, as well as a clear game plan for filling vacancies in an orderly way. Vacancies should not be filled on a one-off basis or by someone simply proposing a candidate thought to be congenial. In my experience chairing the committee at Merck that was responsible for recommending new board members, it proved helpful to consult a matrix that listed the company's ongoing needs, such as individuals with standing in medicine and science, as well as others with strong business experience and still others knowledgeable about public policy issues. Nonprofit organizations have their own lists of needs, which usually include substantive knowledge of the field in which the organization works and, in many cases, investment capabilities and fund-raising ability. Diversity considerations and age distributions need to be taken into account by organizations in both sectors. Whatever the most urgent needs of a particular board are judged to be, it is important that advanced planning and the recruitment of new board members be undertaken with the knowledge of when particular board members will retire and what gaps will be created when they leave the board.

Organizations should work to avoid situations like the one that our nominating committee inherited at Merck when, by coincidence and (admittedly) some lack of advance planning, six board members were scheduled to retire within a two-year period. Recruiting new members in clumps is never desirable. It is much easier to incorporate new members if they are added to the board one by one. New directors/trustees need to be socialized by being introduced to key staff and to their fellow board members, by making site visits, and by familiarizing themselves with the history of the organization and its key policies. All of this is easier to accomplish if vacancies are staggered and board recruitment is an orderly rather than episodic process. At Merck, we learned to pay close attention to the age distribution of the board in recruiting new directors.

More recently, the board of Home Depot has been criticized—in the aftermath of the sudden ouster of Robert Nardelli—for failing to plan ahead to ensure proper board turnover. Three Home Depot board members were scheduled to retire together in the spring of 2007, when they all would have reached the mandatory retirement age of seventy-two, but these board members are now being asked to serve another year to provide expertise to Nardelli's successor. A fourth Home Depot board member and lead director, Kenneth Langone, is already scheduled to retire in the spring of 2008. It would obviously have been better if the Home Depot board had anticipated this bunching of retirements and recruited new members earlier.[17]

In short, the recruitment of board members should be pursued as systematically as the recruitment of a new CEO. A real search process is required. It is unwise to rely solely on word of mouth and friends, but it would be equally foolish not to take advantage of the knowledge of board members who have had experience with outstanding candidates in other settings. To give a personal example, I recommended that the Merck board consider Peter Wendell, general partner at Sierra Ventures and an exceedingly able venture capitalist with whom I had worked closely at both Princeton and the Mellon Foundation. Wendell had no previous experience serving on boards of large corporations and no credentials as a scientist; he would not have come to the attention of the board had I not known him personally. Wendell has already proved to be an outstanding director, and identifying him as a candidate for election to the board—on the understanding that other directors would then conduct their own due diligence—may well be one of the more valuable contributions I made to the building of the Merck board.

However, only a limited number of "Wendells" will be well known to current board members. Search firms can be helpful in developing larger lists of candidates, but it is imperative that those on the board responsible for recommending candidates give the search firm a very clear sense of the needs of the board and of the criteria that it wishes to have applied in building a list. I also believe that, as when using search firms to identify candidates for CEO, the board members leading the recruitment process need to make key contacts themselves. They must explore the potential interest of highly desirable candidates who may be very hard to recruit and vet candidates before offering them a place on the board. In both the for-profit and nonprofit sectors, evaluations of board candidates should focus more than is commonly done on how well an individual has performed on other boards. Not all capable people are good board members.

More generally, systematic and ongoing efforts to build boards should be expected to yield inventories of candidates that can then be reviewed regularly. Nominating committee members and staff should monitor the progress of individuals in the inventory who look promising and to whom they may want to turn at the right moment. Designing and then executing an effective recruitment process can pay very high returns.

Recruiting the Right Individuals

However well conceived the process is for building a board, ultimate success or failure will depend on how wisely the board chooses individuals. The right people can make any process look good, and no system can guarantee positive results. Wisdom, judgment—and some modicum of luck—are required.

In thinking about criteria, it is useful to begin with what I would call "common, core qualifications": integrity, competence, reliability, good judgment, independence of mind, and dedication to the cause. As trite as it may seem to list these seemingly old-fashioned virtues, taking them for granted can be disastrous, as much recent experience demonstrates. In listing core qualifications, I also agree with Larry Bossidy that boards should seek individuals with, in his words, "a demonstrated history of accomplishments in whatever the field . . . Tangible accomplishments are far more important than credentials."[18]

Every director also needs to possess the ability to work with colleagues in settings in which collective decision making is the order of the day. Sometimes very smart, very talented people simply cannot be integrated successfully onto boards, especially boards whose members are already accustomed to working well together. A good example is Marty

Wygod, founder of Medco, the leading pharmaceutical benefits manager, who was invited to join the Merck board after the company acquired Medco. Wygod was an incisive thinker who anticipated better than perhaps anyone else the need for sophisticated systems approaches to the purchase of prescription drugs in managed-care settings. Unfortunately, however, his aggressive style and apparent lack of appreciation for the talents of board colleagues made him an unsatisfactory board member. He resigned after six months as a director.

As Tom Neff, chairman of Spencer Stuart U.S., has argued, boards also need to have a core of individuals who understand how complex organizations work and what is involved in leading them. This is one compelling reason to include some number of CEOs. As Neff goes on to emphasize, organizational "smarts" can also be found among individuals who have been responsible for leading nonprofits, such as large museums, hospitals, and major research universities, and among those who have had high-level governmental experience.

Boards also need outside directors with first-hand knowledge of the genre of the organization. These individuals play a valuable role in helping the board ask key questions. On corporate boards, many believe that this need is met by the presence of other CEOs who have current experience with similar business issues in their own companies. Having made this assumption myself, I was somewhat taken aback by several commentators from the for-profit world who warned me not to exaggerate the extent to which CEOs will understand each other's businesses. Substantive knowledge of particular fields or industries is often more valuable. Nicholas Katzenbach observed that Harold Brown, a distinguished scientist and former head of Caltech, was invaluable on the IBM board because of his ability to identify technical issues that other board members would have missed. Merck's board benefits enormously from the presence of highly qualified scientists with deep knowledge of developments in fields such as molecular biology. Multinational companies benefit from having board members who appreciate the worldwide context in which such companies work.[19]

Nonprofits also need board members who have sufficient experience with the field in which the organization operates to alert the board to new developments, potential traps, and key conventions—who will know enough to ask awkward questions. Neil Rudenstine, former president of Harvard, proved to be exceptionally valuable in helping his colleagues on the Princeton board of trustees understand issues confronting all research universities; and I can attest personally to the frequent contributions to the work of the Denison board made by David Bayley, a respected faculty member and dean at SUNY-Albany. To be sure, "amateurs" are likely to dominate the rosters of nonprofit boards, but this can be fine, since what is needed is not a numerical supremacy of professionals or experts, but the presence of some trustees with a deep knowledge of the field in question. There is just no substitute for professional sophistication on the part of at least some board members.

Nonprofits also use board recruitment to secure professional talent that they may not need on a full-time basis or might not be able to afford if the talent were not volunteered. Lawyers and investors often fall into this category.[20] More generally, I believe that every individual on a board should have some special competence or experience to contribute. Although it is obviously desirable to have individuals with a breadth of experience, it is dangerous, in my view, to recruit people who make careers serving as outside directors. Requiring that potential members have deep roots in another organization or in a particular vocation offers at least partial protection against dilettantism.

Organizations in the nonprofit sector that must raise considerable sums of money from donors have an obvious need for fund-raising capabilities—and for board members who are themselves capable of generosity. This is a primary criterion in recruiting some board members; and presidents or executive directors, along with their development staff, will often have critically important information to contribute to the nominating process.

Sometimes, however, it is surprisingly hard for nonprofit organizations with a strong scholarly or professional focus to give sufficient weight to the importance of recruiting individuals who can help raise money. I know of at least two prominent academically oriented nonprofits whose boards, which were composed almost entirely of highly qualified academics, paid a big price for resisting the election of individuals with fund-raising capacities because those individuals were not thought to possess the proper scholarly qualifications. I consider this attitude foolish, assuming that care is taken to be sure that potential directors understand and respect the mission of the organization. The opposite danger lies in giving so much attention to fund-raising that the board forgets why it is raising money in the first place. As in everything else, a sensible balance of interests and qualifications has to be struck.

Another, very different kind of need is common to both for-profit and nonprofit boards. In his report on the problems at WorldCom, Richard Breeden observed, "Perhaps more than speeches from lawyers, *every board can use a curmudgeon or two*" (my emphasis).[21] He went on to note, "Someone on the board has to be prepared to object if management does not observe rules of good behavior, if management seeks excessive compensation, or if management is creating unacceptable risks." In a similar vein, another commentator stressed the value of having a "pilot fish" on the board, who is unafraid to swim upstream.

I remember well how much I benefited, when I was president of Princeton, from having to respond to pointed questions from independent-minded trustees such as Michael Blumenthal and Paul Volcker about the cost structure of the university and tuition policies. It is critically important, however, to have the right kind of curmudgeon. Both Blumenthal and Volcker were strongly supportive of the university, and of its leadership, at the same time that they vigorously debated the wisdom of one decision or another. In the words of the late John Gardner, distinguished public servant and former head of Common Cause, institutions need to be spared both "uncritical lovers and unloving critics." Collegiality and mutual respect cannot be sacrificed in order to include questioning, if not dissenting, voices in the conversation.

Let me now advance one other proposition in which I have come to believe strongly, and which I will reiterate in the concluding chapter: In the corporate world in particular, *courage and the will to act are often the attributes in scarcest supply*. In my experience, after some amount of time and discussion (to be sure, frequently too much time and too much discussion), it usually becomes fairly obvious what should be done. The trick is marshalling the energy—and especially the courage—to act. It is so much easier simply to wait a little longer for events to unfold. In the American Express saga that culminated in the resignation of James Robinson as CEO and then as chairman, it was Rawleigh Warner who stepped up and said what was on the minds of a number of other directors.[22]

Unfortunately, the problem is deeper than merely finding individuals with the requisite backbone—though that is, I suspect, the most important thing. The less tractable aspect of the problem reflects what one experienced board member has described as the "director's dilemma":

> Executive management must be left free to run the company uninhibited by excessive interference by the board. The issue, of course, is what is excessive interference? I find that most conscientious directors are overly shy about being perceived as rocking the boat. This leads to a broader question. Can directors be more than a purely reactive force? The catch 22 is that the reluctance to be perceived as interfering makes for passive rather than active board participants. The importance of not engaging or interfering in short-term management frequently causes directors to abdicate their responsibility for long-term direction. The "director's dilemma" is a difficult one; I suspect you may have felt it acutely at times.

Another commentator, who exceeds any normal standard of conscientiousness and courage (David Culver, chairman of CAI Capital Corporation, retired chairman of Alcan Aluminium, and a former colleague of mine on the American Express board) starts from what he calls "General Doriot's definition of an organization as a group of individuals helping one person do a job."[23] In his view, directors are there to help the CEO do a most difficult job, and therein lies the tension. As Culver went on to observe,

> There is no problem as long as the organization is "on a roll." But then along comes the day when the CEO, barely disguising his adrenalin, proposes a big bold move. He has done his best to keep his board informed. He has made it abundantly clear to the other party—and to his staff—that the matter is subject to board approval, etc., etc. As a director, you don't like it. It doesn't feel right. However, it is a fast moving world, and if I say "no way," I am pulling the rug out from under the feet of the person I am trying to help "do a job." Thus the director finds himself making comments about the proposed deal—knowing that it is too late to stop it from happening (the other 80% of the board is not going to do anything!)—and yet hoping to have an influence on the CEO's

next idea, not knowing what that next idea could possibly be! It's the essence of indirect influence, not easy to do, and not much fun.

This kind of thing can go on only so long. Eventually the conscientious director has to overrule General Doriot and conclude that new leadership is mandatory.

It is hard to know when simply raising questions, and eyebrows, has become insufficient. Culver is right that being effective, without prematurely pulling the rug out, requires artistry of a high order. Realistically, all that we can hope to accomplish in building boards is to increase the chances that such artistry will be present and exercised. In addition to electing wise individuals who have the will to act, boards need to create a climate, and to set up structures, that will facilitate rather than inhibit courageous decision making.

In selecting members of nonprofit boards, there is another attribute of critical importance that is sometimes overlooked or undervalued: finding individuals who have a genuine understanding of the mission of the organization, combined with empathy and commitment. Ron Daniel, former managing director of McKinsey & Company and an active trustee of nonprofit entities, argues that this qualification is as important for nonprofits as courage is in for-profit settings. As Daniel observes, the boards of nonprofit organizations may include individuals who, while highly competent in some general sense, "simply don't get it."

It is dangerous to have trustees who lack understanding and empathy, who fail to understand how a ballet company functions or how graduate education relates to undergraduate education in a research university. Daniel's blunt assessment is that "such a person will never be of any use." People with no visceral feel for the organization may be clumsily overblown and do real damage, or so insecure that they just do not participate. Trustees should have passion for the institution or great esteem for its leader—and preferably both.

This enhanced need for understanding and empathy is one reason why nonprofits should not simply collect names on their boards. A specific problem is that some high-profile individuals may feel a need to perform at board meetings. When individuals join boards to make a splash or advance a personal agenda, the effects can be disruptive. A board can soon find itself wasting time and missing opportunities for serious discussion. This can be a particularly serious problem when boards are required to meet in open session, a format that invites "performance."

To end this discussion on a rather different note, I will suggest another qualification, albeit not really a professional one, that should be taken seriously in the process of composing boards. Including individuals who make it stimulating and enjoyable—fun—for other trustees or directors to come to meetings can be invaluable. Having interesting colleagues is an important reward for service, and the presence of such people encourages fuller attendance and more active participation in the work of the board. Any number of individuals come to mind as illustrations of this point, but I would mention especially the late Malcolm Forbes, former publisher of *Forbes Magazine*, who was an extremely effective trustee of Princeton. As many will attest, Mr. Forbes was a wonderfully engaging, irreverent spirit who had the capacity to make even the dreariest occasion interesting. His liveliness never detracted from the serious issues of the day; rather, it served to highlight them and to direct energy to the search for solutions to the most mundane problems.

Diversity

Diversity of both backgrounds and perspectives continues to be extremely important in composing boards—so important that it deserves separate consideration. As valuable as it is, diversity must be achieved without sacrificing agreement on a common set of assumptions about the institution and its mission.

In the case of colleges and universities, diversity is necessary if boards are to be effective as questioners and decision makers, if their policy decisions are to be perceived as legitimate, and if they are to be successful in appealing for support from the institution's varied constituencies. In discussing the implications of gender equity for athletic programs, it is obviously desirable to have the viewpoints of women as well as of men. Similarly, discussions of how to handle racial slurs in the context of an institution's commitment to free speech will benefit greatly from the active contributions of trustees who are themselves members of minority groups.

In the case of for-profit boards, "who we are" says a great deal to staff members, vendors, and customers all over the world about the company's values and commitments. Companies that preach the virtues of diversity, and emphasize diversity in recruiting and promoting staff, can hardly claim the high ground if board membership fails to demonstrate the same commitment. As the demography of America continues to change, with white high school graduates projected to make up just 58 percent of graduating classes in 2014, and as more companies become global in their reach, the importance of achieving some real measure of diversity is greater than ever before.[24] It remains true, however, that "there are still many firms without a non-white director."[25]

Many organizations want more diversity on their boards but are unsure how to go about including members of previously excluded groups, especially racial minorities. It can be tempting to earmark positions (for example, the "black seat") on a board, but this practice is both patronizing and an inadequate response to the opportunity to enrich a board by recruiting outstanding individuals of diverse backgrounds. I also believe that no board should be limited to one of anything, even though practical constraints on size preclude giving full effect to this "Noah's Ark" principle. It is much easier for women and members of minority groups to address the full range of issues presented to a board if they don't harbor the suspicion that the board is expecting them to somehow represent the perspective of all women or all minorities—as if a single perspective existed in the first place. Similarly, it may be better if there is more than one corporate CEO—and more than one educator too, especially if the organization is a college or university.

If individuals believe that they are on a board to represent a particular group, or a particular point of view, they will not be what Quakers call "weighty" board members. It is too easy to dismiss their arguments as special pleading. To have influence, individuals must think for themselves and be perceived by others as concerned about the best interests of the organization as a whole. Just as it would be wrong to expect minority group members to speak for their group, it would be wrong for other board members to feel that they have no responsibility to be sensitive to such concerns because others are assumed to feel them more acutely. It is important to reject categorically any notion that individual members represent particular constituencies.

Diversity must be achieved without the loss of essential commonalities. As one commentator put it, "All board members must believe in certain things or it will be impossible for the board to function." Stories abound of well-intentioned efforts to diversify boards that unfortunately ended up by frustrating everyone concerned. Backgrounds, lifestyles, and modes of discourse can become so heterogeneous that it is impossible, as a practical matter, to conduct an informed and focused discussion. In such situations, people lose patience.

One practical way of increasing the odds that a truly diverse board will work effectively is to recruit individuals who are already familiar with the workings of complex organizations and may even have participated in the leadership of such organizations. Generally speaking, board members who have the most difficulty being effective are those who simply do not understand how boards work, the pressures under which a CEO labors, the need to achieve consensus, and so on. Thanks in no small measure to the success of affirmative action programs, pools of well-qualified and experienced candidates from diverse backgrounds are becoming larger all the time.

Diversity is not merely of symbolic importance. Select Comfort Corporation, a mattress company, had only male directors, even though women are much more likely than men to buy mattresses. Moreover, many of Select Comfort's workers were female. A new CEO/chairman, William McLaughlin, was determined to fix this problem, and he did, by immediately recruiting three women directors between 2002 and 2004.[26] More generally, boards need to hear and learn from people conditioned by the experience of having grown up in different circumstances and settings. As a wise friend of mine observed many years ago, "We don't learn much when we are surrounded only by the likes of ourselves."

Independence of Board Members

In the for-profit sector, there is far more awareness today of the importance of having truly independent board members than there used to be. The listing requirements of both the New York Stock Exchange and NASDAQ include detailed definitions of independence, and the ISS has an even more detailed definition of who is and who is not an "independent outside director."[27] The key distinctions are inside directors versus outside directors, and then affiliated outside directors versus independent outside directors. Employees of the company, including of course the CEO, are inside directors. Affiliated outside directors include former executives of the company, relatives of employees, individuals providing professional services to the company, and those employed by a significant customer or supplier. Trustees and employees of nonprofit organizations that receive grants from the company are also sometimes regarded as failing the independence test.[28]

The number of independent directors is on the rise, especially among large companies. According to the *Spencer Stuart Board Index* for 2006, the CEO is now the only non-independent director in 39 percent of S&P 500 companies (up from 27 percent in 2001), and 81 percent of all directors of these companies are independent (up from 77 percent in 2001).[29] These trends represent a definite improvement in governance because the presence of insiders other than the CEO can inhibit discussion. Moreover, insiders must support the position of the CEO and cannot be expected to present independent points of view. I consider it a mistake (one that I myself helped to make on one occasion) to "reward" senior officers other than the CEO for loyal service by electing them to the board. Of course, insiders can and should attend parts of board meetings, but only on an invitational basis. In the nonprofit sector, it is almost unheard of for an insider other than the president or executive director to serve on the board.

The mechanical standards of independence that apply in the for-profit sector remind everyone that the existence of relationships between the company on whose board an individual serves and that board member's other business interests can create awkwardness and raise questions about objectivity. Of course, individuals in the category of affiliated outside directors can, and no doubt usually do, rise above potential conflicts and act with integrity. Nonetheless, more and more weight is being given to appearances, especially when appearances can inhibit the candid discussion of issues.

Compliance with all the specified standards of independence should not, however, be considered a guarantee of true independence. In the case of WorldCom, two key members of the board satisfied the independence standards of the time, and probably the NYSE standard today, but both men had been involved in business relationships with WorldCom's CEO for years and "owed a substantial portion of their net worth to his actions."[30] Most board members of other scandal-ridden companies, such as Tyco and Enron, as well as WorldCom, were technically "independent."

As several wise friends with much corporate experience have pointed out, *"Independence is much more than checking the right boxes. It is a state of mind—the willingness to be honest, to disagree, and to speak up."* One of the worst problems is cronyism. The cascading difficulties at Morgan Stanley resulted in no small part from the fact that Philip Purcell "maintained tight control by putting together a board whose members are from the Chicago area, where Mr. Purcell lives, or have long-standing ties to Mr. Purcell or one another."[31] The same problem is evident in the current situation at Home Depot, with critics referring to the presence on the board of a number of "GE cronies"; and it was a serious source of difficulty at Reader's Digest, when I served on that board. In short, board members need to be at least reasonably independent of one another, as well as independent in other respects.

The most insidious danger, because it is rarely visible, is that boards will include large numbers of individuals tied too closely together—and too closely to the CEO—by other loyalties.[32] One commentator referred to "powerful social links" and another to the consequences of "club-like" relationships, which I have certainly seen operate to the detriment of good outcomes.

In the words of Michael Blumenthal:

> The sense of honor, prestige, and importance people derive from certain types of board service is not to be underrated. You certainly know that from Princeton and it applies to many persons who serve on the most prestigious corporate boards as well . . . It helps your standing in the business community to be a director of, say, GE, GM, IBM, etc. That also means that, once inducted into the most prestigious "club," it inhibits asking the nasty questions. You want to stay a member! It's tough to be the skunk at the garden party (I know!). All that is very much part of the group dynamic of "going along."[33]

This is tricky territory because long associations and friendships can and do contribute to the effective functioning of organizations. Personal relationships often lead people to devote more time and attention to the task at hand than they would do otherwise. Friends are also sometimes more willing to raise hard questions early on and to be more direct in their criticisms than are mere acquaintances, who may fear that their comments will be misunderstood or motives questioned. There is no way to legislate against personal relationships as a potential barrier to independent decision making without simultaneously sacrificing advantages worth more than whatever protection against abuse stricter rules can purchase. On many occasions I have benefited personally from the wise counsel of board members who were also friends. As Ken Lewis, chairman and CEO of Bank of America, has argued, "Independence, like most ideas, is best adhered to in moderation, with a healthy respect for the relationships, the trust, and the teamwork that enable effective boards to do their jobs."[34]

All participants in the governance process should acknowledge openly and explicitly that there is an inescapable tension between maintaining an appropriate distance between board members and the CEO and maintaining trust and collegiality. A sensible balance must be struck. No one should be surprised, or offended, if the need for board members to be simultaneously supportive and critical creates some unease. It should. This is, after all, the essence of the "director's dilemma."

Issues of independence arise in the nonprofit world too—where they can be just as troubling. When I served as a regent of the Smithsonian, it was evident that the political and social aspects of life in Washington made it difficult for some regents to say what they really believed about some issues. Offending others present at the meeting could make life difficult for an outspoken regent. As an absolute outsider I had the great advantage of being able to say whatever I believed without risk of causing trouble for myself or for organizations outside Washington with which I was affiliated. There was no penalty that Chief Justice Burger, who was the chancellor of the Smithsonian at that time, or anyone else could impose on me for speaking my mind—as I did to the chancellor's dismay at several sensitive moments. I would like to believe that this independence increased my usefulness as a regent.

In other nonprofit settings, it can be tempting for board members to suggest that their firms provide business services to impecunious organizations on whose boards they sit—often out of the most altruistic motives. A survey conducted by the Urban Institute found that 45 percent of nonprofit organizations with annual budgets of $40 million or more reported having bought goods or services from companies affiliated with their board members, and that fully one-third of these transactions were not reviewed or approved by other board members. Nonprofits are subject to the same risks as for-profits that personal friendships, and social or political relationships, will influence judgments.[35] Moreover, it can be very awkward to terminate a business relationship—with, for example, a money management firm—when the organization providing a service is led by a board member.

For all of these reasons, nonprofits are now more likely than they used to be to adopt written standards, sometimes tailored to their own circumstances. To illustrate, the trustees of the Mellon Foundation adopted a statement on "The Appearance of Private Benefit," which went through numerous drafts and stimulated much debate. There was no disagreement on the objectives to be served, but it was difficult to find phrasing that captured the spirit of the discussion. The more we talked, the more we realized that rigid proscriptions would do more harm than good, particularly when we left the relatively clear domain of purely business relationships and entered the realm of grant making. The board could have adopted a policy that precluded grants to any organization headed by a trustee, but decided not to do so.

The implications of such a policy for the foundation's program in higher education illuminate the reasons why such a policy seemed unwise. The foundation has always had distinguished university presidents on its board, and the guidance of these individuals has been enormously helpful in fashioning programs that reach across broad sectors of higher education. If the foundation were unable to make grants to the colleges or universities led by these presidents, they would have to resign in order to protect the eligibility of their institutions for foundation support. Other presidents would be unwilling to serve for the same reason, and the foundation would be deprived of the views of the people best positioned to give informed advice.

There are other ways to protect against potential conflicts without cutting the board off from the talent it needs. Managing conflicts appropriately, a subject that will be discussed in more detail in the next chapter, is obviously necessary to avoid the improper exercise of influence.

7

Board Machinery

IN ADDITION to a good mix of able and committed directors/trustees, every board, in both the for-profit and the nonprofit sectors, needs to have at least a modicum of "machinery" (structure and processes) if it is to function effectively. The right combination of able members, proper machinery, and good leadership encourages the development of a healthy dynamic within the boardroom. Good governance depends on "the totality of the system, not [just] its individual parts."[1]

In this chapter I discuss committee structures; board deliberations and board dynamics (including the use of executive sessions, the management of conflicts of interest, and the handling of leaks); when directors/trustees should and should not resign; the removal of dysfunctional directors and the uses of term limits and mandatory retirement to promote board renewal; compensation of directors and trustees; and, finally, board evaluation.

Committees

A well-conceived committee structure is essential to the effective functioning of a board, even as we recognize that the size of the board will dictate the use made of committees. Large boards have no option but to conduct much of their business through committees; small boards can function more frequently in a "committee-of-the-whole" mode. Privately held companies generally have small boards and less need for committees than do their publicly traded counterparts.

The core committees established by charter at most large for-profit companies are the audit, compensation and benefits, and governance/nominating committees. Companies whose businesses involve significant interactions with the public and with congressional/legislative bodies also usually have a committee on public policy/social responsibility. Increasingly, large nonprofits are likely to have a similar set of core committees, in part because the regulatory climate requires it. The frequent appearance these days of audit committees best exemplifies this trend, which I regard as entirely healthy as long as bureaucratic tendencies are kept in check and there is no proliferation of unneeded committees. In the past, the committee structures of the boards of even some large nonprofits have been too casually conceived.

One difference between for-profits and many nonprofits lies in their typical use of an executive committee. As we have seen, nonprofits are much more likely to have large boards than are for-profits, and nonprofits with large boards often rely on executive committees to handle at least some (and sometimes much) of their business. In the for-profit sector, by contrast, executive committees are becoming, in the words of commentators, "atavistic" or "vestigial" creatures. There are two reasons:

(1) In today's world of easily organized telephonic board meetings, it is possible for the full board to meet at least over the phone whenever there is an important matter to discuss between regularly scheduled board meetings. Although not as satisfying as in-person meetings, this kind of machinery can work surprisingly well, especially if materials are mailed out in advance and there is good preparation (no surprises!).

(2) There is real concern about the effects of executive committees on collegiality and maintaining a shared sense that all board members matter.

My experience at American Express underscores the importance of this second reason. During the leadership transition that followed James

Robinson's resignation and the appointment of Harvey Golub as CEO, the board undertook an organizational experiment that failed. A fairly large executive committee—on which I served, along with the chairs of the company's other standing committees—was established to work with Richard Furlaud (the non-executive chairman at the time) and Golub. It wasn't clear exactly what the executive committee was supposed to do, and those directors not on it—roughly half of the board—understandably resented feeling that they were "below the salt." They wondered, as one member asked rhetorically, "What am I, half a director?" It did not take long for the full board to recognize the tensions created by this arrangement and to agree that a large, amorphous executive committee was divisive.

Two-tiered boards are basically a bad idea, certainly in the for-profit sector. I also question the extent to which nonprofits rely on executive committees to make decisions that really ought to be made by the full board. That said, there are mechanisms that nonprofits can use to democratize the executive committee model if, because of board size and the infrequency of meetings of the full board, it simply has to be used. In particular, care should be taken to make sure that (1) the executive committee reports regularly to the full board; and (2) trustees are rotated on and off the executive committee, so that there is no semi-permanent "super board."

Beyond the core standing committees, both for-profit companies and nonprofits utilize more specialized committees. For example, Merck has a research committee because of the centrality of its research function. Nonprofits with sizable endowments and grant-making foundations with substantial financial resources almost always have an investment committee. Colleges and universities generally have committees on academic affairs and student life. They may also have committees on athletics and alumni affairs. Nonprofits that seek contributions usually rely heavily on a development (fund-raising) committee. Large museums may have committees responsible for acquisitions and perhaps de-accessioning.

A question relevant in both sectors is when to establish special committees with limited lifetimes. At Princeton, one of the most important special committees ever formed was the Special Committee on Coeducation. As noted earlier, Merck created a special committee responsible for overseeing an independent investigation of the development and marketing of VIOXX. Colleges and universities almost always form search committees when they need to find a new president. Depending on the circumstances, companies may also use ad hoc search committees to coordinate the process of finding a new CEO. Special committees can be highly useful in focusing attention on issues of immediate, overriding importance, but reliance on such committees can be overdone. The whole board should consider the truly important questions facing the organization, whether they are strategic, operational, or organizational.

This last observation leads directly to a cardinal principle: *Whatever the committee structure is, committees should report to the full board and should not, except in unusual circumstances, themselves exercise the power to decide.* In general, committees should assemble information and frame issues for discussion and then action by the full board. Making decisions for their colleagues is not part of their mandate. Exceptions to this principle include the need for specialized committees, such as investment committees, to act on matters within their purview, and for executive committees to act on what should normally be pro forma matters (final review of the terms of a contract, ratifying an appointment, and so on) between meetings of the board. And, to repeat, all members of the board should be kept informed of the activities of every committee and be given the opportunity to participate in discussions of policy issues.

This norm is violated most frequently, I suspect, by large nonprofit boards facing hard choices. Consider the case of Wilson College, a small liberal arts college for women in Pennsylvania that nearly closed in the early 1970s. Members of the minority on the board who opposed the original decision to close the college criticized a practice that allegedly permitted a small group of trustees, functioning as an executive committee and acting in concert with the president, to make decisions without any real discussion within the board as a whole. Board members who opposed the closing claimed that they were given no real option but to ratify what the president and the executive committee had already decided.[2] In the equally contentious saga of the University of Bridgeport, which was ultimately "rescued," "bailed out," or "acquired" (depending on the connotation one prefers) by a group funded by Sun Myung Moon and his followers, it has been alleged that key decisions to borrow large sums of money were made by the finance and executive committees, and then brought to the board as a whole for ratification only when they were, in effect, irreversible.[3]

In the case of for-profit boards (where, as I have said, executive committees are rarely used anymore), independent directors increasingly make up the entire membership of the so-called Big Three committees (audit, compensation and benefits, and governance/nominating). Management and staff prepare materials and sometimes participate in discussions, but only by invitation and not as voting members. Independent directors customarily meet alone, at least for parts of meetings. These practices seem generally agreed upon and clearly right. Unfortunately, especially in the case of the nominating function, CEOs sometimes drive the process more than they should, even though it is understood, at least in principle, that the independent board members are the decision makers.

How any committee functions depends critically on who chairs it. In my view, the board's governance committee should play the decisive role in determining committee assignments; the CEO should be consulted, but he or she should not dictate assignments. If the board has a separate non-executive chairman, that person should have primary responsibility for determining committee roles. The choice of the committee chairman can be especially consequential in the case of the compensation committee. One commentator observed ruefully that he had served on a board where, for more than a decade, the same person chaired the compensation committee and behaved in a highly predictable manner:

> His ability to defend sizeable increases for the top officers was totally unconnected with how well or how badly the company was doing at any given time. When things went well, the chairman (CEO) had to be rewarded; when disaster struck, his morale had to be protected (dark references to a depressed mood, etc.) . . . I suspect that the norm in the corporate world is for the CEO to find a chairman of executive compensation who can be counted on to behave this way—and then stick with that choice.

I am less skeptical than this commentator about standard practice, although evidence is hard to obtain. Attitudes toward executive compensation are changing, and more emphasis is being given to policies that tie compensation to performance. Still, an overly cozy relationship between the CEO and the chairman of the compensation committee must be avoided.

A more general question concerns the rotation of chairmanships and committee assignments in general. Although I agree with the concept of rotation, I have learned from some bad experiences that this "principle" can be given too much weight. The reality is that some directors are better at handling certain functions than are their colleagues, and it is a mistake to allow an abstract commitment to rotation to put the wrong person in the wrong job at the wrong time. The audit committee is perhaps the best example of a committee that has to be led by someone who is truly financially literate, who has an acute sense of smell, and who is prepared to make every effort to ensure that sound judgments are being made and that the highest standards of integrity are being observed.

Finally, serving on committees must not take up so much of directors/trustees' time that it limits opportunities for the board as a whole to discuss issues of substance. This problem is especially likely to arise if audit committees are encouraged to examine with infinite care every small corner of an organization's activities. Time needs to be husbanded for full consideration of the larger questions for which the board has collective responsibility. Privately held firms understand this proposition very well, and their boards do not waste time on unnecessary committee meetings. Board members representing the sponsors of these firms interact regularly with management, often serving a sounding-board function, but they are not prisoners of the regular schedule imposed by an overly elaborate formal committee structure.

Board Deliberations and Dynamics

The conduct of board meetings is of the utmost importance. What I regard as wise rules of the road are an amalgam of regularized procedures and an intuitive sense of how to stimulate genuine discussion, to encourage the honest expression of differences of opinion, and then to close ranks—or, if that is impossible, to find acceptable ways of dealing with chasms that are just too wide to bridge. Boards need to manage conflicts, and individual board members need to know when—and when not—to resign.

Boards should meet with reasonable frequency, and board agendas should allow adequate time for discussion of the most important topics.

However, no magic formula exists for translating these propositions into specific numbers of meetings or exact time allocations. The number of yearly board meetings should depend on the use made of committees and on how serious the consequences are of waiting significant periods of time for the board to act. Meetings should be frequent enough that members not only remember what transpired when they met last but also gain experience working together.

Adhering to a well-understood schedule of regular board meetings also provides discipline for staff work. As Richard Lyman observed on the basis of his experience as president of Stanford and then of the Rockefeller Foundation,

> I used to think the main benefit from a board meeting was that it forced staff to prepare; questions had to be anticipated, thoughts clarified. If we had cancelled each meeting a day or two before it was to have taken place, we'd have been as well off, and lots of people would have been saved travel time, etc. Of course, once we'd done that a couple of times, no one would believe that we really intended to meet!

It is hard for me to imagine an effective board in either the for-profit or nonprofit sector that meets fewer than four times a year, though I have been told that three meetings can sometimes suffice in the nonprofit sector. In both sectors, frequency should depend on the size and nature of the organization. For large and complex companies, eight to ten meetings a year seems a reasonable range. The WorldCom board was criticized for meeting too infrequently (quarterly) and holding perfunctory meetings; according to the Breeden report, the audit committee "spent as little as 3 to 6 hours per year overseeing the activities of a company with more than $30 billion in revenue."[4] In the nonprofit sector, holding more than three or four meetings per year is desirable if the organization is an entrepreneurial start-up that confronts issues of consequence that have to be decided quickly; Ithaka is a good example of such an organization. Telephonic board meetings can sometimes substitute for in-person meetings.

Boards can also meet too frequently. An excessive number of meetings can encourage directors or trustees to act like managers or staff members, while simultaneously discouraging promising candidates for board membership from being willing to serve. Cause and effect in these situations is not always clear, since board members with intrusive instincts may press for more meetings, and for longer meetings. A colleague has observed that trustees with too much time to contribute can be just as problematic as trustees with too little time. She notes that trustees who have much time available sometimes fail to understand the time pressures under which staff members work—and as a result, they can cause staff time to be misallocated.

The theme of time—how much time is needed, and how the available time can be used most productively—recurs frequently. A number of commentators have recommended that boards set aside enough time to allow directors to consider big issues once, reflect, and then return to them. As the lead director of one major research university explained, his board seeks to build a "rolling consensus" by giving ideas enough time to breathe and develop, sometimes over several meetings and many months. Retreats can offer useful opportunities for board members to talk about longer-term directions in a relaxed way.

The total amount of time that directors/trustees should be expected to contribute must be weighed in conjunction with judgments about the ability of the board to recruit busy candidates, how board meetings will be conducted, and what kinds of information will be provided to board members in advance of meetings. The challenge is to provide sufficient opportunities for small group conversations and ample opportunities for individuals to speak without encouraging tendencies, as one college trustee put it, to "wallow in words."[5]

Time at board meetings must be used well. Efficient use of time requires thoughtful construction of board agendas and careful preparation for meetings, with written materials being mailed out well in advance. Board members should be informed of key topics to be considered so that proper mental preparation is possible. Every effort should be made to avoid surprising board members. The trustees, in turn, have to keep the president apprised of any conversations of consequence that they have with either other officers or other trustees, so that he or she is never caught off guard. Mutual efforts to avoid surprises have the added benefit of building trust. These admonitions notwithstanding, situations continue to arise in which both presidents and board members are taken by surprise. Such oversights are hard to accept if accidental, and impossible to excuse if deliberate.

In constructing agendas, it is necessary to do more than ensure that meetings are not consumed by routine reports, though that can be a problem in its own right. It should be assumed that board members will read materials distributed in advance, and every effort should be made to avoid "show-and-tell" presentations that bore everyone, waste scarce time, and sometimes seem like filibusters. As one commentator observed,

> The desire of management and often even board colleagues leading a discussion to read to the board materials that were provided in advance is maddening. In many cases, the prepared presentation provides the nervous business unit manager or staff member with a security blanket he just can't give up. Not only is this a colossal waste of time, it sends a message to board members that reviewing the materials in advance is unnecessary since they will be read aloud in the meeting. In my experience this pattern can only be broken by repeated coaching and ultimately establishing a culture where the behavior is recognized and called out on the spot.

Taylor Reveley suggests, and I agree, that board members themselves should participate actively in establishing agendas. Reveley's suggestion is that each director/trustee make a list of critical issues that he or she believes will need to be confronted in the course of a year. These lists can then be consolidated, agreement reached on central topics, and plans made to cover the topics in an orderly way. An effective governance committee can coordinate such a process. Board calendars should be developed in analogous ways, with a planned sequence of topics covered each year.[6] Privately held companies have an easier time focusing on substantive issues that really matter. As one commentator put it, they have the luxury of focusing on business strategy, financial plans (and results), and organization and personnel, with less time devoted to process issues.

Within the structure established by well-organized agendas and calendars, genuinely open discussion should be encouraged. However skillfully materials are prepared and meetings are planned, it is the quality of the ensuing discussion that matters most. This can be influenced significantly by the way a meeting is chaired and by the ability and willingness of key board members to ask direct questions and try out ideas. The CEO/president must be open to different points of view, and care should be taken to avoid letting a debate over a substantive issue take on the character of a referendum on the CEO's leadership. The goal should be to have an informed exchange of ideas that may even lead to a new understanding of a complex issue that satisfies all involved.

An example from the Princeton trustees' deliberation on coeducation illustrates this approach. President Robert Goheen asked Harold Helm—a respected senior member of the board and a self-proclaimed skeptic about coeducation at Princeton—to chair the special committee charged with studying the question. The result was an extensive report and then a wide-ranging discussion, both of which reflected a variety of points of view. Eventually, President Goheen's recommendation in favor of coeducation was endorsed by the Helm committee and adopted by the trustees, but with eight dissenting votes (out of thirty-two). The board wisely did not try to impose unanimity on itself, and as a result the entire process had a sense of legitimacy. Mutual respect prevailed, and no trustee resigned in the aftermath of the decision.

In this situation, the Princeton board learned (or relearned) the value of studying carefully all aspects of a sensitive issue. One vignette: Harold Helm had a brother who had also gone to Princeton and who strongly opposed coeducation—even after Harold and his committee had endorsed it. When Harold's wife, Mary Helm, was asked how these two brothers, so much alike in so many ways, could end up disagreeing so strongly about the merits of coeducation, Mary replied simply, "Well, Harold studied the question." How perceptive—and a lesson for the ages!

I have found that there is no good substitute for board leaders who can disagree with each other, and with the CEO/president, without being disagreeable—who can debate contentious issues in a civil manner. Individuals with a sense of humor and a ready smile help a lot. Of course, even if these qualities are present, they will not always carry the day. Sharp disagreements between Carly Fiorina and the HP board that culminated in her firing are a case in point. In the opening paragraph of her book, *Tough Choices*, Fiorina describes her tenure at HP in these words:

In the end, the board did not have the courage to face me. They did not thank me and they did not say good-bye. They did not explain their decision or their reasoning. They did not seek my opinion or my involvement in any aspect of the transition.

Elsewhere in the book, Fiorina writes,

Some board members' behavior was amateurish and immature. Some didn't do their homework. Some had fixed opinions on certain topics and no opinion at all on others.[7]

I have no basis for judging the fairness of this account, but I can attest that there were difficult moments in the American Express boardroom when Robinson's status was being debated.[8] In that case, however, disagreements were subsequently worked out, and today the American Express board functions extremely well.

In reflecting on board dynamics, there is one last general point to note. Ron Daniel, who serves on the boards of both Brandeis and Rockefeller universities, believes that the physical setting for meetings is more important than most people think. If board members have to meet around such a big table or in such a cavernous space that microphones are needed, it is extremely hard to have a real discussion. Rooms designed for easy interactions can be helpful, and sometimes it is wise to sacrifice a tradition of always meeting in "the boardroom" if another venue works better—especially when the objective is to encourage open-ended discussion of large topics that lend themselves to a committee-of-the-whole approach.

EXECUTIVE SESSIONS

One of the most important changes in board operations over the last decade is the much more regular use of executive sessions, especially those with no inside directors in attendance, including the CEO/president. I regard the routine use of such sessions as a healthy development that is overdue. Executive sessions should be held as a matter of course, so that they do not seem awkward, "special," or unnecessarily frightening. At the minimum, the person chairing an executive session can simply ask, "Does anyone have something to bring up that we should discuss now?" The leader of the session can also be more proactive—for example, by tabling the most important questions and framing the discussion. When well handled, executive sessions can encourage directors and trustees to be more open in expressing concerns while simultaneously reducing the risk that they will simply brood over grievances and imagined problems.

However, executive sessions can also be damaging, as several commentators have noted.[9] It is important to avoid using these sessions for extended discussions of topics that require the knowledge of the CEO or president. Such discussions are inefficient, and they can also annoy the CEO or president. Similarly, boards should avoid arriving at premature conclusions in executive sessions, before management and staff have been given an opportunity to comment.

More generally, the CEO/president must be comfortable with the ways in which executive sessions are used. Including the CEO/president in the first part of the session and providing prompt feedback after the conclusion of the board-only part of the discussion can provide reassurance. Some boards prefer to have the non-executive chairman or lead director provide the feedback; others prefer to have more than one director present to reduce the risk of miscommunication. Another approach involves inviting the CEO/president back into the room so that he or she can be debriefed in the presence of the entire board. Any of these methods can work, and the approach should be tailored to the circumstances, including the nature of the issue under discussion and the "chemistry" among the relevant individuals. The one critical requirement is that the feedback be accurate. Much harm can result from failure to inform the CEO/president of concerns when they exist.

In the nonprofit sector, executive sessions are still less common than they should be. One experienced trustee said that she continues to press the boards on which she sits to have an executive session without the president in attendance at every meeting. She reports that when this reform is introduced, board members often feel a new opportunity to contribute, and they sometimes obtain new information. Having an executive session as a regular part of the board meeting raises no red flags and, as this trustee observed, "may well be the most important change instituted by many of these nonprofit boards in recent years."

MANAGING CONFLICTS OF INTEREST

The quality of board interactions is also determined by how successfully the board handles conflicts of interest. Boards can avoid some of the more obvious potential problems simply by not electing individuals when inherent conflicts can be identified in advance. In the corporate world there are established standards for avoiding conflicts (of individuals associated with competitors or major vendors, for example) that are routinely checked in reviewing the qualifications of board candidates.

In the college and university world, I continue to be skeptical that it is wise to elect current students or faculty members to their institution's board of trustees. Electing such individuals poses obvious conflicts when subjects such as tuition increases and faculty salary policies are discussed. Moreover, it is possible to gain these valuable perspectives without facing conflict issues, by electing recent graduates and faculty members teaching at other institutions.[10] Effective channels of communication between the board and the various constituencies of the institution are needed, but using board seats to achieve this objective is not, in my view, the right approach. Having current students or active faculty members represent their constituencies is also awkward for reasons that go beyond the conflict issue. For example, what should a faculty member on a board do when his or her personal views on an issue differ from the official position taken by the faculty at large?

The cases just discussed seem relatively straightforward, but it is not always possible to predict conflicts of interest. A painful experience at TIAA-CREF occurred when a trustee of TIAA and a trustee of CREF sold a product designed to facilitate the rigorous evaluation of the value of stock options to the outside auditor. It was hard for those of us on the board of overseers of TIAA-CREF to understand how this situation could ever have arisen, since the conflict was so obvious. It was equally hard to understand why the auditing firm in question (Ernst & Young) was so slow to recognize the problem. The board of overseers, which is expected to work in concert with the separate boards for TIAA and CREF, commissioned Nicholas Katzenbach to conduct an investigation of this strange episode. Eventually the two trustees who caused the conflict resigned. Katzenbach concluded that TIAA-CREF had relied too heavily on Ernst & Young to address the issues and had been too slow in mounting its own investigation. There were also internal failures of communication that exacerbated relations among trustees of TIAA and CREF, overseers, and officers and staff members.[11]

Mistakes were made—and acknowledged—all around. Two positive outcomes were (1) recognition of the need for much more timely exchanges of information when any potential problem of this kind arises and (2) a clearer understanding of the respective roles of the trustees of TIAA and CREF and the overseers. These outcomes have, I believe, already led to improved board dynamics.

As we saw in Chapter 6, issues of independence and how to handle conflicts of interest arise regularly in the nonprofit sector—perhaps with even greater frequency than they do in the for-profit sector. The quality of board interactions is affected by how openly these issues are addressed and by how skillfully boards manage them, since potential conflicts can rarely be avoided altogether. Indeed, seeking to eliminate all potential conflicts can lessen the ability of organizations to achieve their fundamental purposes. Charles Exley once observed that board members with no potential conflicts of any kind may lack the knowledge or experience needed to be effective directors or trustees!

To cite a specific situation, President John L. Hennessy of Stanford is deeply embedded in Silicon Valley, and his relationships with entities such as Google and Cisco Systems could conceivably cause difficulties because Stanford has so many interactions with these companies. However, Hennessy's relationships are fully disclosed, and the Stanford board has created protections of various kinds to head off problems. The Stanford code of ethics, in addressing problems of this kind (which of course involve faculty members as well as administrators), wisely notes that such conflicts are "common and practically unavoidable in a modern research university."[12]

Moreover, it is not always easy to know when a situation might represent a true conflict. For example, the Mellon Foundation was responsible for creating JSTOR—which is today a highly successful nonprofit, entirely independent of Mellon, that uses digital technologies to provide a searchable file of the back issues of over 650 scholarly journals. Scholars and students at more than thirty-five hundred libraries in over a hundred countries now use the database, which contains more than twenty million pages of content. Acting in the mode of a venture philanthropist, the foundation provided JSTOR with a combination of start-up funding, board leadership, and access to its network of connections. These interacting roles created a web of relationships that could be thought of as involving conflicts, but all were essential to the creation and subsequent success of JSTOR—and all were solely in the service of the foundation's philanthropic mission.[13]

Two comprehensive reports—one focused on college and university boards, and one addressing governance issues in the nonprofit sector more broadly—have noted that many nonprofits now have elaborate new policies in place to handle potential conflicts and other conduct issues.[14] Attention to all the myriad possibilities of conflict can be overdone and even debilitating, but I am convinced that a straightforward statement of basic principles can help nonprofit boards work together more effectively. Smith College, for example, has an exceptionally well worked-out policy on conflicts that focuses on disclosure and recusing oneself from certain discussions.

CONFIDENTIALITY AND THE HANDLING OF LEAKS

Board dynamics are affected powerfully by disputes that rise above the level of mere disagreements. As Joann Lublin and Erin White observed in a *Wall Street Journal* article, "Experts say that some argument can be healthy but warn that boards must learn to manage disagreement constructively or risk becoming dysfunctional."[15] The article cites the experience of the Hewlett-Packard board as a major case in point. Confidential board discussions of strategic directions were leaked to the press, and this breach led to a controversial investigation into the source of the leaks that involved unauthorized access to the personal phone records of directors and reporters. When knowledge of this highly unusual investigation became public, it drew sharp criticism from many quarters and a round of congressional hearings. Eventually Patricia Dunn, chairman of the HP board, along with former HP staff members and outside investigators, were indicted on charges of "using false or fraudulent pretenses to obtain confidential information from a public utility, unauthorized access to computer data, identity theft, and conspiracy to commit each of these crimes." Subsequently, the California court dropped all criminal charges, because of the lack of criminal intent.[16]

Several commentators sympathized with Dunn's irritation at the leaking of confidential information but were mystified by the way in which the HP board handled the matter. As one experienced general counsel put it (in a personal conversation):

> If a board is going to investigate leaks by board members, it needs to get full buy-in by the board up front. Everyone needs to understand what is going to happen, to agree that an investigation is in order, to agree on how the investigation is to be conducted, probably to agree to voluntarily turn over personal phone records, and to agree on the consequences; i.e., if someone is found to have leaked confidential information, that person must leave the board.

Apparently none of this happened at HP. Although debate continues on the legalities in various jurisdictions of obtaining phone records by "pretexting" (pretending to be the person whose records are being sought), there seems little doubt that extremely poor judgment was exercised.

Warren Buffett has been quoted as arguing that sometimes leaking is "the right thing to do." In his words, "After trying to persuade his colleagues, an unhappy director should feel free to make his views known to the absentee owners." But Buffett also agrees that some things should not be divulged, such as new products and new strategies. In the HP case, Buffet concludes, "The leaking was at best questionable; the spying was at best just plain wrong."[17]

One of the more painful experiences I had when presiding over meetings of the Princeton board involved a leak by a trustee, during the emotionally tense days of Vietnam, of the name of someone slated to receive an honorary degree who was sure to be a controversial choice—before the individual in question (George Shultz) even had the opportunity to decide if he would accept. Members of the board were incensed, and I told the trustees how disappointed I was that the leak had occurred and how strongly I felt about respecting confidential matters discussed within the confines of the boardroom. I felt that we had to decide, as a board, how we were going to operate. If leaks were viewed as in any way acceptable, I would simply not be able to be as open with the board as I had always been in discussing personnel matters and other sensitive issues. The board as a whole, with each trustee responding individually, unanimously reaffirmed the principle of respecting confidentiality. For-tunately, there were no other violations of this principle during my time at Princeton, and several trustees later remarked on the beneficial effects that direct consideration of the issue had on board dynamics.

A problem of a somewhat different kind arose at TIAA-CREF. The overseers as a group were not informed of the serious conflict of interest described earlier before it became public and was reported to the SEC. One other overseer, Arthur Levitt (himself a former chairman of the SEC), and I confirmed publicly, in response to direct questions from a reporter, that we had not been informed; and both of us went on to say that we felt strongly that all overseers should have been told right away. Both the CEO of TIAA-CREF and the president of the board of over-seers acknowledged that a serious failure of communication had occurred, and in his report to the overseers, Nicholas Katzenbach agreed that under the circumstances it would have been awkward for Levitt and for me to refuse to say whether we had known of the problem. Not everyone agreed with our position, but it was encouraging to hear from a number of TIAA-CREF participants that our willingness to speak out had strengthened their confidence in the independence and integrity of the board of overseers. In my view, the direct discussion of the conflict, and of the associated questions about the role of the overseers within the TIAA-CREF governance structure, positioned the overseers to be more effective in the future.

When Resigning Is (and Is Not) the Right Thing to Do

As important as it is for boards to try to reach consensus on issues of consequence, that is not always possible. When irreconcilable differ-ences exist, directors and trustees have to decide if they should resign. The decision is always a matter of judgment and, ultimately, of personal conviction; in general, however, I believe that dissenting directors/trustees should try to convince themselves to stay on as board members. There is little to recommend forced unanimity, and boards often benefit from continuing debates over complex issues. I have already referred to the continued service on the Princeton board of the eight trustees who voted against coeducation. Their subsequent participation in discussions of admissions policies and the size of the undergraduate college demonstrated the value of having a variety of viewpoints represented in the boardroom. It was also encouraging to see how the actual experience with coeducation, which was overwhelmingly positive, led some of the original dissenters to conclude that the board had made the right decision. Years later, one trustee said to me that he believed every trustee should be given the right to change one vote he had cast, and that if he were given that right, he would change his vote in opposition to coeducation.

Such gratifying outcomes do not always occur. Trustees and directors can feel so strongly about an issue that they see no recourse but to resign. This is what happened at Hewlett-Packard when Tom Perkins resigned in protest at the handling of the investigation into board leaks. It was Perkins' resignation, and how it was reported to the SEC, that brought the entire debate over leaking and spying into the public domain. At American Express, in the aftermath of the closely divided vote that allowed Robinson to remain chairman when Golub was elected CEO, the board member who had spearheaded the attempt to remove Robinson from both positions, Rawleigh Warner, resigned from the board. I tried to convince Warner to remain as a director, but he believed strongly that, having failed in his effort to oust Robinson altogether, he should resign. In part, he hoped to signify publicly how strongly he felt about the need for a complete revamping of the American Express leadership. He also thought that his continuing presence on the board would make it harder to have a constructive debate about the company's future. In retrospect, I think that, given these circumstances, Warner was right to resign. As Warner noted at the time, he had played the role he thought he had to play, and he believed that it was time for him, as well as for Robinson, to move on.

As a director of American Express at the time, I, too, had opposed Robinson's continuing as chairman (though I had supported the election of Golub as CEO), but I decided to stay on the board. My reasoning, which was shared by some of the other directors who agreed with my point of view, was that this drama was not over. I felt that some of the dissenters might play a useful role in facilitating a further change in leadership—a change that, as noted earlier, occurred within a week's time, when Robinson resigned in response to mounting pressures from many quarters. The secretary of the American Express board, Steve Norman, subsequently observed that there need to be "bridges" between "before and after," and that it would have been unfortunate if all the dissenters had left the board.

In another situation I made the opposite decision. Having failed to convince my colleagues on the board of the Reader's Digest Association (RDA) that a fundamental change in direction was needed and that the company should be sold, I resigned when the other directors disagreed with my arguments and decided to ask the former chairman and CEO, George Grune, to return. As I said to my colleagues on the board at the time, I had made the same speech about strategic directions so often that I was boring myself as well as them, and I did not see that I had anything more to contribute. Furthermore, I thought it was only fair to allow Grune to resume his leadership of the company without my presence on the board as a confirmed dissenter with no new ideas to offer. At that time, companies were not required to tell the SEC the reasons why a director resigned, and my reasons were not made public. Today Sarbanes Oxley would require that my reasons be reported to the SEC, and it is conceivable that such a disclosure might have stimulated more debate among investors as to the future of Reader's Digest.

I will conclude this discussion by relating another of my own experiences with the question of when to resign. I resigned from the Denison University board of trustees in 1975, after nine years of service, not because of any disagreement, but simply because I felt that I had served long enough. I thought that my departure might encourage the board to recruit new talent and add fresh perspectives. When I re-joined the Denison board some seventeen years later, following the election of Michele Myers as president, I was pleased to see how much stronger the board had become. I would like to think that my earlier departure played at least a small part in bringing new leadership to the fore.

In reflecting on these varied experiences, mine and others, I think that any decision concerning one's further service on a board should depend on (1) the presumed effects of a decision to stay or to leave on the dynamics of board deliberations, (2) the ability of the director or trustee to work effectively with both other board members and the president or CEO, and (3) the individual's own sense of his or her ongoing capacity to contribute a useful perspective.

Dysfunctional Board Members, Term Limits, and Mandatory Retirement

To function effectively, boards need to think carefully about how to renew themselves. It will not do to rely on individual directors and trustees to decide, one by one and on their own, when they should retire. Corporate boards and nonprofit boards alike face the recurring problem of how to replace directors who are not performing or who simply have served too long. At the minimum, members who fail to meet a reasonable attendance requirement should not be kept on boards. The SEC requires corporations to publish the names of directors who attended less than 75 percent of all meetings of the board and relevant committees, and nonprofits should be every bit as serious about monitoring this measure of trustee commitment.

Mere attendance does not, however, come close to measuring performance. It almost goes without saying that directors or trustees who fail to contribute to the work of the board should be replaced. The qualifier "almost" is needed because in too many situations a combination of courtesy and inertia prevents remedial action. One approach is to ask individual board members to conduct self-reviews, so that they can help answer the question of whether electing them to another term is appropriate. Experienced board members report that surprisingly good results can be achieved by well-phrased letters and skillfully handled conversations that encourage self-assessments. In the corporate world, boards often focus on changes in an individual's circumstances. Where there is a significant change (for example, the director shifts vocations, makes a major geographic move—or is fired by his primary employer or even indicted), the board can expect the individual to submit a pro forma resignation, which the relevant board committee then considers.

The importance of collegiality makes it harder, though not impossible, to impose a more stringent standard related directly to substantive aspects of performance. Does the individual think hard about issues, contribute ideas, and share in the collective responsibility for making decisions? Or, at the other extreme, is the board member disruptive? Would the board be better off if this individual were not reelected? In recent years I have seen a greater willingness to apply tougher standards, but it would be hard to argue that boards have done well in addressing this problem. One commentator was unusually blunt: "It is shameful that boards do not review the performance of their directors and get rid of those who need to be replaced."[18]

Since such matters are almost always handled quietly, it is hard to know whether this is a fair assessment. It is essential to distinguish unwanted directors from dissenting directors because the latter can be very valuable board members. Boards must actively protect idiosyncratic members and freethinkers, assuming that such members in turn respect board processes and the views of their colleagues. But boards should not tolerate inadequate performance by directors, never mind disruptive behavior.

The assertion that boards are incapable of "getting rid of those who need to be replaced" certainly does not apply to all organizations. I have served on both for-profit and nonprofit boards that have acted to terminate the service of board members. In one instance, a nonprofit board simply needed the place occupied by someone who was not making contributions. In another instance, a member of a nonprofit board was so clearly at loggerheads with the president and with the rest of the board on a pivotal issue that the board finally asked the individual to resign. In one for-profit setting, an individual's health was preventing the member from contributing fully. In another situation, a board member who was overly fractious and made orderly discussion difficult was asked to leave. I agree with Larry Bossidy, who says simply, "You basically don't tolerate a bad director, because his behavior influences the rest."[19]

From a governance perspective, it should be a representative of the board, *not* the president or CEO, who speaks with the board member in question and addresses the problem. This is an important process point that is often overlooked. The CEO works for the board; the board does not work for the CEO, and it is inappropriate to ask the CEO to handle delicate and difficult resignations. The process followed in all of the situations in which I have been involved consisted, first, of informal one-on-one conversations with other board members to confirm that there was a clear consensus in favor of the action to be taken and that the action was being taken for the right reasons. Then, as chairman of the relevant board committee in three of the examples cited in the preceding discussion, I had candid conversations with the individuals who needed to step down. These conversations were much less difficult than one might have expected. When there is a real problem, the individual in question often recognizes it and may even welcome the opportunity to leave the board quietly and with dignity.

As essential as it is, reviewing the performance of individuals in a rigorous way may not always provide sufficient turnover to keep a board "fresh." Richard Breeden argues persuasively in his report on World-Com that "a static board membership can be dangerous." However, he goes on to propose an approach that I think is unwise and unworkable—namely, that boards should be required to elect at least one new director each year, and that, if necessary, a lottery would determine which sitting director should resign to make room for the newcomer.[20] A better alternative, in my view, is some system of terms or term limits with appropriate degrees of flexibility built in. Term limits also make it easier to select relatively young members, since there is no risk that someone will serve uninterruptedly for decades.

Colleges and universities have had good experiences with such arrangements. One model limits the terms of "charter trustees" to ten years and requires that a charter trustee who has served for ten years sit out for one year before being eligible for reelection. I am increasingly inclined to think that this approach, or some variant of it, has merit in the for-profit world as well. Patty Stonesifer, CEO of the Bill & Melinda Gates Foundation and an Amazon board member, has observed that if directors serve too long, it becomes very difficult for them to discharge their watchdog function. After many years on the board they can become so associated with the management ("co-opted," as someone else put it) that they are the ones who need to be watched! Sam Sachs echoed this thought in his reflections on the consequences of having museum boards led by directors who may have served for twenty-five or thirty years.

Failure to find an effective mechanism for ensuring turnover contributes to the problem of overly large nonprofit boards. The chairman of one such board with more than fifty members agreed that his board was too large, but then explained that it has been adding members nonetheless because of a pressing need for new people who could raise money. The lack of a mechanism for removing members is causing this board to pay an exorbitant price to renew itself.

There is, however, another side to this discussion of term limits, as several commentators have pointed out. All of us are familiar with special situations in which a long-serving director provided institutional memory and leadership at a critical moment. In the American Express case, Rawleigh Warner's twenty-six years of service, his standing, and his deep understanding of the company contributed greatly to the election of a new CEO and the eventual resolution of differences within the board. Rigid term limits can be especially problematic for small boards and for nonprofit boards that, with less pulling power than a Princeton, need to hold on to board members whose loss would be inordinately damaging.[21]

The arguments for term limits as a way of achieving board renewal need to be evaluated in the context of the specific circumstances of an organization and the availability of other means of achieving renewal. Transitions also must be managed carefully. In organizations contemplating the adoption of term limits, the new policy should be put in place carefully and perhaps gradually in order to prevent the disruption that could accompany a sudden change in board membership. As always, it is wise to avoid strictly mechanistic approaches to complex issues, to pay attention to context and timing, and to exercise common sense.

Mandatory retirement at a specified age has been the traditional way of dealing with these problems, and I favor it—even as I recognize that it may not always produce sufficient turnover, which is why I believe that organizations should consider a combination of mandatory retirement and a flexible system of term limits. In corporate America, the fraction of S&P 500 boards with a mandatory retirement age has increased from 58 percent in 2001 to 78 percent in 2006. At the same time, the most common age at which mandatory retirement occurs has gone up from seventy to seventy-two.[22] Both of these "directional changes" seem appropriate.[23]

The long-standing philosophical debate over mandatory retirement has always centered on why boards should deprive themselves of the services of a seventy-two-year-old who is still performing superbly. The best answer to this question that I know was provided to me years ago. When I was a young graduate student in economics at Princeton, I took a course in the history of economic thought taught by Jacob Viner, one of the greatest economists of his or any generation. As it happened, Viner was about to retire because of the then mandatory retirement provision for faculty (no longer in effect). I summoned all of my courage and went to see Professor Viner to complain that future students would be deprived of the opportunity to study with him, for no good reason. Viner smiled, gave me one of his piercing looks, and replied, "Mr. Bowen, most of what you say is true but your conclusion is wrong. Yes, you are right: I am at the peak of my powers, I am smarter than all of my colleagues, and future Princeton graduate students will lose out by not being able to study with me. But I know my colleagues," Viner continued, "they are good and compassionate people. They will never distinguish me from the others who should have retired 10 years ago! Either all of us go, or none of us goes, and it is better that all of us go."

The postscript is that Viner was invited to teach at Harvard, Oxford, and any number of other places until the day he died, so students in general were not denied the privilege of studying with him. But the Princeton faculty was able to benefit from the turnover that mandatory retirement provided, and the market ensured that only the ablest faculty had other attractive opportunities.[24]

The dangers inherent in regularly making exceptions to mandatory retirement provisions were illustrated dramatically by the problems experienced by the Hewlett-Packard board. One of the HP directors who appears to have been exceptionally strong-willed, Tom Perkins, served well past the mandatory retirement age, and making an exception year after year for Perkins may well have contributed both to Perkins' own sense of entitlement to his board seat, and to the difficulties experienced by the HP board in trying to work together. Eventually, the mandatory retirement provision at HP was simply waived altogether—an acknowledgment that the policy was not working, but surely a problematic way of resolving the problem.[25]

Compensation of Directors and Trustees

We come now to the sometimes vexing subject of board compensation. In the case of business boards, compensation of directors should both reflect the responsibilities involved in serving on a for-profit board and be high enough to attract the requisite talent. Some have argued that compensation for service on corporate boards does not recognize adequately the time commitment required and the liabilities accepted.[26] I am skeptical, however, that the level of compensation is critical in determining most corporate directors' willingness to serve. I recognize that reasonable compensation can be important for recruiting directors who come from academia and other less well compensated fields (as I did), and it is desirable that such people serve on corporate boards. Still, I am not persuaded that existing compensation—which averages slightly over $200,000 a year in the case of boards of large companies—is too low.[27]

Indeed, paying too much might tempt directors to "hold their fire," lest they jeopardize their positions as directors by offending the CEO or other powerful board members. Michael Blumenthal once referred to those who come to meetings simply to collect their fees as "rice-bowl directors." In some ways the *form* of compensation is as important as the level. I continue to believe that a large share of the compensation provided to directors should be in the form of company stock, and that directors should be required to hold that stock until after their retirement. A major reform would be to put much more of the compensation of directors of publicly traded for-profit companies in the form of equity in the companies for which they are responsible—as is the case today with directors of privately held companies.

Compensation for trustees of nonprofit entities is—surprisingly—a slightly more complex issue. My perhaps iconoclastic position is that the problem in this sector may be too little tangible reward in certain circumstances rather than too rich a gruel. Predictably, there are occasional outrages, including the annual compensation of, at times, more than $1 million paid to trustees of the Bishop Estate until the state intervened in 1999.[28] The much more common pattern is for directors of nonprofit entities to serve without any compensation at all. We should think hard about whether this convention makes sense in all contexts.

Confronting the compensation question raises the most fundamental issues concerning service on nonprofit boards: why individuals serve, and what responsibilities go with board membership. We need to distinguish between two types of nonprofits: (1) providers of services of various kinds, such as health care and other insurance plans, which do not rely on philanthropic contributions to carry out their work; and (2) the "charitable nonprofits," such as universities, orchestras, and museums, which depend heavily on the generosity of donors. I believe that the directors of the first class of nonprofits should be compensated, but that the directors (or trustees) of charitable nonprofits should contribute their services.

Private foundations constitute a third class of organizations, which in these respects resemble institutions in the first category more than they do those in the second. Thus, it is not surprising that foundations, especially the large ones, typically compensate their trustees—a practice which seems appropriate. As Richard Lyman, former president of the Rockefeller Foundation, explains, "At Rockefeller, we felt it necessary to pay trustees . . . who had to forego other possible ways to make money to spend time on the RF board. For them, there were real opportunity costs." In addition, foundations frequently match charitable contributions that trustees make to eligible organizations.

The main reason that I favor compensating the directors of the service-providing nonprofits is that the absence of compensation can encourage the feeling that whatever they do or don't do is fine, since they are "only volunteers."[29] Paying directors of this class of nonprofits at least a nominal fee would make it clear that they are expected to render significant services. The *New York Times* endorsed this position in the aftermath of the problems some years ago with Empire BlueCross BlueShield: "The pay wouldn't cost very much and would send a signal heard by members of other corporate boards: You're hired to do an important job, so get to work."[30]

Compensating directors of service-providing entities that fall outside the domain of charitable nonprofits makes sense for a related reason. Legal accountability depends on the presence of compensation: Section 720(a) of New York's Not-For-Profit Corporation Law causes compensated directors of New York not-for-profits to be held to a higher standard of accountability than their uncompensated counterparts.[31] Providing direct compensation may also discourage the substitution of less visible "perks." In the Empire BlueCross BlueShield case, government investigators unearthed evidence of lavish gifts purchased for directors. Apparently the corresponding Maryland plan paid $300,000 for a sky box at Oriole Park in Baltimore, and an executive of the Washington plan is said "to have traveled to Bermuda, Portugal, and Switzerland to see whether certain resorts were appropriate for Blue Cross meetings."[32]

Why don't the same arguments apply to compensation for directors

of all nonprofits, including those that depend on philanthropic contributions? In principle, I think they do. Trustees of "charitable" nonprofits should know that they, too, have real responsibilities, and they
should feel accountable. But certain offsetting considerations seem
more powerful. Providing even token compensation to these trustees
could have the perverse effect of reducing their sense of *financial*
obligation—their generosity—to the organizations they serve. Although
directors of grant-seeking nonprofits could give back any nominal fees
that they were paid, just as they normally make other contributions, it is
hard to know how many would elect this option. Moreover, some
trustees might feel that, by returning their fee, they had done all that
they should be expected to do. The existence of an opportunity to give
back modest fees might make it harder to extract meaningful contributions from all board members.

The perilous financial state of many nonprofits also argues against
compensating their trustees. As Taylor Reveley observes,

> When there's not enough money to pay the staff a living wage, or
> to have decent office space and equipment, or to keep creditors
> easily at bay . . . , it would be hard to explain even trifling fees for
> trustees.

The argument of principle and purpose is finally the most powerful
of all. Robert Goheen echoes the views of many:

> I frankly do not like the notion of pay for trustees of nonprofit
> institutions like universities, museums, and research organiza-
> tions. In my view trustees should serve because they believe in
> what the institution is doing (or trying to do) and want to help it
> do it well (or better). If they don't have that commitment, I doubt
> a modest fee will make them more zealous.

The combined force of these points explains why board compensation is so uncommon among charitable nonprofits—and why, in my
view, it would be unwise to alter the present convention.

Board Evaluation

The last piece of board machinery to be discussed consists of the methods used to evaluate how well the board itself is performing. These are separate from evaluations of the performance of individual directors/trustees and of the CEO. Many agree that board evaluation is necessary and can be valuable, but it is not clear that most boards have a well-established and effective program of evaluation. There is a tendency to just go through the motions, even though perfunctory reviews of board performance that simply meet NYSE listing requirements offer little value.[33]

Internal survey instruments are often employed to solicit the directors' views on questions such as, Is the board giving the right degree of attention to strategic issues? Is the flow of information in advance of meetings adequate? Is there enough opportunity in board meetings for a serious exchange of ideas? Does the board have enough executive sessions, and how useful are these sessions? How satisfied are the directors with the way the various board committees work? Many more questions can be posed, but directors may be less than candid when answering questions like these, out of a concern that incriminating findings discovered through honest reviews may be used against the board in litigation. To avoid this danger, some firms use outside lawyers to lead the evaluation process in the hope that claims of client privilege will protect the confidentiality of their findings. Firms may also engage outsiders to conduct informal interviews with board members because they believe that directors will be more forthcoming when speaking with someone they consider objective.[34]

The search for best practices remains a work in progress as companies experiment with different approaches. At Merck, a decision was made to replace paper questionnaires with one-on-one interviews of individual directors. The director who serves as chairman of the Committee on Corporate Governance and also as lead director conducts the sessions. The secretary of the board sits in on most of each interview to take notes, but she then excuses herself near the end so that the director can speak only to the fellow director conducting the interview. The interviews are based in part on written questions about aspects of board performance distributed in advance. This seems a promising approach, and its results should be studied carefully.

I am persuaded that most boards want to do a better job of self-evaluation than they do at present, but that they need help in fashioning effective procedures. Furthermore, whereas for-profit boards can and should do a much better job of self-evaluation, nonprofit boards in general have an even greater need for improvement in this area. Many (most?) simply assume that they are doing fine.

* * * * *

A NUMBER OF THE aspects of board operations discussed in this chapter may seem, and in fact may be, mundane. But careful attention to committee structures, board agendas, the conduct of board meetings, "rules of engagement" for board members, and some understanding of how to handle conflicts are important determinants of the ability of boards to provide strategic guidance and oversight. Similarly, a well-conceived approach to board renewal (including recognition of situations in which board members should step down), sensible compensation policies, and an agreed-on process for board evaluation can be important ways of improving board performance.

8

Themes

IN THIS CONCLUDING chapter, I identify five themes that have come to guide my thinking about boards and their effectiveness:

(1) Understanding the centrality of the partnership between the board and its chief executive/president, and finding ways to strengthen this relationship

(2) Recruiting board members who possess the key attributes needed for effective board leadership—especially courage and the will to act

(3) Making up-front investments of time and resources in mechanisms that can promote good governance

(4) Distinguishing ways in which governance in the for-profit and nonprofit sectors should and should not converge

(5) Recognizing the rewards of board service in both sectors

The CEO–Board Partnership

The quality of the working relationship between the CEO/president and the board is *the* most important factor determining organizational effectiveness in both sectors. Successful governance is difficult, if not impossible, to achieve without a mutually rewarding partnership between the board and the organization's chief executive.

When I wrote my first book on boards, the overarching issue in the for-profit sector was how to achieve a sensible balance between mechanisms that encouraged crisp executive decision making and mechanisms that encouraged the right kinds of oversight by governing boards. At that time (1994), this balance was generally tilted too much in the direction of the CEO. The "imperial CEO" was very much in vogue.

I did not believe then, and I certainly do not believe now, that the right way to redress this balance is to "defang" the chief executive. CEOs need to be strong leaders. They should be expected to come to clear conclusions, to advocate decisive steps, and to act. It was the other side of the equation that required attention: boards needed to be less supine. Boards should be reliable sources of probing questions, and board members should be good critics as well as compatriots. Strong CEOs and strong boards can complement each other in any number of ways, and a healthy, friendly tension is appropriate. The experiences of many nonprofit organizations have demonstrated convincingly that more of a partnership approach is beneficial.

In the intervening years, and especially in the post-Enron era, progress has been made in strengthening the role of the board and building more productive partnerships between business CEOs and their boards. As the *Spencer Stuart Board Index* for 2006 notes in its introductory statement, "The Board's relationship with the chief executive officer is shifting, as the greater representation and involvement of independent directors is changing the balance of power and rules of engagement."[1]

There is growing interest in the separate non-executive chairman model, which, at the level of general principle, has a great deal to be said for it. Nonetheless, practical problems—of perceived loss of status for the CEO and the challenge of finding outstanding individuals willing to serve as non-executive chairman—often prevent the adoption of this model, at least right now. The lead director model has become the favored alternative and is now the norm, at least for large US companies. This is a step in the right direction. I suspect, however, that adoption of the lead director model will prove to be a transitional stage and that, over time (perhaps, to be sure, a considerable amount of time!), ways will be found to overcome the practical barriers to institutionalization of the position of non-executive chairman.

Other important developments include the practice, now widespread, of making regular use of executive sessions and expecting independent directors to be responsible for selecting new board members. More care is given to periodic evaluations of the CEO, and there is a greater willingness than before to terminate CEOs who are not performing well. In addition, it is becoming more and more evident that former CEOs should not continue to serve on the boards of the companies they once led.

Despite these profound changes, business boards can still be too timid and too slow in addressing fairly obvious problems. Bringing about changes in leadership at the CEO level is complicated by the fact that the very companies that need new CEOs often have boards that are themselves ill suited to seeing the need for change and to acting on it. As one commentator put it, "Strong CEOs tend to nurture strong boards; weak ones not."

Another generic problem is that many compensation committees are less successful than they need to be in establishing credible performance-based compensation systems for chief executives, though here, too, I see signs of progress. There is also room for improvement in the way that corporate boards manage succession planning and the search for new leadership.

Last on this brief list of unfinished tasks is the need to devote continuing attention to the systematic building and renewing of the board itself—with a willingness to deal forthrightly with dysfunctional directors and to consider the use of a combination of mandatory retirement and flexible term limits to ensure an appropriate degree of turnover.

Undoubtedly, a number of the changes in governance have been stimulated by growing pressures on boards exerted by activist shareholders, intense media scrutiny, government regulators, and the courts. There is significantly more disclosure and transparency than there used to be in both the for-profit and nonprofit sectors. Of course, any fundamentally healthy development can be taken to extremes, and some commentators (especially Martin Lipton) believe that "we cannot afford continuing attacks on the board of directors." Lipton raises the question, "Will the migration from director-centric governance to shareholder-centric governance overwhelm American business corporations?" Among Lipton's specific worries are activist investors who will pressure boards to manage for short-term share price appreciation, overuse of executive sessions, and a dearth of good directors to recruit because of time demands and the potential for embarrassment from media coverage of scandals.[2]

I agree with Lipton that care must be taken not to overwhelm boards with bureaucratic requirements that can become so onerous that they distract as well as annoy, and that boards need to resist foolish proposals from any quarter. But I am more optimistic that reasonably sensible balances will be found. In my view, Lipton is overly inclined to defend past board practices that need improvement.[3] Overall, the structure and functioning of corporate boards is much healthier than it was a decade ago, and working relationships between most CEOs and their boards have improved markedly.

The right distribution of power between the president or executive director of a nonprofit and his or her board can also raise concerns, but the "direction" of this problem, if there is one, is likely to be opposite that in the for-profit sector. In the nonprofit sector, finding the appropriate balance between executive authority and board oversight is more likely to require strengthening the hand of the chief executive than building up the powers of the board. On occasion, presidents or executive directors are not even given the status of ex officio board members and can be made to feel that they are simply paid help, carrying out programs set by the board. Of course, all involved share the blame for such unsatisfactory relationships. Presidents and executive directors in the nonprofit sector are sometimes too reluctant to lead and to take on their boards if necessary. At the same time, nonprofit boards, with their long history of separate board chairs and considerable board authority, are much more likely than their for-profit cousins to become too involved in the management of their organizations.[4]

In both sectors, what is needed—and, fortunately, what is often found—is a healthy partnership. I can testify, on the basis of personal experience, that the relationships between presidents of nonprofits and their boards, especially their board chairs, can be enormously productive and satisfying. As president of both a research university and a large foundation, I was privileged to work with outstanding trustees. From my vantage point, the leaders of those boards were close colleagues and partners. I learned so much from them.

Courage and the Will to Act

By far the most important attributes of a director/trustee are *courage and the will to act*. This is the thesis articulated repeatedly by several commentators (most notably Bruce Atwater and Larry Bossidy). I could not agree more strongly. The reality is that, in the absence of directors with courage, no hard decisions will be made. It can be so tempting just to wait patiently for problems to somehow disappear on their own. I have seen too many instances in which it was fairly obvious what needed to be done, but devilishly difficult to get action. In some of these situations, I fault myself, as well as my board colleagues, for having been too patient. At the minimum, directors and trustees need to raise the most challenging questions—the ones that no one may want to hear—and then pursue them relentlessly until satisfactory answers are in hand.

In nonprofit settings, the temptation to just go along can be even more deadly because there are no markets to cast their own votes. Prolonged inaction in a corporate setting is likely to lead to a falling share price, irate investors, and hostile media scrutiny. There is no close analogy in many parts of the nonprofit sector, though declining revenues, falling enrollments or declining attendance, fund-raising shortfalls, and shrinking endowments should be seen as important indicators of trouble.[5]

In the nonprofit sector more generally, I am a strong advocate of death with dignity when an organization has accomplished its purpose, lost its sense of mission, or simply run out of energy. The cases of Wilson College and the University of Bridgeport, cited earlier, and the more recent (possible) demise of Antioch College,[6] illustrate the difficulty of taking decisive action. Because performance in the nonprofit sector often defies easy assessment, lackluster leadership can go unnoticed for considerable periods of time, with mere survival the objective—which never should be the case. The long lists of charitable nonprofits maintained by the IRS, including many that are inactive de facto, demonstrate how hard it is to prune the nonprofit tree.

Another key attribute of directors and trustees is the ability to keep one's ego under control. No one should attempt to occupy center stage too much of the time. Governance through the board mechanism is a team sport, par excellence, and individual members must understand that boards have a *collective* oversight responsibility. It is just as important for all board members to recognize that they make every decision as a group, as it is for individuals to speak out. The ablest board members are open-minded, able to listen to others and to change their own minds when there are persuasive reasons for doing so. They possess the capacity to work in organizational settings in which the distribution of authority is ambiguous and personal relationships can be complex. Managing an organization is generally much easier.

Investing in Governance

Appropriate governing arrangements can enable the CEO-board partnership to operate smoothly, and they can also facilitate both the exercise of courage and effective forms of collective decision making. Well-conceived mechanisms give independent directors the opportunity to nominate and replace colleagues, influence board agendas, participate actively in setting strategic directions, monitor the performance of management, handle conflict issues, address any compliance matters, and discuss candidly both the leadership provided by the CEO and their own stewardship.

Experience has helped me overcome an ingrained distaste for spending time thinking about matters of process when substantive issues are more interesting. I have learned that process problems are generally harder to handle after the fact, and I have come to believe that the up-front investments of the time and energy needed to put good mechanisms in place can pay large dividends. Once sound structures have been adopted, and once directors and management have become accustomed to using them, concern about governance can assume its rightful place in the background. The whole point, after all, is to create machinery that allows directors and trustees to focus on substance. Governance is a means to an end, not something to be admired in and of itself. Ironically, lack of attention to governance often creates situations in which debates about decision-making processes are time-consuming, intense, and debilitating. The objective should be to have in place a system of governance that satisfies reasonable norms and that operates routinely and more or less effortlessly.

Guiding principles and established practices must be more than implicit, however. It should be difficult for board members to forget to do the right thing. I have been in meetings of nominating committees in which the CEO remained throughout the deliberations because no one remembered that the outside directors were supposed to have an opportunity to talk alone about potential nominees. In most instances, this bow to formality is unimportant, but being explicit about conventions reduces awkwardness and increases the odds that responsibilities will be discharged appropriately. As a physicist friend (the late Aaron Lemonick) used to say in another context, "If it goes without saying, it should definitely be said." His alternative phraseology was, "If you think everyone already knows it, be sure to write it on the blackboard."

Small matters like the timely distribution of materials, advance notice of important subjects coming up for discussion, the routine use of executive sessions, and carefully coordinated schedules of the meetings of key committees can be very helpful. At the same time, as I have said, no one should celebrate the beauty of the nearly invisible machinery. The distinguished architect Robert Venturi is fond of saying "Never let de-tail wag the dog!" Fine, but the details need to be well in hand, although unobtrusive.

Venturi's admonition to keep "de-tails" in their proper place leads directly to a broader concern about situations in which excessive attention has to be given to issues of compliance and due diligence. Marty Lipton states the danger this way: "Proliferating lawsuits, certification requirements, and governance rules, as well as the increased threat of personal liability, are forcing boards to spend more time and energy on compliance, due diligence and investigations, and less on the actual business of their companies."[7] A closely related danger is that boards will become too cautious and risk-averse. Protecting oneself is a natural tendency, but a director/trustee can become too self-protective, too inclined to think about every issue from the perspective of how best to avoid the possibility of criticism. As one report warns, "Minimizing risk, rather than managing risk, seems to have become a board's mantra."[8] I agree with this general proposition, but I would also note that, in the case of private-equity companies, there is an opposite risk: the appeal of leverage can be so great as to encourage taking on too much debt and too much risk, with real dangers for bondholders of companies taken over and other investors.

Are For-Profit and Nonprofit Board Practices Converging?

Nonprofit boards and for-profit boards have much to learn from each other—even as we recognize that external constraints operate very differently in the two sectors. Both sectors can benefit from transfers of knowledge, and such transfers are encouraged by the high degree of overlap in board rosters: in particular, many directors of for-profits serve on nonprofit boards as well.[9] During the last decade, board practices in the two sectors have converged in two significant respects.

First, in defining their structures, for-profit boards have moved a considerable distance in the direction of the nonprofit world. It is far less common today for a large company to be strongly CEO-centric. The widespread adoption of the lead director model, alongside the gradual adoption of the separate non-executive chairman model, means that for-profit companies can now benefit from a more explicit sharing of responsibility for decisions affecting the board itself and how it discharges its duties. More generally, well-run nonprofits have much to teach their profit-making cousins about the marshalling of resources, how to do much with little, and the advantages of collegial decision making.

Second, governance in the nonprofit sector has become more formal, mirroring practice in the for-profit sector in healthy ways. There is more emphasis on accountability, and nonprofit boards are moving rapidly to create audit/compliance committees and to adopt other practices, such as regular review of presidential performance and routine use of executive sessions. "Strategic planning" has become something of a buzzword in the nonprofit sector, and more use is made today of benchmarking and other techniques long familiar to the boards of for-profit companies.

It is possible, however, for nonprofit boards to become too "business-like." There are fundamental differences between the sectors related to both their distinctive missions and the very different "markets" in which they operate. Simple transplants of what are thought to be best practices may not work well. It may be wise, as argued in Chapter 4, to allow the leaders of nonprofits to operate on a longer leash than their brethren in the for-profit world. Nonprofit boards also need to be comfortable working with more nuanced measures of performance than are common in the business world. The very mission of the enterprise can be difficult to define with precision and is often seen differently by various influential participants and supporters. Relevant data and analyses are frequently either unavailable or, if available, slippery to the touch. At the end of the day, trustees must be prepared to exercise their own judgment concerning both strategic directions and performance.

Rewards for Service on Boards

Both for-profit and nonprofit boards can have more impact on the success or failure of an organization than most people realize, and rewards have to be at least roughly commensurate with obligations and the "market rate" for the time of outstanding individuals. In the for-profit sector, the payment of appropriate stipends and fees is the principal way in which board members are compensated. Even in this sector, however, the reasons why an individual of ability serves on boards almost always transcend financial considerations.

Prestige is certainly a factor (sometimes too much of a factor), as is the interesting nature of the issues to be considered, the multiple opportunities to learn about substantive matters, and the wisdom gained through close interactions with colleagues from varied backgrounds. At Merck, I felt privileged to participate in what seemed like an ongoing seminar on molecular biology, the life sciences, and issues of health care around the world. At American Express, all members of the board had opportunities to learn a great deal by observing how an exceedingly well run company addresses issues associated with rapidly changing financial markets and payment patterns worldwide.

Nonprofit boards rarely pay their board members, so the rewards in this sector have to take other forms. Again, both prestige and learning opportunities are clearly consequential. In many nonprofit contexts, there is substantial room for judgments to be made, both good and bad. Active involvement in setting directions, making choices, and attracting outstanding individuals who are deeply committed to good causes can be both stimulating and satisfying. Service on boards of all kinds should be enjoyable as well as challenging. One commentator told me that one reason he enjoys serving on the boards of privately held companies is that there is less hassle, his work is more substantive, and it is just "more fun."

The even greater reward that comes from serving on nonprofit boards is, I believe, that such service can provide an opportunity to contribute to something that is more important than you are and that will last longer than you will. As Gene Likens, the discoverer of acid rain, said on the occasion of his retirement as president of the Institute of Ecosystem Studies (IES), "There are so few opportunities in the world to really make a difference."

Hallmarks of American society are the number and vitality of its voluntary associations—organizations that serve purposes that in other societies fall within the public sector. The success of this typically American way of addressing societal needs depends directly on the willingness of busy, talented individuals to work diligently as trustees. Because monetary rewards are modest at best, and usually nonexistent, we can be grateful that so many people seem genuinely to believe that working hard for a good cause is its own highest reward—and a privilege. That is, let me say emphatically, my own view.

Notes

Preface

1. See the lead editorial in the *New York Times*, "The Sound of Snoring at Empire" (Editorial), August 21, 1993. More recently, the board of regents of the Smithsonian Institution has been described as "AWOL for too long." See "The Regents' Reckoning: The Smithsonian Board, AWOL for Too Long, Is Back" (Editorial), *Washington Post*, June 22, 2007.

2. The number of articles in which the term "corporate governance" appeared in the *New York Times* has remained above two hundred since 2002 (the time of the Enron debacle). The count since 1990 has been as follows: 1990: 153, 1995: 93, 2000: 69, 2001: 98, 2002: 426, 2003: 304, 2004: 257, 2005: 222, 2006: 263. The pattern in *BusinessWeek* is similar, with the peak number of articles mentioning "corporate governance" (173) occurring in 2002, compared to 32 in 1990, 55 in 1995, 58 in 2000, 52 in 2001, 117 in 2003, 84 in 2004, 68 in 2005, and 41 in 2006. (Article counts derived from Nexis search for "corporate governance" in the *New York Times* and in *BusinessWeek*.)

3. For an influential early commentary employing these concepts, see Sir Adrian Cadbury, "Reflections on Corporate Governance," Ernest Sykes Memorial Lecture, March 11, 1993 (London: Chartered Institute of Bankers, 1993), 1.

4. One product of that process was a report issued by a special committee chaired by Professor Stanley J. Kelley Jr. at Princeton University—Special Committee on the Structure of the University, *The Governing of the University: Final Report of the Special Committee on the Structure of the University* (Princeton University, April 1970)—that was not only highly consequential at the time it was written

but has continuing value for those especially interested in the governance of colleges and universities.

5. Major publications from recent years include Ram Charan, *Boards That Deliver* (San Francisco: Jossey-Bass, 2005); and two books by William A. Dimma— *Tougher Boards for Tougher Times: Corporate Governance in the Post-Enron Era* (Mississauga, ON: J. Wiley & Sons Canada, 2006), and *Excellence in the Boardroom: Best Practices in Corporate Directorship* (Etobicoke, ON: Wiley, 2002). Two earlier book-length studies of the for-profit sector, each containing many references to earlier work, are Jay W. Lorsch, *Pawns or Potentates: The Reality of America's Corporate Boards* (Boston: Harvard Business School Press, 1989); and Charles N. Waldo, *Boards of Directors: Their Changing Roles, Structure, and Information Needs* (Westport, CT: Quorum Books, 1985). Of course, much of the current literature on corporate governance appears in journals and episodic publications. Publications on the nonprofit sector include, among many others, Brian O'Connell, *The Board Member's Book* (Washington, DC: Foundation Center, 1985); Cyril O. Houle, *Governing Boards: Their Nature and Nurture* (San Francisco: Jossey-Bass, 1989); and a most useful series of pamphlets published by the National Center for Nonprofit Boards as its "Governance Booklets." Some studies also focus on individual fields. One example is the comprehensive study of boards of trustees at independent liberal arts and comprehensive colleges by Richard P. Chait, Thomas P. Holland, and Barbara E. Taylor: *The Effective Board of Trustees* (Phoenix, AZ: Oryx Press, 1993).

6. These entities are described in various annual reports of the Mellon Foundation (especially the reports for 2003 and 2004), which are posted on the foundation's Web site at www.mellon.org. In brief, JSTOR is a highly searchable digital library of the back files of more than 650 scholarly journals; it is used by approximately thirty-five hundred libraries in over a hundred countries. ARTstor is a digital library of art images (544,000 as of May 2007) and related scholarly material, along with software tools that facilitate using the images; it is already being used by over 750 participating institutions in the United States and in select countries around the world. Ithaka has the broad mission to "accelerate the productive uses of information technology for the benefit of higher education worldwide" (www.ithaka.org/about-ithaka); it is now incubating new entities with highly focused missions, including one that is assembling digital content from the developing world starting in Africa, one that is creating an electronic archive of born-electronic journal content, and one that is dedicated to serving the needs of clusters of liberal arts colleges.

7. From a speech given on Wall Street on January 31, 2007, and reported in Jim Rutenberg, "Bush Tells Wall St. to Rethink Pay Practices," *New York Times*, February 1, 2007.

Chapter 1

1. For an excellent discussion of what nonresident boards can contribute in a university setting, see Special Committee on the Structure of the University, *The*

Governing of Princeton University: Final Report of the Special Committee on the Structure of the University (Princeton University, April 1970), also known as the "Kelley Report," 53ff. This incisive report was written at a time when the Vietnam War and other issues provoked many on campuses to question the need for (or the desirability of) a board of trustees.

2. From *The English Constitution*, originally published in the *Fortnightly Review* 1865–1867; first edition as a book published in 1867 (London: Chapman and Hall).

3. Fund accounting, needed in the nonprofit sector to ensure that donors' intentions are respected, can be extremely puzzling to trustees who come from for-profit organizations and are used to thinking that revenue is revenue. More generally, the confusion between operating statements and what are (or should be) capital accounts that is encouraged by the odd construction of IRS reporting forms can lead to highly misleading conclusions concerning financial trends and even the underlying financial health of an organization. For an extended discussion of this important and complex subject, see my book *Inside the Boardroom: Governance by Directors and Trustees* (New York: Wiley, 1994), 120–124. More recently, Doug Lederman has noted the problems posed for financial officers seeking to present understandable figures and for trustees trying to grasp the content of reports that they have been given (see "Cost and the College Trustee," *Inside Higher Ed*, March 6, 2007, online edition, http://insidehighered.com/news/2007/03/06/agb— which describes a talk given at the annual meeting of the Association of Governing Boards of Universities and Colleges).

4. The intense controversy over coeducation at Princeton involved members of the staff, especially the development staff, as well as alumni. I remember vividly the use made of the trustees' decision by the then financial vice president, Ricardo Mestres. Immediately after the decision was made, on a Friday afternoon, Mestres met with the business and development staff members, some of whom were opposed to coeducation on grounds of principle and some of whom thought that coeducation would damage permanently the university's ability to raise money. The message delivered by Mestres was simple and to the point: "The trustees of the university have made a decision. Those of you who can embrace it and work hard to make it succeed, should come back to work on Monday." The meeting adjourned.

5. Kevin Guthrie is also the author of an excellent study of the New-York Historical Society—*The New-York Historical Society: Lessons from One Nonprofit's Long Struggle for Survival* (San Francisco: Jossey-Bass, 1996)—in which he demonstrates the problems that that organization faced over many decades in part because it kept accepting "gifts" (of books and manuscripts, in particular) that it lacked the resources to care for.

6. William Shanklin, "Fortune 500 Dropouts," *Planning Review*, May 1986, p. 13.

7. Julie Schlosser and Ellen Florian, "The Biggest Moneymakers! The Best Investments! The Hall-of-Famers and the One-Hit-Wonders! The Triumphs, the Failures, the Milestones! Fifty Years of . . . AMAZING FACTS!" *Fortune*, April 5, 2004, p. 152.

8. See Daniel L. Kurtz, *Board Liability: Guide for Nonprofit Directors* (Mount Kisco, NY: Moyer Bell, 1988), especially ch. 1 and 4. The duty of *care* concerns a director's competence in performing directorial functions and typically requires directors to use the "care that an ordinarily prudent person would exercise in a like position and under similar circumstances." The duty of *loyalty* requires the director's faithful pursuit of the interests of the organization rather than the financial or other interests of the director or another person or organization. The objective is to avoid self-dealing and conflicts of interest.

9. Kurtz, *Board Liability*, 4. In addition, a nonprofit considering a major change in its mission is required to notify the IRS. Notification is all that is required as long as it is clear that charitable purposes are still being served.

10. Hanna Gray, quoted in Bowen, *Inside the Boardroom*, 22.

11. In addition to the extensive press coverage, see Kurt Eichenwald, *Conspiracy of Fools: A True Story* (New York: Broadway Books, 2005); the movie *Enron: The Smartest Guys in the Room*, based on the book *The Smartest Guys in the Room* by Bethany McLean and Peter Elkind; and Richard Breeden's 2003 report on WorldCom ("Restoring Trust: Report to the Hon. Jed S. Rakoff, the United States District Court for the Southern District of New York on Corporate Governance for the Future of MCI, Inc.," *Corporate Monitor*, August 2003). The Breeden report says that the WorldCom bankruptcy was caused in large part by "what appears to be the largest accounting fraud in history," but commentator Charles Exley, himself an astute observer of the business scene, disagrees. Exley writes, "It is simply impossible for a profitable company with a strong balance sheet to be put into bankruptcy by accounting errors, however huge. The bankruptcy of both companies [Enron and WorldCom] was caused by the investment of billions of dollars in assets which proved of virtually no value at the time of bankruptcy. Both companies invested heavily in fiber optic cable . . . The accounting fraud in both cases was an attempt to cover up these calamitous investments—an effect, not a cause." (Personal correspondence with the author, March 17, 2007.)

12. See the speech by Joann S. Lublin of the *Wall Street Journal* titled "Journey of 1,000 Steps: One Journalist's Long Look at Corporate Governance," delivered at Stanford University Law School, May 24, 2005, in which Ms. Lublin notes major improvements in corporate governance over the last two decades at the same time that she identifies continuing issues, such as excessive corporate pay. Salamon and Geller at Johns Hopkins report that their recent survey of what nonprofit boards actually do found that overall performance is quite good. See Lester M. Salamon and Stephanie L. Geller, "Nonprofit Governance and Accountability," Communiqué no. 4 (Baltimore: Johns Hopkins Center for Civil Society Studies, October 2005). Similarly, a book on foundations by Joel L. Fleishman—*The Foundation: A Great American Secret; How Private Wealth Is Changing the World* (New York: PublicAffairs, 2007)—details the accomplishments of foundations over many years at the same time that it notes shortcomings.

13. *Sarbanes-Oxley Act of 2002*, HR 3763, 107th Cong., 2d sess., 2002.

14. For a positive assessment of SOX, see the article "Stop Whining about SarbOx!" (*CNNMoney.com*, August 1, 2006) by Andy Sewer, *Fortune* editor-at-large, who concluded his review of the arguments pro and con as follows: "And now that I've waded through the jungle of competing claims about [SOX], I'm here to say that net-net, it is unassailable that SarbOx has been a positive for our markets and our economy." See also William J. Holstein, "Rethinking Sox," *Directorship*, June 2006, for a long interview with Michael Oxley that discusses ways in which the legislation might be "fine-tuned."

15. The argument that SOX has been mainly responsible for the growth of private equity is undermined by the rise of private equity elsewhere in the world. See David Wessel, "Closing the Door: Going Private Offers Rewards," *Wall Street Journal*, May 17, 2007.

16. "The Enron Verdicts . . . ," *Wall Street Journal*, May 26, 2006, online edition, http://online.wsj.com/PA2VJBNA4R/public/article/SB114860578243163811.html.

17. See Chris Young, comment titled "Settlement Fever," Institutional Shareholder Services Corporate Governance Blog, posted August 16, 2006, http://blog .issproxy.com/2006/08. Activist shareholders in Europe, and especially the United Kingdom, are also flexing their muscles and having an impact (Julia Werdigier, "Boards Feel the Heat as Investor Activists Speak Up," *New York Times*, May 23, 2007). One highly experienced board member, Hanna Gray, has observed that there is also, she believes, growing hostility between boards and their shareholders.

18. Eichenwald, *Conspiracy of Fools*, 620.

19. Thomas Kostigen, "Read All about It: Media Coverage May Be What Holds Companies to Account," *MarketWatch*, July 21, 2006, www.marketwatch.com/ news/story/media-best-keeping-businesses-line/story.aspx?guid=%7B170D9BE0 %2D8CD2%2D4AE9%2DAF95%2DE744BE4380F4%7D.

20. See the comments by John Snow, the former public-company CEO and treasury secretary, who is now the public face of Cerberus ("Closing the Door: Going Private Offers Rewards," *Wall Street Journal*, May 17, 2007).

21. Here is Exley's account of such a situation: "At one index fund, their position was explained to me this way: 'Mr. Exley, we are against this takeover and think it would be a bad thing for both companies. However, we are told by AT&T that this takeover is inevitable. We have 18 times the investment in AT&T that we have in NCR. That being the case, we think it is in our interest to have the deal completed at the lowest possible cost to AT&T . . .' I felt that I had stepped through the looking glass. I wondered what the other NCR shareholders would think of this exercise of shareholder rights."

22. James Bailey and Douglas Macauley at Cambridge Associates, working with data assembled by UBS Global Asset Management, as well as their own database, estimate that at the end of 2006, private equity totaled $1.5 trillion and venture capital $0.5 billion. Hedge funds accounted for another $1.5 trillion. These are huge numbers, and by the end of 2007 both the private-equity and hedge fund amounts could well be half again as large as they were at the end of 2006. Still, to gain perspective, note that equities worldwide were $43 tril-

lion at the end of 2006, and the total investable capital market, which includes nearly $50 trillion of bonds, was $106 trillion. Various observers have suggested that it would be a mistake to assume continued growth of private equity at anything like the recent rate. Stock markets are unlikely to continue to be as buoyant as they have been over the last decade, and if debt were to become more expensive and less available (as is now the case), the buyout movement would be slowed. (See Henny Sender, "Private Equity: Is Deal Frenzy Nearing End?" *Wall Street Journal*, May 29, 2007.)

23. Robert McCabe, a venture capitalist and member of many start-up boards, provides this revealing example, having to do with the now unpopular "poison pill." Here are McCabe's reflections: "Many companies still use Marty Lipton's curious invention, particularly smaller ones that are more easily subject to a coercive takeover. I have never quite understood how something like the pill has been found to be valid. But it is in fact a very useful device to protect shareholders. The governance rankers don't seem to understand the dynamics of takeovers, and assume that anyone who has a pill simply wants to stay independent. I have chaired the poison pill committees of companies that would have been delighted to evaluate a serious fair offer to their stockholders. Without the pill, a raider or green mailer has the upper hand. I believe that the pill, which is certainly a bizarre creation, is a very valid device for protecting the interests of all the shareholders. This assumes that it is not being abused and used with the intent to protect and enrich management . . . In the hands of directors who are working for the best interests of their shareholders, it can be a weapon to help assure that shareholders are treated fairly and the price is the best obtainable." (Personal correspondence with the author, March 12, 2007.)

24. It would be a mistake, however, to think that all issues of right behavior in the nonprofit sector are compensation related—or that all examples of abuse of authority are recent. A useful case from the past is that of the Heye Foundation and the collection of Native American art now under the care of the Smithsonian. The prolonged neglect of the foundation's extraordinary collection of Native American art by the Heye trustees in the 1970s led to the eventual intervention by the attorney general of New York, who reconstituted almost the entire board of the foundation. But by then the difficulties of caring for the collection, and exhibiting it properly, had become overwhelming. After much debate, arrangements were made to transfer responsibility for the collection to the Smithsonian Institution, and it is housed today in Smithsonian museums in Washington and New York. The Red Cross is another organization that has had a contentious history, related to its odd governance structure and some of its operating policies (see Chapter 6).

25. One review of reactions from the higher-education sector concluded that, "while many institutions have introduced elements of Sarbanes-Oxley into their governance and financial-reporting structures, few have embraced it fully." (Alexander E. Dreier, "Sarbanes-Oxley and College Accountability," *Chronicle of Higher Education*, July 8, 2005, online edition, http://chronicle.com/weekly/v51/i44/44b01001.htm.) Some auditors have urged colleges and universities to see

SOX as creating opportunities to improve communications around the financial reporting process. See John Mattie and Jack McCarthy, "The Substance of Transparency," *NACUBO Business Officer*, February 2003, pp. 39–43.

26. See Panel on the Nonprofit Sector, *Strengthening Transparency, Governance, Accountability of Charitable Organizations: A Final Report to Congress and the Nonprofit Sector* (Washington, DC: Panel on the Nonprofit Sector, June 2005). The president of one large foundation observed (in a private conversation) that she feels caught between pressures to hold down administrative expenses and pressures to do more monitoring and provide more reports.

27. Jonathan A. Small, e-mail message "More Nonprofit Panel Recommendations— May 19 comment deadline" to author and others, May 14, 2005. Small refers to the following statement of Senator Richard J. Santorum: "I got a letter recently from an organization that looked at the 94 instances of, quote, 'abuse' that were cited in the June 22nd, 2004 hearing and I'm told that all but two actually are illegal under current law." (Senate Finance Committee, *Charities and Charitable Giving: Proposals for Reform*, 109th Cong., 1st sess., April 5, 2005.) Senator Grassley also threatened legislative action against American University's governing board in the aftermath of "damaging audit findings on lavish spending by the university's former president . . . and proposed retribution against a whistle-blower." (Paul Fain, "U.S. Senator Threatens Legislative Action against American University's Governing Board," *Chronicle of Higher Education*, May 26, 2006, online edition, http://chronicle.com/weekly /v52/i38/38a03301.htm.) In the foundation world, a report titled "Proposed Governance Principles: Large Foundation Discussions," drafted in June 2004 by the presidents of a group of large private foundations, illustrates the approach that I favor. These guidelines are available at www.cof.org/Content/ General/Display.cfm?contentID=1753.

28 Stephanie Strom, "Donors Sweetened Director's Pay at MoMA, Prompting Questions," *New York Times*, February 6, 2007.

29. In his lengthy report on the WorldCom scandal, Richard Breeden proposes to use articles of incorporation (which can be modified only with prior shareholder consent) to constrain the activities of the board of directors by requiring them to follow rather elaborate rules in electing directors, compensating executives, and listening to shareholders. Sympathetic as I am to the need to correct abuses found at WorldCom, I regard Breeden's proposals for more process constraints as overly mechanistic, impractical in some respects, and likely to inhibit the wise use of judgment by directors. See Breeden, "Restoring Trust," especially pp. 3–4 and 19. See also the critique of the Breeden report by Martin Lipton and his colleagues: "Restoring Trust or Losing Perspective," memo distributed by Wachtell, Lipton, Rosen & Katz, August 27, 2003.

30. See Eichenwald, *Conspiracy of Fools*, 4, 391.

31. See the report by Business Roundtable and the CFA Centre for Financial Market Integrity on the alleged corrosive effects of short-term thinking on American business, exemplified by too much focus placed on quarterly results and too little strategic thinking (Dean Krehmeyer, Matthew Orsagh, and Kurt N.

Schacht, "Breaking the Short-Term Cycle," CFA Centre for Financial Market Integrity and the Business Roundtable Institute for Corporate Ethics, July 2006). See also Joe Nocera, "In Defense of Short-Termism," *New York Times*, July 29, 2006, for a good discussion, citing pros and cons, of a complex issue.

32. The significance of multiple objectives can be illustrated by examples cited from the field of higher education. In seeking to understand pronounced shifts in the arts-and-sciences share of BA degrees conferred by educational institutions in the 1960s, a colleague and I found that one important group of colleges and universities—historically vocational and preprofessional institutions whose enrollments grew significantly during the 1950s and 1960s—chose to "spend" increased student demand on efforts to enhance their academic standing. They did so by increasing their offerings in the arts and sciences, and they apparently gave greater weight to this objective than to increasing enrollment in more vocationally oriented fields—thereby forgoing the opportunity to earn higher net revenues, at least in the short run. (See Sarah E. Turner and William G. Bowen, "The Flight from the Arts and Sciences: Trends in Degrees Conferred," *Science*, October 26, 1990, pp. 517–521, especially 517–518.) For-profit educational institutions would almost surely have responded quite differently to the enrollment boom of the 1960s; the educational institutions, without shareholders expecting increased earnings, had more choices. More recent decisions by a number of colleges and universities to substitute grants for loans in the financial aid packages offered to students from low-income families reflect judgments that this way of expanding educational opportunity (one part of institutional mission) has a greater claim on these resources than would devoting the same funds to advancing a different part of the institutional mission—again, a choice that a for-profit provider might not have thought was available to it. (See Karen W. Arenson, "Harvard Says Poor Parents Won't Have to Pay," *New York Times*, February 29, 2004; and Marisa Schultz, "U-M Financial Aid Program Benefits Low-Income Students; The School's Goal Is to Offer an Opportunity to Talented Applicants Discouraged by the Cost," *Detroit News*, March 1, 2005.) Failure to recognize that educational institutions may well choose to invest in financial aid because such outlays serve their educational missions can lead to great confusion about the likely effects on tuition charges of reducing governmental support for student aid. For-profit educational institutions, focused on the financial bottom line, could be expected to respond very differently to changes in governmental support of financial aid programs. See William G. Bowen, "The Student Aid/Tuition Nexus," in *Ever the Teacher: William G. Bowen's Writings as President of Princeton* (Princeton, NJ: Princeton University Press, 1987), pp. 538–543; and William G. Bowen and David W. Breneman, "Student Aid: Price Discount or Educational Investment?" *Brookings Review* 11, no. 1 (Winter 1993): 28–31.

33. The attorney general in the state of New York did address problems at the Wallace-Reader's Digest Funds beginning in 1998 because of concerns by institutional beneficiaries of these funds that investments managed by supporting organizations established by the funds were not invested to the optimal benefit of the institutions, but may have favored Reader's Digest. Following the efforts

of two attorneys general—Dennis Vacco and then Eliot Spitzer—an agreement whereby funds formerly managed by Wallace Funds supporting organizations were transferred directly to the institutions, was reached in 2001. (Mark Sidel, "The Nonprofit Sector and the New State Activism," *Michigan Law Review* 100, no. 6 [May 2002]: 1312–1355.) In addition, the former attorney general in California, Bill Lockyer, issued a major report on the Getty Trust: "Report on the Office of the Attorney General's Investigation on the J. Paul Getty Trust" (Office of the Attorney General, California Department of Justice, October 2006).

34. See "A Statement from the Board of Regents on the Report and Recommendations of the Governance Committee" (June 18, 2007); the "Report of the Governance Committee to the Board of Regents" (June 14, 2007); "A Report to the Board of Regents of the Smithsonian Institution" (Independent Review Committee, June 18, 2007); and the extensive coverage in the *Washington Post* of these important reports ("The Regents' Reckoning; The Smithsonian Board, AWOL for Too Long, Is Back," June 22, 2007; and other articles). The specific issues examined in these reports are discussed in subsequent chapters. The point here is that a combination of congressional scrutiny and media coverage had a large impact on the governance of the Smithsonian.

35. Guthrie, *New-York Historical Society*. See also Bowen, *Inside the Boardroom*, 162–164.

Chapter 2

1. John Gapper, "The Trouble with the Two-Title Guys," *Financial Times*, September 18, 2006. The *FT* has run a number of stories on this theme, reflecting the general preference in the United Kingdom for splitting the roles.

2. Paul Volcker, personal correspondence with the author, March 14, 2007.

3. See Claudia Deutsch, "Fewer Corporate Chiefs Are Also Serving as Chairmen," *New York Times*, March 17, 2006. Other commentary in the next few paragraphs draws on Deutsch's perceptive column.

4. Quoted in Patricia Beard, *Blue Blood & Mutiny: The Fight for the Soul of Morgan Stanley* (NY: William Morrow, 2007), p. 340. Beard's account of the power struggle at Morgan Stanley is limited by the fact that Purcell would not speak with her. Still, there is no reason to doubt the accuracy of quoted comments such as this one by Debs.

5. It is easy to cite examples. A shareholder revolt at Disney forced a decoupling of the roles following the controversy over the huge severance package awarded to Michael Ovitz, whom Michael Eisner, as CEO-chairman, first hired and then fired. At AIG (American International Group), the unchallenged power of Hank Greenberg was evident in the events that precipitated the intervention of the New York attorney general, the forced departure of Greenberg, and the decision to elect an independent chairman to work alongside a new CEO.

6. Deutsch, "Fewer Corporate Chiefs."

7. In the leadership transition at American Express following the resignation of

James Robinson as chairman, Richard Furlaud, as non-executive chairman, handled this role exceptionally well, explaining to one and all how the board was handling the transition.

8. Damon Darlin and Miguel Helft, "H.P. before a Skeptical Congress," *New York Times*, September 29, 2006; and US Congress, House of Representatives, Committee on Energy and Commerce, Subcommittee on Oversight and Investigations, *Hewlett-Packard's Pretexting Scandal*, 109th Cong., 2nd sess., September 28, 2006, Serial No. 109-146 (Washington, DC: US Government Printing Office, 2006), 744. Note, however, that later discussions of what happened at HP suggest that Hurd was more involved in the spying decisions than initially appeared to be the case. (James B. Stewart, "The Kona Files," *New Yorker*, February 19 & 26, 2007, pp. 152–167.)

9. A brief chronology: Dunn became chairwoman when Fiorina was fired, and she retained that title after Mark Hurd was named CEO. At the time, Dunn echoed the views of others when she said, "It is just harder to achieve independent oversight of a CEO who's also the chairman" (Deutsch, "Fewer Corporate Chiefs"). The widely publicized spying activity aimed at board members and journalists then led, in one of the great ironies in corporate governance, to the dismissal of Dunn herself and the recombining of the roles of chairman and CEO.

10. David Kimbell and Tom Neff, "Separating the Roles of Chairman and Chief Executive: Looking at Both Sides of the Debate," *Point of View: Perspectives on Leadership* no. 1 (2006): 14–24. See also William A. Dimma, *Excellence in the Boardroom: Best Practices in Corporate Directorship* (Etobicoke, ON: Wiley, 2002), for a discussion of this issue in the Canadian context.

11. Chuck Lucier, Steven Sheeler, and Rolf Habbel, "The Era of the Inclusive Leader," *strategy+business* 47 (Summer 2007): 4.

12. See Chuck Lucier, Paul Kocourek, and Rolf Habbel, "CEO Succession 2005: The Crest of the Wave," *strategy+business* 43 (Summer 2006): 1–14, especially 11–12; and Lucier, Sheeler, and Habbel, "Era of the Inclusive Leader," 2, 6.

13. Kenneth D. Lewis, "The Board: Independent and *Inter*dependent," *Directors and Boards*, Third Quarter 2006, p. 22.

14. Gapper, "Trouble with the Two-Title Guys," 19.

15. One person who has recognized—and emphasized—the importance of this consideration is Tom Neff, perhaps in part because his work at Spencer Stuart has involved him directly in the search for board talent of all kinds, including candidates for non-executive chairman and lead director.

16. Gapper, "Trouble with the Two-Title Guys," 19.

17. See Tom Neff's contribution in Kimbell and Neff, "Separating the Roles," 22. See also "2006 Route to the Top" (Spencer Stuart, 2006), http://content.spencer stuart.com/sswebsite/pdf/lib/RTTT_CEO_study_2006.pdf; "Chief Executives Average Longer in Office: Findings of the Fifth Cantos FTSE Leadership Survey" (Cantos, 2006), http://w3.cantos.com/cantos/abt/press/Cantos_FTSE_lead ership_survey_30-6-06.pdf. There is reason to believe that the tendency for British CEOs to retire early is actually accelerating, and that it is connected to the availability of opportunities to serve as the part-time chairman of another

company. If this trend continues, the pool of candidates to be considered for the position of non-executive chairman will continue to deepen. See Jean Eaglesham, "US Executives Prove Less Retiring," *Financial Times*, March 11, 2006.

18. *The Changing Profile of Directors: Spencer Stuart Board Index 2006* (Spencer Stuart, 2006), 3, http://content.spencerstuart.com/sswebsite/pdf/lib/SSBI-2006.pdf. Lead directors are less commonly found in smaller companies, but the lead director model can be expected to spread "downward," as it were, over time. Heidrick & Struggles found that 75 percent of the directors at 660 of the two thousand largest publicly traded companies included in their *10th Annual Corporate Board Effectiveness Study: 2006–2007* (Chicago: Heidrick & Struggles, 2006, www.heidrick.com/NR/rdonlyres/723D125E-9746-4486-829A-D49A8AF0832B/0/HS_BoardEffectivenessStudy0607.pdf) have an independent director who serves as a lead or presiding director. In the United States, lead directors are generally seen as alternatives to non-executive chairmen, and it would be highly unusual for a company to have both a lead director and a non-executive chairman. In the United Kingdom, however, where the separate chairman model is commonplace, there is also the position of senior independent director (SID). This person is an independent director who has the additional responsibility of overseeing an annual evaluation of the performance of the non-executive chairman—a role that can normally be handled in an unobtrusive fashion. (See David Kimbell's contribution in Kimbell and Neff, "Separating the Roles," 17–18.)

19. I have served on several corporate boards in which a single CEO-chairman has performed superbly, and I know that many other directors could readily provide similar testimony. To be sure, these have tended to be successful companies on a proverbial roll. Still, in at least one situation of which I have personal knowledge (the takeover of NCR by AT&T), life was far from calm; and the CEO-chairman, Charles Exley, was nothing less than masterful in his struggles on behalf of NCR shareholders. But I am compelled to add that, even in this instance, when the CEO had a well-deserved reputation for competence and integrity (and also owned a large number of shares personally), some institutional investors snidely suggested that Exley might be putting the interests of management ahead of the interests of shareholders. In retrospect, a supportive, non-executive chairman might have helped somewhat with the issue of appearances, even though it would have been impossible, in my judgment, to have improved on the results that Exley delivered. Moreover, a separate chairman might well have made it more difficult for Exley to handle the negotiations in the way that he did. But we also need to recognize that NCR's shareholders might not have been blessed with a CEO who identified so strongly with their interests.

20. Julie Hembrock Daum, Tom Neff, and Jule Cohen Norris, "A Closer Look at Lead and Presiding Directors," *Cornerstone of the Board* 1, no. 4 (March 2006): 3.

21. The lead director model is much less common in the nonprofit sector, because there is almost always a non-executive chairman who is separate from the president or executive director. But the model can also work well in the nonprofit sector. John Kenefick, former president of the Union Pacific Railroad, describes

his work as de facto lead director at Princeton University in practical terms that apply to both the for-profit and the nonprofit sectors:

> To work at all, of course, the "lead director" must be formally recognized with some sort of title; and he must be prepared to give the job some time so that he will know generally what is going on, but without intruding in or interfering with the responsibilities of the chief executive officer. In any event, in addition to the obvious functions, I believe he and only he can play certain very important roles:
>
> First, act as an intermediary between the outside directors and the CEO. On occasion an outside director will be reluctant to ask what might be a sensitive question publicly but can be comfortable asking that question of the lead director, who is a colleague. The lead director can answer the question himself or get an answer. He can pass on to the CEO ideas or opinions which come to him from individual outside directors and also, of course, do the reverse: explain to individual directors the policies of the administration.
>
> Second, detect possible problems early on, consult with the CEO and, when appropriate, discreetly warn outside directors. He can offer a comfort factor to his colleagues who know someone on their side is watching the shop.
>
> Finally, if worst comes to worst and it appears a change of CEO must be made, provide the mechanism, first to evaluate the situation and then, if necessary, to make the change in a timely and efficient way.
>
> It is a delicate role, but it can work.

22. For a good statement of this concern, see the commentary by George M. C. Fisher in the *Spencer Stuart Board Index 2005* (Spencer Stuart, 2005), 12, http://content.spencerstuart.com/sswebsite/pdf/lib/SSBI-2005.pdf.

23. Empirical evidence makes clear that companies are most likely to elect a separate chairman when one of a number of moments in time is at hand. In particular, the split-roles model is especially likely to be adopted in two specific situations: (1) during a transition in executive leadership, especially when the new CEO is either young or lacks relevant experience (such as actually having run a major company); and (2) in the presence of turmoil, evident danger, or vexing strategic issues that require an absolute focus by the CEO on core business issues and that usually also entail the need to provide reassurance to varied constituencies (investors, rating agencies, employees, and the board itself). Of course it would be better if a sound structure were in place ahead of a crisis, because implementing structural change can be an added complication that is not needed when other issues are pressing.

24. The recent experience of the Smithsonian underscores, in the nonprofit context, the need for a strong chairman. The Independent Review Committee (IRC) charged with reviewing the work of the regents and of the Smithsonian more generally during the tenure of Lawrence M. Small as secretary (CEO), con-

cluded that the failure of the regents to provide proper oversight was due in part to the lack of a chairman who could devote substantial time to the operations of the board. At present, the chief justice is the presiding officer, and it is unrealistic to expect him to provide the leadership and direction that the regents require. There is a separate chairman of the executive committee of the regents, but it would be better, the IRC concluded, if there were a chairman of the governing board. ("A Report to the Board of Regents of the Smithsonian Institution" [June 18, 2007], p. 17, www.smithsonianirc.org/images/FINAL_IRC_REPORT.pdf.)

25. *Spencer Stuart Board Index 2006*, 20.

26. See Chuck Lucier, Steven Sheeler, and Rolf Habbel, "The Era of the Inclusive Leader," *strategy+business* 47 (Summer 2007): 4.

27. At the May 2007 annual meeting of Home Depot, 34 percent of the votes on a shareholder proposal to split the roles of chairman and CEO were in favor. (See Patti Bond, "Home Depot Annual Meeting: Calm after '06 Storm; Unlike Last Year, Most from Board Attend; CEO Answers Questions," *Atlanta Journal-Constitution*, May 25, 2007.)

28. In this instance, by a striking coincidence, the news that the Merck board had elected a three-person executive committee to function in lieu of a separate chairman was announced immediately after the defeat at the annual meeting of a resolution (opposed by management) that would have mandated separating the roles. The main proponent of the resolution, Father John Celichowski, was quoted in the *New York Times* the next day as being "very surprised" by the timing of these outcomes and by the decision of the board not to ask one person to be both CEO and chairman. (Patrick McGeehan, "A Friar Speaks, and Lightning Strikes," *New York Times*, May 8, 2005.) Those of us on the board obviously failed in our effort to explain to shareholders such as Father Celichowski that we agreed that there were circumstances in which splitting the roles was the right thing to do, but that we did not think it was wise to adopt a permanent mandate.

29. Kenneth N. Dayton, *Governance Is Governance* (Washington, DC: Independent Sector, 2001), 4.

30. I was then able to work cheerfully and effectively with Whitehead until he retired and was succeeded as chairman by another exceedingly able person, Hanna Gray, then president of the University of Chicago. Whatever I was able to accomplish at the foundation was made possible in no small measure by the highly collegial relationship I had with these two effective chairmen (and later with Anne Tatlock, former chairman of Fiduciary Trust, who succeeded Hanna Gray).

31. Frederick Rudolph has described in detail the rise of "academic man" in the latter part of the nineteenth century, when faculty hierarchies and departments were established, publication was emphasized, learned journals and university presses were created, and sabbaticals for research became common. He writes, "All this apparatus, all of these manifestations of organization, would be a tremendous boon to the academic itinerant, for whom a reputation in his profession was more important than any commitment to a particular institution. The tendencies of the new scholarship and of organization would make such a man

loyal to professional standards . . . , but indifferent to the fate of the institution to which he might temporarily be attached." Rudolph then goes on to suggest implications for governance: "The professionalization of the professors had not brought them any new authority in college and university affairs; actually, it had only helped to widen the gap between them and the university board . . . The structure of the colleges and universities in the end made room for an extremely professionalized faculty and for a governing board whose professional competence lay outside the main interest of the institution itself." (Frederick Rudolph, *The American College and University: A History* [1962; repr., Athens: University of Georgia Press, 1990], especially ch. 19 and pp. 408, 427.)

Chapter 3

1. Kenneth Langone, lead director of Home Depot, may be an exception to this generalization. See his spirited defense of Robert Nardelli's compensation at Home Depot (as quoted in Joe Nocera, "Speaking Up in Fresh Air at Home Depot," *New York Times*, May 26, 2007) and his earlier defense of Richard Grasso's pay at the New York Stock Exchange (Thomas Landon Jr., "Ex-Director of N.Y.S.E. Defends Chief's Pay, Again," *New York Times*, June 15, 2004).

2. As cited in Eric Dash, "Off to the Races Again, Leaving Many Behind," *New York Times*, April 9, 2006. See also a major *Fortune* article by Rik Kirkland titled "The Real CEO Pay Problem," July 10, 2006, pp. 78ff.

3. See Joann Lublin and Phred Dvorak, "The Insiders: How 5 New Players Aid Movement to Limit CEO Pay; Mainstream Figures Mix with Activists; A Fix 'from Within,'" *Wall Street Journal*, March 13, 2007.

4. Eric Dash and Milt Freudenheim, "Chief Executive at Health Insurer Is Forced Out in Options Inquiry," *New York Times*, October 16, 2006. See also Eric Dash, "Who Signed Off on Those Options?" *New York Times*, August 27, 2006, for an extensive account of how executive compensation was manipulated at Mercury Interactive (now HP Mercury, a Silicon Valley software company) by the backdating of options. The SEC and the IRS have continued to investigate hundreds of cases of this kind.

5. Geraldine Fabrikant, "G.E. Settles S.E.C. Case on Welch Retirement Perks," *New York Times*, September 24, 2004; Andrew Hill, "Welch Asks GE to Cut His Package," *Financial Times*, September 17, 2002; David Cay Johnston with Reed Abelson, "G.E.'s Ex-Chief to Pay for Perks, but the Question Is: How Much?" *New York Times*, September 17, 2002.

6. *New York Times*, July 13, 2005.

7. Dash, "Off to the Races Again."

8. A statement attributed to Carl Reisner, a lawyer at Paul, Weiss who works with buyout firms. See David Carey, "Deliver and You Get Paid," *Deal*, June 1, 2007, online edition, www.thedeal.com.

9. Dash, "Off to the Races Again." In a study done for the Conference Board, the compensation consultant, Fred Cook, has criticized the methodology of other

studies of similar ratios and has concluded that the median CEO–worker ratio in 2004 was "only" 187 to 1, not 400 to 1 as some argued.

10. The study is Xavier Gabaix and Augustin Landier, "Why Has CEO Pay Increased So Much?" *Quarterly Journal of Economics*, forthcoming. The quotes here come from David Wessel's discussion of that study: "With CEO Pay, Size Does Matter," *Wall Street Journal*, November 2, 2006

11. These two sets of data were reported in, respectively, the *New York Times* (Eric Dash, "More Pieces. Still a Puzzle," April 8, 2007), and the *Wall Street Journal* (Joann S. Lublin, "The Pace of Pay Gains," April 9, 2007). Both papers also published, in these issues, elaborate tables showing compensation of individual CEOs as reported in company proxies under the new disclosure requirements. At one time, large pay packages were a purely American phenomenon, but CEOs of the top 100 companies in the United Kingdom received £3 million in 2005 (almost $6 million), a 30 percent increase over the prior year, in part because of greater use of incentive pay components. (See Kate Burgess, "Top Chief Executives See Pay Rise 30% to £3m," *Financial Times*, November 23, 2006.) It is evident that, for better or worse, the US model of executive compensation is spreading.

12. Woolard's views are described in Gretchen Morgenson, "How to Slow Runaway Executive Pay," *New York Times*, October 23, 2005. The Bogle quotation is from Dash, "Off to the Races Again"; the Munger and Immelt quotations are from Rik Kirkland, "The Real CEO Pay Problem," *Fortune*, July 10, 2006, pp. 81 and 84. See also the comments by James Robinson, chairman of Bristol-Myers Squibb and former CEO of American Express, in William J. Holstein, "Staying Focused on the Big Picture: A Conversation with Jim Robinson," *Directorship*, February–March 2007, p. 16

13. See Schacht's talk "The Distribution of Wealth in the New Millennium: Challenges and Opportunities." Seventh Annual William R. Laws Peacemaking Lecture, April 3, 1999, First Presbyterian Church, Columbus, IN.

14. Quoted in Morgenson, "How to Slow Runaway Executive Pay."

15. David Wessel, "Democrats Target Wealth Gap and Hope Not to Hit Economy," *Wall Street Journal*, November 21, 2006.

16. Jim Rutenberg, "Bush Tells Wall St. to Rethink Pay Practices," *New York Times*, February 1, 2007.

17. "House Votes to Give Investors Say on Executive Pay," *New York Times*, April 21, 2007.

18. Irving Shapiro, "A Personal Performance Review of the Board" (Summer 1984; repr. in *Directors and Boards*, Fourth Quarter 2006, p. 48).

19. Dan Ryterband, "Boards Take the Reins on Compensation," in *The Changing Profile of Directors: Spencer Stuart Board Index 2006* (Spencer Stuart, 2006), 24, http://content.spencerstuart.com/sswebsite/pdf/lib/SSBI-2006.pdf.

20. *Spencer Stuart Board Index 2005* (Spencer Stuart, 2005), 11, http://content.spencerstuart.com/sswebsite/pdf/lib/SSBI-2005.pdf.

21. The suggestions that follow in this section of the chapter are similar in many respects to the excellent list of proposals by Joann Lublin in "Ten Ways to Restore Investor Confidence in Compensation," *Wall Street Journal*, April 9, 2007.

22. Ryterband, "Boards Take the Reins," 24. See also the long story by Gretchen Morgenson titled "Gilded Paychecks" (*New York Times*, October 15, 2006), which focuses on the role of Fred Cook in advising boards on CEO compensation.

23. "Berkshire Hathaway Inc. 2005 Annual Report" (Warren E. Buffett, 2006), 16, www.berkshirehathaway.com/2005arn/2005ar.pdf.

24. William J. Holstein, "Staying Focused on the Big Picture," 17.

25. Richard C. Breeden, "Restoring Trust: Report to the Hon. Jed S. Rakoff, the United States District Court for the Southern District of New York on Corporate Governance for the Future of MCI, Inc.," *Corporate Monitor*, August 2003, pp. 82–99. One of Breeden's conclusions is that ill-conceived compensation practices, more than anything else, are what "seemed to lay the foundations for the fraud that ultimately transpired, and that represented the worst manifestation of WorldCom's governance failures" (p. 26). A recent Mercer study shows that less use is being made of options, with more direct stock grants. Stephen Taub's report ("Study: Director Pay Hikes Slowing Down," CFO.com, August 8, 2006) on the Mercer study quotes Peter Oppermann, of Mercer, explaining this shift: "Ownership, or having a stake in a company's shareholder value, is more appropriate than a 'leveraged' award for increasing stock price."

26. Quoted in David Wessel, "Capital: Closing the Door: Going Private Offers Rewards," *Wall Street Journal*, May 17, 2007.

27. Quoted in Carey, "Deliver and You Get Paid."

28. See Joann S. Lublin, "Adding It All Up," *Wall Street Journal*, April 10, 2006. Ms. Lublin cites specific examples in which the use of tally sheets had a real impact.

29. See Gretchen Morgenson, "Weird and Weirder Numbers on Pay Reports," *New York Times*, March 11, 2007. For example, total compensation can be reported as negative if market movements reduce the value of options granted in previous years, even though the executive in question may have taken home substantial cash.

30. See Claudia Deutsch, "Behind Big Dollars, Worrisome Boards," *New York Times*, April 9, 2006; and Stephen Labaton, "Spotlight on Pay Could Be a Wild Card," *New York Times*, April 9, 2006. See also "CEO Pay and SEC Disclosure Requirements," *BusinessWeek*, August 22, 2006. These stories list a variety of viewpoints on the disclosure debate. The quote is by Charles M. Elson, from the Deutsch article.

31. Gretchen Morgenson, "McKinnell Fumbled Chance to Lead," *New York Times*, August 6, 2006.

32. See "Investigators Secretly Mined Munitz's Records," *Los Angeles Times*, September 2, 2006; and much earlier coverage, as well as the final "Report on the Office of the Attorney General's Investigation of the J. Paul Getty Trust" (summarized in "California Attorney General Appoints Overseer of Reforms at J. Paul Getty Trust," *New York Times*, October 3, 2006).

33. See "Report of the Governance Committee to the Board of Regents" (June 14, 2007). The Governance Committee has now established a procedure whereby "expenses for travel, representational activities, and special events incurred by or on behalf of the Office of the Secretary will be subject to review by the Audit and Review Committee for reasonableness and compliance with standard Smithso-

nian policy. The Audit and Review Committee will report to the Board at least annually on the results of the review" (p. 13).

34. In the university world, a widely discussed story in the *Wall Street Journal* indicated that the trustees of Vanderbilt University did not pay sufficiently close attention to expensive renovations of Chancellor Gordon Gee's house or to his very sizable housing and entertainment allowances. Following a review by a special board committee, these practices were changed substantially to provide closer oversight and full disclosure to the entire board. See Joann Lublin and Daniel Goldin, "Vanderbilt Reins in Lavish Spending by Star Chancellor," *Wall Street Journal*, September 26, 2006.

35. Reason should also prevail. Robert Atwell, former president of the American Council on Education and a frequent critic of presidential pay, has pointed to instances in which "there may have been excessive media coverage of small potatoes." One example is a $140 dinner paid for by a community college president. See Paul Fain, "High Pay Makes Headlines," *Chronicle of Higher Education*, November 24, 2006, p. B6.

36. See the special report "Executive Compensation," *Chronicle of Higher Education*, November 24, 2006, section B. This report provides elaborate detail on all aspects of compensation in different sectors of higher education, but it is important to recognize (as the report does) that in some instances reported compensation for a single year is misleading in that it includes deferred compensation and the payout of retirement benefits earned over many years. For this reason, the reported compensation of presidents who are retiring is particularly subject to misunderstanding. The Form 990s used to report salaries in higher education and in other parts of the nonprofit sector suffer from a double counting problem: deferred pay *earned* in a particular year is included in total compensation for that year and then is included again in total compensation in the year that the individual retires and the deferred amounts are paid out.

37. See Scott Jaschik, "Gee's Take on Gee," *Inside Higher Ed*, July 19, 2007, online edition, http://insidehighered.com/news/2007/07/19/gee.

38. For detailed data on compensation of the leaders of the largest and best-known nonprofits, see Noelle Barton, Maria Di Mento, and Alvin P. Sanoff, "Top Nonprofit Executives See Healthy Pay Raises," *Chronicle of Philanthropy*, September 28, 2006, pp. 39ff.

39. See "A Report to the Board of Regents of the Smithsonian Institution" (Independent Review Committee, June 18, 2007), 3–5.

40. See Stephanie Strom, "Donors Sweetened Director's Pay at MoMA, Prompting Questions," *New York Times*, February 16, 2007.

41. United States. Internal Revenue Service, "Report on Exempt Organizations Executive Compensation Compliance Project—Parts I and II," March 2007, www.irs.gov/pub/irs-tege/exec._comp._final.pdf. See also Kenneth Bertsch, "Trends for Non-executive Chairs and Lead Directors," *Corporate Board*, November–December 2006, pp. 5–9.

42. For a good discussion of the demand–supply situation, see Thomas J. Tierney, "The Nonprofit Sector's Leadership Deficit" (Bridgespan Group, March 2006),

www.bridgespangroup.org/PDF/LeadershipDeficitWhitePaper.pdf; and references to this work in the *Chronicle of Philanthropy*'s survey (quoted in Barton, Di Mento, and Sanoff, "Top Nonprofit Executives See Health Pay Raises").

43. "The Leadership Imperative: The Report of the AGB Task Force on the State of the Presidency in American Higher Education" (Washington, DC: Association of Governing Boards of Universities and Colleges, 2006).

44. See Scott Jaschik, "Should U.S. News Make Presidents Rich?" *Inside Higher Ed*, March 19, 2007, www.insidchighered.com/news/2007/03/19/usnews.

Chapter 4

1. See the 2007 annual Booz Allen Hamilton report on CEO turnover, written up in Chuck Lucier, Steven Sheeler, and Rolf Habbel, "The Era of the Inclusive Leader," *strategy+business* 47 (Summer 2007): 1–14; "More CEO Heads Are Rolling," *Directorship*, June 2006, p. 7; "CEO Heads Rolling Faster than Ever," *Governance News Watch*, Directorship.com, September 22–28, 2006; Kevin Orland and Leslie Gersing, "Executives Switch Jobs More Often This Year amid Added Pressure" Bloomberg.com (www.bloomberg.com/apps/news ?pid =20601103&sid=aw5qcrqZBf6o&refer=news#), August 22, 2006, citing a study by Liberum Research; Jason Kelly, "'Hypervigilant' Boards Ousting U.S. Executives in Droves," *International Herald Tribune*, September 27, 2006, online edition, www.iht.com/articles/2006/09/26/bloomberg/bxceos.php, citing a study by Challenger, Gray & Christmas; and "Why Corporate Board Rooms Are in Turmoil," *Wall Street Journal*, September 16, 2006, citing the 2006 Booz Allen Hamilton CEO turnover study and other sources.

2. *American College President: 2007 Edition* (Washington, DC: American Council on Education, 2007), 86.

3. G. Thomas Sims, "Siemens Chief Agrees to Quit in Scandal," *New York Times*, April 26, 2007.

4. Fiorina rejects this explanation for her demise. See Carly Fiorina, *Tough Choices: A Memoir* (New York: Portfolio, 2006). Joe Nocera ("Carly Fiorina's Revisionist Chronicles," *New York Times*, October 14, 2006) disagrees with Fiorina's interpretation of events and emphasizes poor performance. I find Nocera's account credible and consistent with the views of many others.

5. Ricke's resignation came after a weak quarter and pointed discussions with the Blackstone Group, a big institutional investor. See Katrin Bennhold, "Chief of Deutsche Telekom Leaves after a Weak Quarter," *New York Times*, November 13, 2006.

6. The O'Connell case illustrates that, "while increasingly assertive corporate directors are ousting more chief executives, . . . it's harder to say goodbye without a big check." An arbitration panel ruled that the Massachusetts Mutual Life Insurance Company board did not have grounds to dismiss O'Connell for cause, and insisted that he be paid more than $40 million (a decision that is under appeal). See Joann S. Lublin and Scott Thurm, "How to Fire a CEO," *Wall Street Journal*, October 30,

2006, online edition, http://online.wsj.com/ article/SB116217755560707504.html ?mod–us_business_biz_focus_hs, as cited in *Directorship*.

7. Quoted phrases are from Ann Davis and Randall Smith, "Delayed Reaction: At Morgan Stanley, Board Slowly Faced Its Purcell Problem," *Wall Street Journal*, August 5, 2005.

8. See Joe Nocera, "In Business, Tough Guys Finish Last," *New York Times*, June 18, 2005. This case also illustrates the growing importance of major institutional investors (here T. Rowe Price and Highfields Capital Management) in pressing for the removal of a CEO. Nocera's theme was reiterated in Booz Allen Hamilton's 2007 report (Lucier, Sheeler, and Habbel, "Era of the Inclusive Leader"). In the words of the report, "Today's inclusive CEOs must be willing to engage in dialogue with investors, employees, and government; to surround themselves with managers and advisors who complement their own capabilities; and to maintain transparency in their communications about financial results and compensation" (pp. 1–2).

9. To elaborate briefly on the "academic freedom" point and its lack of relevance here, the president of a university cannot expect to enjoy an unfettered right to say whatever he or she chooses on any topic—as, within broad limits, a faculty member without comparable governance responsibilities can. The reason is simply that people in general are not going to separate the president's personal views from the views of the institution that the president represents. Judge Richard Posner put it well when he said that there is a "fiduciary responsibility" on the part of a president to think carefully about the consequences for the institution of whatever the president says. Richard Posner, "Larry Summers and Women Scientists: Posner," *Becker–Posner Blog*, January 30, 2005, www .becker-posner blog.com/archives/2005/01/larry_summers_a.html. For a more general discussion of the deliberations of the Harvard Corporation leading to Summers' resignation, see Javier C. Hernandez, "Houghton Says It's Time," *Harvard Crimson*, June 7, 2006, online edition, www.thecrimson.com/article.aspx ?ref=513844.

10. See "A Report to the Board of Regents of the Smithsonian Institution" (Independent Review Committee, June 18, 2007), 8.

11. For an extensive account of this troubled history, see Elizabeth Farrell, "How Student Protestors Toppled a Would-Be President at Gallaudet U.," *Chronicle of Higher Education*, November 3, 2006, online edition, http://chronicle.com/ daily/2006/11/2006110301n.htm.

12. See "Cooper Reflected, Decided to Step Aside: Resignation Announcement Followed Year Filled with Controversy for UR President," *Richmond Times Dispatch*, January 15, 2006.

13. See Paul Fain, "Ladner Resigns as President of American U., Agrees to $950,000 Settlement," *Chronicle of Higher Education*, October 25, 2005, online edition, http://chronicle.com/daily/2005/10/2005102501n.htm; and Paul Fain, "American U.'s Board Apologizes Publicly in Wake of Furor over Ladner," *Chronicle of Higher Education*, October 28, 2005, online edition, http://chronicle.com/ daily/2005/10/2005102806n.htm.

14. Rutgers is another example of a university in which strong athletic interests have affected governance, priority setting, and presidential oversight. See William C. Dowling's study of the history of efforts at Rutgers to improve football performance: *Confessions of a Spoilsport: My Life and Hard Times Fighting Sports Corruption at an Old Eastern University* (University Park: Pennsylvania State University Press, 2007).

15. In contrast, poorly drafted agreements can cause great difficulty. See Paul Fain, "Dos and Don'ts of Writing Presidential Contracts," *Chronicle of Higher Education*, November 24, 2006, online edition, http://chronicle.com/weekly/v53/i14/14b00801.htm.

16. For accounts of President Dye's resignation and related events, see Jennifer Gonzalez, "Oberlin President Leaving College after 12 Years; Dye's Decision Follows Email from Professors Suggesting Change," *Cleveland Plain Dealer*, September 12, 2006; Scott Jaschik, "Invisible Review at Oberlin," *Inside Higher Ed*, June 14, 2006; and Ben Leubsdorf and Piper Fogg, "Peer Review: Trustee Is Ousted after Dispute over Oberlin College's President," *Chronicle of Higher Education*, June 23, 2006. Disagreements over the college's new strategic plan, the handling of budgetary problems, and the timing of a bonus paid to the president also played parts in the debate over the president's performance.

17. See Joe Nocera, "A Defense of Short-Termism," *New York Times*, July 29, 2006: "For many of the executives back then [in the 1980s], the argument that they were managing for the long-term was bogus. There was too much lethargy in too many companies, and a desire by too many executives to avoid making tough decisions. Having sailed through the post-war era without much in the way of global competition, there were plenty of American industries that desperately needed to be shaken up in a tougher, more competitive era. Whatever their flaws, the raiders helped spur that process—in no small part by forcing executives to pay more attention to the stock price."

18. Alan Murray, "Leash Gets Shorter for Beleaguered CEOs," *Wall Street Journal*, August 23, 2006.

19. See my book *Inside the Boardroom: Governance by Directors and Trustees* (New York: Wiley, 1994), ch. 6, for an elaboration of this argument and a number of examples.

20. Subsequently, Lord Browne decided to step down even earlier than planned because of newspaper reports alleging that he had spent company funds on a Canadian man with whom he had had a relationship. BP concluded that the allegations of misused company funds were "unfounded or insubstantive." Nonetheless, Browne resigned on May 1, 2007, so that the focus on his private life would not distract from the business of running the company. Ed Crooks, Carola Hoyos, and Nikki Tait, "Browne Quits BP after Lies to Court over Lover," *Financial Times*, May 2, 2007. These later developments are, however, unconnected to the decision about mandatory retirement at a set date, which is our focus here.

21. Brett D. Fromson, "American Express: Anatomy of a Coup; Bitter, Seesaw Feud Unseated CEO," *Washington Post*, February 11, 1993.

Chapter 5

1. "What Directors Think: The 2006 *Corporate Board Member*/Pricewaterhouse-Coopers Survey," supplement to *Corporate Board Member*, 2006; *The Changing Profile of Directors: Spencer Stuart Board Index 2006* (Spencer Stuart, 2006), 25, http://content.spencerstuart.com/sswebsite/pdf/lib/SSBI-2006.pdf; and Ram Charan, "Ending the CEO Succession Crisis," *Harvard Business Review* 83, no. 2 (February 2005): 72, 74.

2. *Chronicle of Higher Education* 2005 survey, quoted in "The Leadership Imperative," *The Report of the AGB Task Force on the State of the Presidency in American Higher Education* (September 2006), 16.

3. See Thomas J. Tierney, "The Nonprofit Sector's Leadership Deficit" (Bridgespan Group, March 2006), especially pp. 13–23, www.bridgespangroup.org /PDF/ LeadershipDeficitWhitePaper.pdf.

4. Dennis M. Barden, "Moving Up: To Market, to Market," *Chronicle of Higher Education*, December 15, 2006, online edition, http://chronicle.com/weekly/v53/ i17/17c00101.htm.

5. See "Why They Said No to Harvard," *Chronicle of Higher Education*, February 16, 2007, online edition, http://chronicle.com/daily/2007/02/2007021602n.htm, for an informative discussion of the reasons that a number of possible candidates for the Harvard presidency declined to be considered.

6. W. Arthur Lewis, a Nobel Prize–winning economist, spoke about the importance of humility (and character) in a splendid talk that he gave while being installed as chancellor of the University of Guyana on January 15, 1967: "Excellence is achieved not only by intellect; it derives even more from character . . . To achieve excellence, one must have self-discipline; to practice the same thing over and over again, while others are enjoying themselves; to push oneself from the easy part to the hard part; to listen to criticism and use it; to reject one's own work and try again. *Only the humble achieve excellence, since only the humble can learn.*"

7. It is revealing that the character problems of Andrew Fastow, former CFO of Enron, were apparently not limited to his handling of the Raptors. He is reported to have used some of the proceeds from the Raptor transactions to establish the Fastow Family Foundation, for the unstated purpose of avoiding taxes and charging family vacations to a 501(c)(3) entity. See Kurt Eichenwald, *Conspiracy of Fools: A True Story* (New York: Broadway Books, 2005), pp. 355 and 468–469. In one sense, this was a small offense, but it can be seen as indicative of a particular mind-set and of a willingness to cut corners of all kinds.

8. See the seventeen-hundred-page "Martin Report," on the Merck Web site (www.merck.com/newsroom/vioxx/martin_report.html), for the detailed findings of what I consider a model investigation carried out by highly competent people.

9. Larry Bossidy, "The Job No Leader Should Delegate" (Spring 2002), reprinted in *Directors and Boards*, Fourth Quarter 2006, p. 59. See also the best-selling book by Bossidy and Ram Charan: *Execution: The Discipline of Getting Things Done* (New York: Crown Business, 2002).

10. See Chuck Lucier, Steven Sheeler, and Rolf Habbel, "The Era of the Inclusive Leader," *strategy+business* 47 (Summer 2007): 6, for a strong indictment of the idea of keeping the former CEO as chairman.

11. From an interview with Charles Burck, published in Larry Bossidy, "'I Don't Agree with the Idea of Lead Directors,'" *Corporate Board Member* 8, no. 3 (May/June 2005), online edition, www.boardmember.com/issues/archive.pl?article_id=12198.

Chapter 6

1. *The Changing Profile of Directors: Spencer Stuart Board Index 2006* (Spencer Stuart, 2006), 12, http://content.spencerstuart.com/sswebsite/pdf/lib/SSBI-2006.pdf. In its 1993 proxy report, the *Spencer Stuart Board Index* showed that the average size of a board in its universe had declined to thirteen from fifteen five years earlier (in 1988).

2. For private colleges and universities, see the following survey: Merrill P. Schwartz and Louis Akins, *2004 Policies, Practices, and Composition of Governing Boards of Independent Colleges and Universities* (Washington, DC: Association of Governing Boards, 2005). Broader surveys have been conducted by the National Association of Corporate Directors (NACD), BoardSource, and Grant Thornton. The data for orchestras are from Heather Noonan, "Under the Microscope: Public Scrutiny of Tax-Exempt Institutions Affects Orchestras by Definition," *Symphony*, July–August 2006.

3. Major donors sometimes insist on board seats. Having donors on the board, while unavoidable in most situations, can be tricky, especially if their presence inhibits discussion by causing other trustees to avoid comments that might offend them.

4. Michael Klausner and Jonathan Small argue that there are positive advantages to having "bifurcated boards," with some members responsible for governing and others for fund-raising. See "Failing to Govern? The Reality of Nonprofit Boards," *Stanford Social Innovation Review* 3, no. 1 (Spring 2005): 42–49. Under this approach, those not responsible for governing are relieved of legal and fiduciary responsibilities that they may not wish to shoulder. They may be happy just fund-raising. The authors also recognize, however, the problem of deciding which board members belong in each category, as well as potential problems of status. I am highly skeptical that this is a good idea.

5. Harvard has a small Corporation with decision-making power and a large Board of Overseers that is mainly advisory. The Harvard Corporation may well be an example of a governing board that is too small, given all the demands made on it.

6. *Memorial Sloan-Kettering Cancer Center 2006 Annual Report*, www.mskcc.org/mskcc/shared/graphics/AR_2006.

7. The average has increased from 10.3 in 1992, 9.9 in 1990, and 9.5 in 1988. See *Foundation Governing Boards and Administrative Expenses in Private Foundations*

and the Council on Foundations, Foundation Management Series, 12th Ed., vol. I-II (Washington, DC: Council on Foundations, 2006), 18; *Foundation Management Report*, 7th Ed. (Washington, DC: Council on Foundations, 1993), 2.

8. Ian Wilhelm, "Stern Warnings for the Red Cross," *Chronicle of Philanthropy*, March 9, 2006.

9. Martin Lipton, *Deconstructing American Business II and Some Thoughts for Boards of Directors in 2007*, Briefly . . . Perspectives on Legislation, Regulation, and Litigation, vol. 10, no. 12. (Washington, DC: National Legal Center for the Public Interest, 2006), 1, www.nlcpi.org/books/pdf/BRIEFLY_Dec06.pdf.

10. See *Spencer Stuart Board Index 2006*, 10 and 12. ISS guidelines recommend withholding support for director nominees who are CEOs of publicly traded companies and serve on more than two public boards other than their own. See also the 2007 report by James Drury Partners that documents the rapid decline in service on outside boards by active CEOs: Jim Drury, "The Flight of the American CEO" (James Drury Partners, 2007).

11. See Ellen Rosen, "Female Lawyers Set Sights on Yet One More Goal: A Seat on a Board," *New York Times*, April 6, 2007, for an extended discussion of efforts to identify and promote promising women candidates for service on corporate boards. Unfortunately, this article contains a serious error. It says, "Only 14.6 percent of Fortune 500 companies counted women among their directors in 2006, according to Catalyst." But the Catalyst release says that women hold 14.6 percent of Fortune 500 corporate board *seats*. Obviously the number of companies having at least one woman on the board is much higher than 14.6 percent. Still, even in its correct form, the 14.6 percent figure is much lower than it should be, or will be over time.

12. Joan Warner, "Who Will Sit on Tomorrow's Boards?" *Directorship*, October 18, 2006.

13. See Beard, *Blue Blood & Mutiny*, 97–98.

14. "Standard Instructions for Filing Forms under Securities Act of 1933, Securities Exchange Act of 1934 and Energy Policy and Conservation Act of 1975—Regulation S-K," *Code of Federal Regulations*, title 17, pt. 229.407, Corporate Governance, reads as follows: "With regard to each nominee approved by the nominating committee for inclusion on the registrant's proxy card (other than nominees who are executive officers or who are directors standing for re-election), state which one or more of the following categories of persons or entities recommended that nominee: security holder; non-management director; chief executive officer; other executive officer; third-party search firm, or other specified source."

15. See Joan Warner, "Agenda 07: Proxy," *Directorship*, December 2006. For a detailed discussion of the variety of majority rule provisions, including the so-called Pfizer model (whereby directors not receiving a majority vote have to tender their resignations, which are then considered by the board's corporate governance committee before being submitted—with their recommendation—to the entire board), see Elizabeth Amon, "Will Majority Rule Prevail in Electing Corporate Boards?" *Corporate Counsel*, July 21, 2006.

16. Marcella Bombardieri, "College Trustees Clash on Key Values, Dartmouth Alumni Funding Both Sides," *Boston Globe*, April 3, 2007; Paul Fain, "Alumni Defeat Governance Change," *Chronicle of Higher Education*, November 17, 2006, p. A31. In September 2007, the Dartmouth Trustees voted to expand their board and to increase the number of trustees chosen by the board while keeping the number of alumni trustees the same. In making this change, the trustees emphasized the need to recruit board members who can support the college financially and who have special skills the board needs. Trustees elected by alumni following contested campaigns may well not meet these criteria. See Scott Jaschik, "Dartmouth Approves Controversial Board Changes," *Inside Higher Education*, September 10, 2007, and Tamar Lewin, "Dartmouth Expands Board, Reducing Role of Alumni," *New York Times*, September 10, 2007.

17. Julie Creswell, "Home Depot Board Faces New Outcry," *New York Times*, January 10, 2007.

18. Larry Bossidy, "'I Don't Agree with the Idea of Lead Directors,'" *Corporate Board Member*, 8, no. 3 (May/June 2005), online edition, www.boardmember .com/issues/archive.pl?article_id=12198.

19. For a good discussion of the value of international perspectives, see the Spencer Stuart publication "Adding International Expertise: Opening the Board's Window on the World," *Cornerstone of the Board*, 2, no. 1 (2007), http://content .spencerstuart.com/sswebsite/pdf/lib/Cornerstone_Opening_the_boards_window _on_the_world12_06.pdf.

20. Here is one example from years ago of a powerful insight contributed by a board member at Princeton: In the years immediately after World War II, the investment committee of the Princeton University board was led by a trustee named Dean Mathey (he was a sophisticated Wall Street investor, most assuredly not an academic "dean"). Mathey persuaded his colleagues to invest a significant portion of the university's endowment in common stocks—and even in start-up ventures such as McDonald's—at a time when much of the conventional wisdom regarded bonds as the only prudent investment for a college or university. That one decision had an enormous impact. More than any other single factor, it is responsible for the relatively large size of the Princeton endowment today. Dean Mathey convinced his fellow trustees to make a strategic decision that, to many of them, must have seemed—at best—ahead of its time. A staunch conservative, Mathey took great satisfaction in telling those who thought he was deserting his principles, "The only true test of conservatism is to be right in the future." Of course, today, because of conflict rules, a Dean Mathey could not make the buy-and-sell decisions he did decades ago.

21. Richard C. Breeden, "Restoring Trust: Report to the Hon. Jed S. Rakoff, the United States District Court for the Southern District of New York on Corporate Governance for the Future of MCI, Inc.," *Corporate Monitor*, August 2003, p. 44.

22. See Brett D. Fromson, "American Express: Anatomy of a Coup; Bitter, Seesaw Feud Unseated CEO, *Washington Post*, February 11, 1993, for a detailed account of what transpired, and of the role that Warner played.

23. General Doriot was a distinguished professor at Harvard Business School, a position he held for forty years (with an interruption for service with the US military during World War II). Doriot is sometimes said to have been the first venture capitalist, having served as president of the American Research and Development Corporation.

24. *Knocking at the College Door: Projections of High School Graduates by State, Income, and Race/Ethnicity, 1988–2018* (Boulder, CO: Western Interstate Commission for Higher Education, December 2003), 6.

25. See Clayton S. Rose, "Race at the Top: Organizational Response to Institutional Pressures and the Racial Composition of the Corporate Elite." PhD diss., University of Pennsylvania, 2007. This is the most thorough empirical study of this subject of which I am aware, and Rose performs a real service by both assembling the relevant data and then testing hypotheses designed to explain the patterns he finds.

26. See "How the Board Put the Bounce Back in Select Comfort," *Corporate Board Member*, May/June 2007.

27. The ISS system of classifying directors can be found at http://issproxy.com /pdf/2007%20US%20Policy%20Update.pdf. The ISS definition of "independent" is more restrictive than the definitions used by the exchanges.

28. See David Bank and Joann S. Lublin, "Giving at the Office on Corporate Boards," *Wall Street Journal*, June 20, 2003.

29. *Spencer Stuart Board Index 2006*, 10. The definition of "independent" used by Spencer Stuart appears to be less restrictive than the definition used by the ISS and focuses primarily on the distinction between inside and outside directors.

30. Breeden, "Restoring Trust," 28.

31. Thomas Landon Jr., "3 Morgan Stanley Dissidents Met Directors," *New York Times*, April 29, 2005.

32. One commentator reported that he had "watched the board of a company whose chairman was a convert to a particular religious denomination. He [the chairman] assembled a board that appeared to comprise only highly involved members of the same denomination. They were very slow in acting on the deficiencies of their CEO. It could have been any form of cronyism but in this case it was religion. The company ended up in hot water." A related threat to real independence arises when the CEO acts as a patron of board members—a situation that is alleged to have existed to at least some degree at Enron. If board members become too enamored of their own perks, their willingness to call into question the performance (never mind the ethical standards) of the patron could well be affected.

33. I should add that Blumenthal demonstrated by his actions, not just his words, his own capacity for independence on the Princeton board when he challenged long-established investment policies that depended too much on personal connections. Those policies were changed.

34. Kenneth D. Lewis, "The Board: Independent and *Inter*dependent," *Directors & Boards*, Third Quarter 2006, pp. 20–24.

35. See Francie Ostrower, *Nonprofit Governance in the United States: Findings on Performance and Accountability from the First National Representative Study* (Washington, DC: Urban Institute, 2007), especially pp. 7–10.

Chapter 7

1. Richard C. Breeden, "Restoring Trust: Report to the Hon. Jed S. Rakoff, the United States District Court for the Southern District of New York on Corporate Governance for the Future of MCI, Inc.," *Corporate Monitor*, August 2003, p. 9.
2. See Elisabeth Clarkson's response to the Beeman report in "Wilson College: A Case Study," [a report prepared for discussion at Lilly Endowment, October 10, 1979, by Alice L. Beeman, with comments by Elisabeth Hudnut Clarkson] (Harrisburg: Pennsylvania Association of Colleges and Universities, 1979).
3. See my book *Inside the Boardroom: Governance by Directors and Trustees* (New York: Wiley, 1994), Appendix B, pp. 165–166.
4. Breeden, "Restoring Trust," 32.
5. For a good discussion of this tension, see the Harvard Business School case on governance at Wellesley: Zach First, "Wellesley College" (Harvard Business School Case Study, President and Fellows of Harvard College, 2005), especially p. 12.
6. See Martin Lipton and Jay W. Lorsch, "A Modest Proposal for Improved Corporate Governance," *Business Lawyer*, November 1992, pp. 69–70.
7. Carly Fiorina, *Tough Choices: A Memoir* (New York: Portfolio, 2006), xi, 293; and John Markoff, "Fiorina Pursued Leaks at H.P., Too," *New York Times*, October 5, 2006.
8. See Brett D. Fromson, "American Express: Anatomy of a Coup: Bitter, Seesaw Feud Unseated CEO," *Washington Post*, February 11, 1993. Accounts of debates within the General Motors board over the years also suggest acrimonious moments, including the allegation that Ross Perot, speaking to Roger Smith, the CEO at that time, ridiculed some board members as "pet rocks." More recently, Jerome York, an associate of Kirk Kerkorian, has been publicly critical of the GM board. See Nick Bunkley and Micheline Maynard, "Dissident Quits Board at G.M.," *New York Times*, October 7, 2006.
9. Ram Charan has a particularly good discussion of this topic in his book *Boards That Deliver* (San Francisco: Jossey-Bass, 2005), 39–40.
10. Wellesley and Princeton both have well-articulated policies of this kind (as do many other colleges and universities). See the Harvard Business School case discussing governance at Wellesley (First, "Wellesley College"); and the "Kelley Report" at Princeton (Special Committee on the Structure of the University, *The Governing of Princeton University: Final Report of the Special Committee on the Structure of the University* [Princeton University, April 1970]), 60–63.
11. See Nicholas deB. Katzenbach, "Report to the TIAA Board of Overseers," April 29, 2005.
12. A long and informative discussion of this set of issues, focusing on the Hennessy–Stanford example, can be found in John Hechinger, "Golden Touch of Stanford's President," *Wall Street Journal*, February 24, 2007. See also Stanford University, *Research Policy Handbook*, ch. 4: "Conflicts of Commitment and Interest," especially 4.3 ("Outside Consulting Activities by Members of the Academic Council") and 4.4 ("Conflict of Commitment and Interest for Academic Staff"), www.stanford.edu/dept/DoR/rph/Chpt4.html.

13. For a history of JSTOR, see Roger C. Schonfeld, *JSTOR: A History* (Princeton, NJ: Princeton University Press, 2003); as well as Mellon Foundation annual reports for the years 1994, 1995, 1999, and 2002. Subsequently, the foundation sponsored the creation of other entities providing electronic resources to the educational community, including ARTstor and Ithaka (described on their Web sites). The multiple roles played by the foundation in establishing each of these start-ups were fully disclosed and, more than that, "advertised"; they were widely seen as signaling to the scholarly world that these entities could be trusted to deliver the services they offered on a continuing basis. At the same time, as JSTOR matured, it became more and more independent of the foundation, and ARTstor and Ithaka are likely to follow similar paths. There is an obvious analogy with venture capital firms operating in the for-profit sector, in that such firms customarily take one or more seats on the boards of companies in which they invest and also provide organizational help and strategic guidance.

14. See Association of Governing Boards of Universities and Colleges, "AGB Statement on Board Accountability," January 18, 2007; and the Grant Thornton survey of governance policies in the nonprofit sector, described in Harvey Lipman, "Many Nonprofit Groups Are Tightening Governance Policies, Study Finds," *Chronicle of Philanthropy Update*, December 12, 2006, http://philanthropy .com/free/update/2006/12/2006121201.htm.

15. Joann S. Lublin and Erin White, "Drama in the Boardroom," *Wall Street Journal*, October 2, 2006. See also other stories on the HP board published on October 5, 2006, in the *Wall Street Journal* ("California Charges Dunn, 4 Others in H-P Scandal") and the *New York Times* ("Ex-Chairwoman among 5 Charged in Hewlett Case" and "Fiorina Pursued Leaks at H P, Too").

16. Damon Darlin, "Adviser Urges H P. to Focus on Ethics over Legalities," *New York Times*, October 4, 2006; and Matt Richtel, "Charges Dismissed in Hewlett-Packard Spying Case," *New York Times,* March 15, 2007.

17. Justin Fox, "The Curious Capitalist: When Leaking Is the Right Thing to Do," *Time Blog: The Curious Capitalist,* September 21, 2006, http://time-blog.com/ curious_capitalist/2006/09/when_leaking_is_the_right_thin.html.

18. Another commentator who has served on many boards, including the boards of a number of start-ups, sent me a copy of a form that he and several colleagues developed in order to assess directly, and without equivocation, the performance of fellow directors. The questionnaire includes questions such as, "How do you rate the director's financial competence/acumen? . . . Please grade the director's ability to bring critical thinking and questions designed to help the company select sound strategies . . . What degree of respect do you have for the director's ability to assess the talents, capabilities, and skills of the board itself and top management?" and, finally, "If you personally owned 51% of the company's shares, would you invite this director to be a member of the board?" As much as I admire this effort to be direct and to the point, I am doubtful that most board members would be comfortable answering (even anonymously) such pointed questions.

19. Larry Bossidy, "'I Don't Agree with the Idea of Lead Directors,'" *Corporate Board Member*, May/June 2005.

20. Breeden, "Restoring Trust," 55–56.
21. Here I am reflecting on my experience on the Denison University board, which, though an excellent board, simply could not afford the loss of two or three key trustees. And even in Princeton's case, where the pool of outstanding candidates was unusually deep, special arrangements were made on at least one occasion to allow a trustee recently chosen as chairman to serve extra years.
22. *The Changing Profile of Directors: Spencer Stuart Board Index 2006* (Spencer Stuart, 2006), 10, http://content.spencerstuart.com/sswebsite/pdf/lib/SSBI-2006.pdf.
23. Full disclosure requires that I repeat something said earlier about my own history—namely, that I was asked to serve one extra year, past mandatory retirement, by the Merck board because I was in the midst of chairing the special committee charged with reviewing the handling by management of the development and marketing of VIOXX. But an artful formula was found, whereby I relinquished all of my other committee responsibilities when I reached the mandatory retirement age. I retired from the American Express board at the specified time, and I think that making exceptions to mandatory retirement provisions is, in general, unwise.
24. Commentators were eager, not surprisingly, to relate stories of absolutely extraordinary people who contributed to boards on which they served well past any conceivable mandatory retirement age. It is hard to contemplate giving up the wealth of wisdom and experience that such individuals possess. Still, although I understand these situations and sympathize with individuals caught up in them, I am less inclined to favor exceptions here than I am in the case of term limits.
25. See James B. Stewart, "The Kona Files," *New Yorker*, February 19–26, 2007, p. 157.
26. For a strong statement of this position, see William A. Sahlman, "Why Sane People Shouldn't Serve on Public Boards," *Harvard Business Review* 68, no. 3 (May–June 1990): 28–30, 34–35.
27. *Spencer Stuart Board Index 2007*, 31, provides detailed information on forms of director compensation, but it is hard, from the table presented there, to estimate an average "all-in" figure.
28. Stephen G. Greene, "Trustees Ousted in Hawaii," *Chronicle of Philanthropy*, May 20, 1999. Both the process for appointing trustees and the governance structure were overhauled following the removal or resignation of five trustees in 1999. Stephen G. Greene, "Insurer to Pay $25-Million to Settle Dispute in Hawaii," *Chronicle of Philanthropy*, October 5, 2000.
29. The reference to "volunteers" is from an account of the Empire BlueCross BlueShield debacle that occurred in the early 1990s. Salvatore R. Curiale, the New York State insurance superintendent, harshly criticized the board of Empire for having "sat on its hands." In response, Harold E. Vogt explained, "Every one of the Board members is a *volunteer*" (my emphasis). (Jane Fritsch, "Top Regulator Assails Board of Blue Cross," *New York Times*, April 17, 1993.) Although Empire BlueCross BlueShield is now a for-profit subsidiary of Well-Point, a publicly traded company, some BlueCross BlueShield health plans remain nonprofit. The Alliance for Advancing Nonprofit Health Care counts

among its members BlueCross BlueShield of Alabama, Blue Cross Blue Shield of Michigan, and Rocky Mountain Health Plans. In addition, many, many other nonprofit service providers exist outside the "charitable" orbit. It is sometimes assumed that the charitable nonprofits—the 501(c)(3) organizations—dominate the nonprofit sector. In fact, there are at least as many nonprofits outside the charitable orbit. See William G. Bowen et al., *The Charitable Nonprofits* (San Francisco: Jossey-Bass, 1994), especially pp. 4–7.

30. "The Sound of Snoring at Empire" (Editorial), *New York Times*, August 21, 1993.

31. Jeffrey Brinck, esq., former partner, Milbank, Tweed, Hadley & McCloy, memorandum to the author. Another attorney, Daniel Kurtz, concurs: "Courts tend not to impose harsh penalties on volunteer directors for their actions or inaction." (Daniel Kurtz, *Board Liability: Guide for Nonprofit Directors* [Mount Kisco, NY: Moyer Bell Limited, 1988], 94.)

32. Jane Fritsch, "At Empire, the Glow of Greed," *New York Times*, July 11, 1993.

33. A 2006 survey by PricewaterhouseCoopers found that almost nine of ten responding boards report that their performance is now formally evaluated on a regular basis. In the words of the survey report, "Board evaluations have been ratcheting up over the past few years, as all boards have generally implemented the NYSE requirements in this area . . . Those boards that conduct their board evaluation seriously, versus looking at it as just a compliance task . . . , have found it to be a very valuable tool." "What Directors Think: The 2006 *Corporate Board Member*/PricewaterhouseCoopers Survey" (*Corporate Board Member* 2006 Special Supplement, October 2006), www.boardmember.com/PDFs/WDTResearch2006.pdf.

34. For further discussion of these issues, see Ram Charan, *Boards That Deliver*, 13; Dimma, *Excellence in the Boardroom*, 18–20, 51–56; and David Anderson, "Using Board Evaluation to Develop Strength," *Directorship*, June 2006, pp. 21ff. The 2006 PricewaterhouseCoopers survey cited in Note 33 reports that six in ten of the boards surveyed use internal general counsel to perform the evaluations, and 13 percent use an outside counsel.

Chapter 8

1. *The Changing Profile of Directors: Spencer Stuart Board Index 2006* (Spencer Stuart, 2006), 3, http://content.spencerstuart.com/sswebsite/pdf/lib/SSBI-2006.pdf.

2. Martin Lipton, "Shareholder Activism and the 'Eclipse of the Public Corporation,'" Keynote address to the 25th Annual Institute on Federal Securities, February 7, 2007, Miami, FL.

3. For a vigorous critique of Lipton's position, see Gretchen Morgenson, "Memo to Shareholders: Shut Up," *New York Times*, February 11, 2007.

4. The Smithsonian has been an exception to many of the points made in this discussion of relations between boards and chief executives in the nonprofit sector. In the case of the Smithsonian, the board of regents has not been given, in recent years, the information it needed to participate effectively in the governance of the institu-

tion. The secretary, who is the chief executive of the Smithsonian, has had too much control over agendas and information. The "Report of the Governance Committee to the Board of Regents" (June 14, 2007), issued in the aftermath of Secretary Small's resignation, advocates a number of reforms intended to "promote a constructive partnership between the Board and the Secretary" (p. 7). The Governance Committee that issued this report, and the Independent Review Committee, in its separate report—"A Report to the Board of Regents of the Smithsonian Institution" (Independent Review Committee, June 18, 2007)— called for giving "gatekeepers" such as the general counsel direct access to the regents and for a much freer flow of information to the regents.

5. See Kevin Guthrie's case study of the New-York Historical Society for an excellent discussion of this set of issues: *The New-York Historical Society: Lessons from One Nonprofit's Long Struggle for Survival* (San Francisco: Jossey-Bass, 1996).

6. Scott Carlson, "A House Divided: How Antioch College Fell into Straits It Could No Longer Ignore," *Chronicle of Higher Education*, June 21, 2007. See also Ralph Keyes, "Present at the Demise: Antioch College, 1852–2008," *Chronicle of Higher Education*, July 20, 2007. In the text, I wrote "possible demise" because of the continuing debate over whether Antioch can somehow be resuscitated. Keyes' account of how Antioch became dysfunctional, appealing only to a narrower and narrower set of students who "knew the truth," makes one wonder why it took so long for the trustees to recognize what was happening. It is sad that they seem to have been unable to arrange for a more dignified way of contemplating the closing of what was once a pioneering institution that had a constructive impact on American higher education.

7. Martin Lipton, *Deconstructing American Business II and Some Thoughts for Boards of Directors in 2007*, Briefly . . . Perspectives on Legislation, Regulation, and Litigation, vol. 10, no. 12. (Washington, DC: National Legal Center for the Public Interest, 2006), 1, www.nlcpi.org/books/pdf/BRIEFLY_Dec06.pdf.

8. See Jim Drury, "The Flight of the American CEO" (James Drury Partners, 2007), 8. The report goes on to say, "The growing structure of governance policies, procedures, reviews and approvals is believed by many to be lowering the level of risk that boards and CEOs seem willing to embrace in the interest of progress."

9. Gwen Moore et al., "Elite Interlocks in Three U.S. Sectors: Nonprofit, Corporate, and Government," *Social Science Quarterly* 83, no. 3 (September 2002): 726–744.

Index